Being a Teacher in the 21st Century

Leon Benade

Being a Teacher in the 21st Century

A Critical New Zealand Research Study

 Springer

Leon Benade
School of Education
Auckland University of Technology
Auckland
New Zealand

ISBN 978-981-10-3781-8   ISBN 978-981-10-3782-5   (eBook)
DOI 10.1007/978-981-10-3782-5

Library of Congress Control Number: 2017930800

© Springer Nature Singapore Pte Ltd. 2017
This work is subject to copyright. All rights are reserved by the Publisher, whether the whole or part of the material is concerned, specifically the rights of translation, reprinting, reuse of illustrations, recitation, broadcasting, reproduction on microfilms or in any other physical way, and transmission or information storage and retrieval, electronic adaptation, computer software, or by similar or dissimilar methodology now known or hereafter developed.
The use of general descriptive names, registered names, trademarks, service marks, etc. in this publication does not imply, even in the absence of a specific statement, that such names are exempt from the relevant protective laws and regulations and therefore free for general use.
The publisher, the authors and the editors are safe to assume that the advice and information in this book are believed to be true and accurate at the date of publication. Neither the publisher nor the authors or the editors give a warranty, express or implied, with respect to the material contained herein or for any errors or omissions that may have been made. The publisher remains neutral with regard to jurisdictional claims in published maps and institutional affiliations.

Printed on acid-free paper

This Springer imprint is published by Springer Nature
The registered company is Springer Nature Singapore Pte Ltd.
The registered company address is: 152 Beach Road, #21-01/04 Gateway East, Singapore 189721, Singapore

Acknowledgements

The research work on which this book is based was made largely possible by the generous funding of the Faculty of Culture and Society and the School of Education of the Auckland University of Technology. This support was invaluable in helping to bring the various elements of the research to fruition.

In a study of this nature, there is no research without participants, and a large number of participants who gave generously of their time over the past three years are gratefully acknowledged. I hope I have accorded their voices and words the respect and dignity they deserve. They, like so many other teachers and school leaders, deserve praise for their unstinting efforts. I focus my work on resisting the movement of teachers' work into the shadow-lands of education.

My thanks to my publisher, Nick Melchior of Springer, and his colleagues, who have supported the publication of this important work. Special thanks to my colleague, Andrew Gibbons, of the School of Education at the Auckland University of Technology, who participated in certain aspects of this research, both in the initial '21st-Century Learning' (2013/2014) and in the later 'Being a Teacher' (2015) studies. Special thanks too are extended to the two anonymous reviewers, whose helpful insights and some incisive commentary have helped sharpening this book.

Last but not least, I acknowledge my wife and professional friend, Gina, who is a constant companion in these endeavours, and has had to put up with my distracted attention and seemingly endless 4 am starts.

Contents

1	**Introduction**	1
	Context	1
	Conceptual Framework	3
	A Bricolage of Critical Theory, Critical Hermeneutics and Post-Intentional Phenomenology	3
	A Personal Note	9
	Division of Content	10
	References	11
2	**Presenting the Research**	13
	Introduction	13
	Design and Participants	15
	Ethics	20
	The Four Schools	21
	Innovation Primary	21
	Angelus School	21
	Millennial College	21
	Holyoake College	22
	Conclusion	22
	References	22
3	**The Future Is Now: What '21st-Century Learning' Means for Teaching**	25
	Introduction	25
	Futures Discourse and the Status of Knowledge	26
	Character of the Digital Age	27
	Technological Determinism	27
	Digital Natives	28
	21st-Century Learning	29
	Skills Students Need for the 21st Century	29
	Lifelong Learning	31
	Learning at the Centre	31

	21st-Century Learning and Modern Learning Practices............	32
	Personalised Learning.......................................	33
	Culturally Responsive Pedagogy..............................	33
	Authentic Learning...	35
	Project-Based, Problem-Based and Design-Based Approaches to Learning...	36
	Time..	36
	'Stage, Not Age'...	37
	Innovation..	38
	Collaborative Teaching.....................................	38
	Learning Environments...	39
	The Imperative of Workspaces	40
	Design Initiative	41
	The Place of Learning......................................	42
	Learning Space Design Principles...........................	44
	Furniture...	46
	Influence of Environment on Teaching and Learning	47
	Critical Perspectives on the Technology of Space..................	50
	Materiality..	50
	Lefebvre..	52
	ICT in Schools/BYOD	53
	'Digital Revolution'	53
	Student Access	54
	Infrastructure...	54
	Staff PD/L..	55
	Integrating ICT in Schools	55
	Digital Pedagogy...	56
	ICT and Student Learning...................................	57
	Teachers' Reflective Practice...................................	59
	Definition	59
	Becoming Reflective.......................................	60
	Being Reflective	60
	Implications for Practice	62
	Change Management...	63
	Teacher Stress and Work Intensification	63
	Change Management for Leadership.........................	64
	Staff Development and Learning............................	65
	Conclusion	66
	References..	67
4	**The Impacts on Teachers' Work: 21st-Century Learning**	75
	The Demands of Modern Teaching and Learning Practices: A Critical Perspective	76
	The Practical Studies...	79
	Modern Teaching and Learning Practice.......................	79

	Approach to Curriculum	80
	Integrated Curriculum	82
	Personalised Learning	85
	Tracking and Reporting	90
	Assessment	91
	Classroom Management	93
	Student Agency and Engagement	94
	Student Attitudes and Opinions	97
	On Reflection	99
	Personalisation and the 'Knowledge Problem'	99
	Intentionality	100
	In Conclusion	102
	References	103
5	**The Impacts on Teachers' Work: Working in Flexible Learning Environments**	**107**
	Flexible Learning Environments and Space: Some Critical Perspectives on Policy	108
	AC Nielsen Study: Best Practice in School Design	109
	Ministry of Education: Learning Studio Pilot Review	111
	The Practical Studies: Working in Flexible (Innovative) Learning Environments	115
	Innovation Primary	116
	Angelus School	116
	Millennial College	116
	Design and Set-Up of the Working Space	117
	Student Work and Attitudes	119
	Classroom Management	121
	Teachers' Work and Attitudes	122
	On Reflection	124
	Spatiality	124
	Design	126
	Intentionality	129
	In Conclusion	131
	References	132
6	**The Impacts on Teachers' Work: ICT/BYOD and Digital Pedagogy**	**135**
	Digital Technology Implementation in Education: Critical Perspectives	136
	The Practical Studies: The Challenge of Undertaking a BYOD Implementation	139
	Holyoake College	140
	The BYOD Policy at Holyoake: Arguments for and Against	140

BYOD at Innovation Primary, Millennial College and Angelus
School.. 142
Digital pedagogy: Holyoake College........................ 142
Digital pedagogy at Innovation Primary, Millennial College
and Angelus School 146
The Relationship Between Device Use and Student Learning:
Holyoake College 147
The Relationship Between Device Use and Student Learning:
At Innovation Primary, Millennial College and Angelus School..... 149
Strategic and Management Considerations: Holyoake College 149
Strategic and Management Considerations: Innovation Primary,
Millennial College and Angelus School 151
On Reflection: Critical Perspectives on Technology and ICT
in Education 152
   Materiality.. 153
   Technology.. 153
   Intentionality... 157
In Conclusion 159
References... 161

7 The Impacts on Teachers' Work: Practitioner Attitudes and Reflective Transitions..... 163
Critically Reflective Practice, Trust and Teaching as Inquiry 164
   Teachers' Critical Reflective Practice in the Context of Twenty-First
   Century Learning 164
   The Role of Trust in Reflective Practice...................... 165
   Teaching as Inquiry: Well Intentioned, but Fundamentally Flawed.... 166
The Practical Studies.. 167
   Introduction... 167
   Open to New Learning 168
   Reflection–In, –On and For–Action.......................... 169
   The Changes that e-Learning Demands...................... 170
On Reflection 171
   Intentionality... 171
In Conclusion 174
References... 176

8 Responding to 21st Century Learning Policy Demands 177
Policy: The New Zealand Context 177
Critical Considerations 179
   The Policy Framework: A Critical Perspective 179
   How Might Change be Effected? Theory and Practice 181
The Practical Studies.. 185
   Introduction... 185
   Vision of, and Support for, Progressive Practices 185

	Recruitment and Team Construction	187
	Supporting Staff	192
	Looking Outward—The Community	194
On Reflection		197
	Intentionality	197
In Conclusion		201
References		202
9	**Lessons to Be Learned?**	**205**
	Lessons for Practitioners in Schools	205
	Lessons for Teacher Educators	206
	Lessons for Policy-Makers	208
	Lessons for Designers	209
	The Final Word	210
	References	210

Chapter 1
Introduction

> Once again, there is no such thing as teaching without research and research without teaching. One inhabits the body of the other. As I teach, I continue to search and re-search. I teach because I search, because I question, and because I submit myself to questioning. I research because I notice things, take cognizance of them. And in so doing, I intervene. And intervening, I educate and educate myself. I do research so as to know what I do not yet know and to communicate and proclaim what I discover (Freire 1998, p. 35).

Context

The past five to ten years have witnessed the increasing use of the somewhat nebulous term, '21st-century learning'. This implies learning and teaching that prepares students to engage with the 21st century world, and while an imperfect term, it is one many policy-makers have latched onto, although terms like 'modern learning', 'innovative learning' and 'modern teaching and learning' are also heard amongst practitioners. Internationally, schooling systems have been motivated for some time to ensure that teachers are able to provide school-leavers with appropriate life-long and 21st century skills.

There is value in understanding how teachers and leaders are making the shift from transmission models of teaching to modern and innovative approaches that develop such skills as critical thinking and problem solving; collaboration and leadership; agility and adaptability; initiative and entrepreneurialism; effective oral and written communication; accessing and analysing information; and curiosity and imagination (Wagner 2008, cited in Saavedra and Opfer 2012, p. 8).

Being a Teacher in the 21st Century traverses the space between being a research report and being a conventional book. It is not exclusively about changes to the spaces in which teachers work, the digital tools they use or the pedagogies they develop in response to these changes. It is rather more about what all these changes do to teachers' heads (to put it bluntly), and thus to teachers' conceptions of their work.

The book is not intended to be a practitioner book of 'how to', or practical suggestions for what to do in flexible space or with digital technology. What it does do is draw on the findings of a qualitative study of teachers and leaders in several New Zealand schools over three years to take stock of some of the central manifestations of 21st-century learning. In particular, these are the collaborative practices associated with teaching and learning in flexible learning environments, and digital pedagogies. This book reflects on the mental shifts and sometimes-painful transitions teachers and leaders are making and experiencing, as they move through uncharted waters, from traditional classroom practices to ones emphasising collaboration, teamwork and the radical de-centring of their personal roles. It demonstrates how they navigate these changes, describing and explaining the nature of pedagogical shifts apparent in digital classrooms and modern learning environments, which, according to international schools' architect, Nair (2011), make the classroom obsolete.

The purpose of this book is to provide scholars, teacher educators, and reflective school leaders and teachers a valuable insight to what it is to be a teacher in the 21st century. The book achieves this aim by presenting original research based on my study of several New Zealand schools between 2013 and 2015, and in particular, my focussed study of four of those schools in 2015.

This book has particular benefits:

1. For teacher educators who may have long since left the classroom, the notions of digital technology and pedagogy, flexible learning spaces, ergonomic furniture and developing critically reflective practice may not be familiar territory. This text will support their efforts to prepare their student teachers for a rapidly changing school environment.
2. For New Zealand scholars and reflective school practitioners, this book contributes by addressing the paucity of relevant, critical, New Zealand education literature in relation to the concept of flexible (or innovative, modern or new generation) learning environments. It does so through its carefully analytical and critical consideration of 21st-century learning, modern pedagogy, teacher reflective practice, and the strategic actions of school leaders in responding to these discrete elements.
3. While drawing on examples that have a New Zealand focus, and reflecting on fieldwork in some New Zealand schools, this book has international relevance. Scholars, teacher educators and reflective school practitioners will recognise the experiences of their New Zealand counterparts described and interpreted in these pages.

Conceptual Framework

Here I will engage in discussion concerning the conceptual underpinnings of this book, which is framed by an ontology that emphasises the lived experience of individuals working in an evolving and emerging educational environment. These individuals seek to make sense of this experience, and this book is an attempt to convey and interpret this sense-making. The analyses in this book are framed by a critical and rationalist epistemology that emphasises the importance of uncovering underlying patterns of thought and practice in discourses, found in daily work practices and texts such as policies. Of particular interest is to uncover discourses that oppress, disadvantage or marginalise whilst simultaneously shaping identities and manufacturing consent. The ontological discoveries and findings are contextualised and embedded in the critical analyses, which in turn are informed by social democratic political influences.

The human experience, while bound to specific contexts, offers valuable lessons across contexts. Why researchers approach their study of human experience the way they do is shaped by multiple historical and cultural influences, giving rise to and deriving from particular ways of seeing the world. These ways of seeing the world influence *how* researchers conduct their investigations, and, in particular, what they do with the results of their efforts.

A Bricolage of Critical Theory, Critical Hermeneutics and Post-Intentional Phenomenology

Denzin and Lincoln (2005) and Steinberg and Kincheloe (2010) wrote of *bricolage*, that is, a bringing together of elements from different and varied sources. Denzin and Lincoln (2005) called the qualitative researcher a *bricoleur*, showing the term to have wide use among many researchers. The *bricoleur* ranges freely, but carefully and intentionally, across a wide range of approaches to research, deploying practices that are pertinent to the particular research task at hand. These practices may not necessarily be worked out beforehand, but emerge from the complexities of the task, as they unfold (2005).

Steinberg and Kincheloe, in keeping with the notion of the *bricoleur*, sought to combine several streams of critical theorising besides the critical theory of the Frankfurt School, including Foucault's genealogy, poststructuralist practices of deconstruction, and critical cultural studies and critical pedagogy (2012). Hermeneutics, they argued, provided this bridge.

Hermeneutics

Hermeneutics is a methodology of interpretation (Mantzavinos 2016). It is the process that allows human beings to interpret what is perceived and to make sense of their perceptions (Ramberg and Gjesdal 2009). Although hermeneutics has a long history, as a method of sceptical critique of Biblical Scripture, it has been associated in modern times particularly with Hans-Georg Gadamer. His approach to hermeneutics, with its emphasis linking interpretation to human interests makes it an ontological project.

Hermeneutic practitioners (such as Gadamer) regarded interpretation as contextual and closely related to the one who interprets. Researchers and their participants are products of history and tradition, and this is likely to influence researcher interpretations. Texts then, are viewed from within each individual perspective, and interpretations are therefore partial (Kinsella 2006). Not only is it the researcher who is historically located, but the texts themselves, and the language in which they are expressed (2006). Therefore, language is fundamental to interpretation. In fact, Gadamer claimed credit for placing the linguistic at the centre of hermeneutics. Human language is essential not only to their humanness, but to their ability to learn from each other. Gadamer noted, in his interview with Carsten Dutt: "We do not need just to hear one another but to *listen to* one another. Only when this happens is there understanding" (Gadamer et al. 2001, p. 39. Emphasis in the original).

Gadamer's point suggests conversation, a further dimension of his hermeneutics, is an invaluable concept in understanding the interpretation of research. Conversation is not a monologue, but a dialogue with another. The process of research entails using language to better understand, even translate, the message the researcher receives. To do so, requires researchers to step over their boundaries and personal limits (2001). In hermeneutic conversation, the researcher becomes a translator of texts in search of a common(ly understood) language. Kinsella (2006) called for a Bakhtinian notion of polyphonic voices to underpin a researcher's understanding of this search for meaning. Certainty is thus replaced with ambiguity, which is consistent, according to Kinsella, with Gadamer's own understanding of how to approach texts. Multiple conversations replace a single, universal intent, thus reducing the prospect of an authoritative reading of text (2006).

Critical Theory

Critical theory originated from the work of the Frankfurt School, which included Theo Adorno, Walter Benjamin, Max Horkheimer and Herbert Marcuse. Jurgen Habermas is an influential 'second generation' member of the Frankfurt School (Farganis 2011). The Institute for Social Research was established at the University of Frankfurt in Germany in 1923, though its founding members were forced to migrate to the United States after 1933 when Hitler's Nazi government outlawed the Institute.

The original members of the Frankfurt School developed a social reconstructive perspective and a commitment to social justice (Bohman 2005). Critical theory draws on several disciplines (Bohman 2005; Farganis 2011) in the human and social sciences. This allowed its founding thinkers to bring together "empirical and interpretive social sciences… [with] normative claims of truth, morality and justice" (Bohman 2005, p. 5). Critical theory is therefore practical, in a moral, not instrumental sense, and normative. Its normative orientation is mainly pointed towards "the transformation of capitalism into a 'real democracy'" (Bohman 2005, p. 3), deploying the knowledge it generates to achieving just social outcomes (Farganis 2011). Critical theory is an epistemological project that proposes rational interests, and its practical effect is to bring about enlightenment and emancipation (Geuss 1981).

Critical theory can thus be distinguished from a traditional (scientific) theory by an explicit agenda for a change of society. A major challenge facing these theorists was the growing influence of a materialist, capitalist economic ethos of instrumentality and technological development, which negated social change (not unlike the influence of neoliberalism today). Horkheimer, in *Eclipse of Reason* (2004), argued that instrumental reason, driven by technological progress, was supplanting independent thought and action. Moral reasoning, which seeks truth and meaning, by focusing on moral ends, had been replaced by irrationality that focussed on means whereby desired practical ends (rather than desirable ones) could be attained.

Writing in 1941, Marcuse spoke of "a new [technological] rationality and new standards of individuality [that] have spread over society" (1998, p. 42). Marcuse argued that technological rationality was characterised by compliance and automatic behaviour: "Rationality is being transformed from a critical force into one of adjustment and compliance…Reason has found its resting place in the system of standardized control, production and consumption" (p. 49).

Therefore, what both thinkers were arguing is that humans were losing their ability to think and act critically, due in significant measure to the economic and technological development of capitalism, but also because of the rise of Fascist ideologies. This compliant attitude exists in ironic relation to so-called open and democratic societies, which ought to be open to critique, but are actually closed to any dissenting opinion (Farganis 2011).

Critical Research and Education

Steinberg and Kincheloe (2012) suggested five requirements of critical research:

- a rejection of positivistic rationality;
- making and keeping explicit the value position (social justice and democracy) of the researcher or practitioner in relation to the field of practice;
- making explicit the tacit cultural and professional understandings that shape the thinking of researchers and practitioners;
- exposing power structures that are dominant in society; and

- maintaining a conscious link to practice, with a view to improving its social justice and democratic potential.

Positivistic rationality can be rejected by recognising the constraints in place over teachers and education researchers. A significant constraint is the singular focus on student achievement. This focus is an example of the 'instrumental rationality' referred to earlier, where teaching and its associated areas of interest are reduced to mere technicalities. Similarly, this mentality is evident in the 'evidence-led' dogma that underpins so much educational policy and practice (see, in this regard, Biesta 2007).

It is helpful for researchers to have a self-conscious sense of their research identity, and to be able to define their positionality. Being a critical researcher and practitioner requires "the attempt to free oneself from the tacit controls of racial, class-based, and gendered discourses and lived practices" (p. 1489). Culture in all its forms is deeply contested terrain in education, and particularly in critical education studies. Culture is "a domain of struggle" (Steinberg and Kincheloe 2010, p. 144), and is a key determinant in shaping perspective. Therefore, the critical educator and researcher must be able to acknowledge the role their own cultural positioning plays in shaping their attitudes. This means recognising the roles class, gender, race and religion play in shaping attitudes, not to mention the role played by the popular culture of cinema and music, for example.

Developing research strategies to counteract the technical determinism inherent in a 'what works', 'evidence-led' policy and practice framework, and to do the work of emancipation could include empirical work. What critical researchers do with that empirical data is what will set them apart from positivistic researchers, by going beyond description and 'objective' reporting, to searching for contradictions and patterns that explain power relationships, for example. The critical researcher eschews the notion of a fact–value divide in empirical work: "The knowledge that the world yields has to be interpreted by men and women who are a part of that world. What we call information always involves an act of human judgment" (Steinberg and Kincheloe 2012, p. 1493).

Power does not hit us in the face, as it were. It is somewhat subtler, yet the critical researcher must seek it out and expose it for what it is—often sophisticated policy announcements and positions designed to encourage a technological determinism, for example. Giving education practitioners the language to identify and 'name' instances of power has an emancipatory effect. So too can be the exposure of the ways in which "citizens are regulated by the forces of power operating in a general climate of deceit" (Steinberg and Kincheloe 2010, p. 140). This requires some understanding of the symbolic language of society, which often acts as a vehicle to convey images of power (such as extolling material affluence in popular media). Uncovering the winners and losers in society is another example of revealing power and how it works. Yet other examples would include instances of gendered power, or issues of sexuality in schools.

To avoid the determinism inherent in 'what works' and effect-size research does not automatically imply that critical theoretic researchers are not interested in bringing about improved practice, though their first concern would be to bring about improved situations and contexts. Giving teachers frameworks on which to construct coherent value positions of their own will be an important first step to supporting their practice. It is not only the practice of teachers that should be of concern here, but the practice of researchers too. Through self-reflexive activity, they are able to confront challenges in their own research practice, especially in such areas as personal cultural context or unintended displays of power.

Developing a Critical Hermeneutics

Although critical theory and hermeneutics do not appear to sit well together, Steinberg and Kincheloe (2010) argued that their reading of Gadamer led them to the view that interpretation is an act of moral reasoning and action (and therefore allied to the aims of critical theory). The time is right, they suggested, for a dialogue between critical theory and the *bricolage* of postmodern and poststructural theories, such as feminism, Foucauldian genealogy, complexity theory and discourse analysis, amongst others. Drawing together this amalgam of approaches to research is consistent with the fuzziness of the contemporary 21st century world. A critical reading of hermeneutics, they suggested, creates the bridge between the *bricolage* of theories that reject boundary setting and Cartesian rationality on the one hand, and critical theory on the other.

An understanding of Gadamerian hermeneutics reminds a critical theorist and researcher "that meaning making cannot be quarantined from where one stands or is placed in the web of social reality" (2010, p. 148). To this view of meaning, Roberge (2011) added that ideology plays a major role: ideology is filled with meaning (rather than meaning something), thus inquiries must seek out the links between groups and their beliefs. Coupled with the impetus to moral action, research will interpret according to the context and the social forces at play over that context, and will seek to point to appropriate action in relation to the phenomena-in-context (Steinberg and Kincheloe 2010). Roberge (2011) too regarded critical hermeneutics as a theory of action responding to 'ideology, domination and violence' (p. 13), by developing, for example, participation and solidarity.

Steinberg with Kincheloe noted that the 'critical' addition to hermeneutics brings a concern with power and justice, and it requires the ethnographic researcher to seek to expose the "concealed motives that move events and shape everyday life" (2010, p. 148). Gadamer's notion of historical context now includes researcher self-awareness, the place and significance of culture in a research context, the construction of research design and the significance of human subjectivity and its construction. The voices of the subjugated are brought forth, and the hermeneutic circle engages the researcher in conversation with those voices, in the pursuit of deeper understanding. Not only are the voices raised and heard, but also they are located in their unique historical, socio-economic, political and cultural contexts.

Critical hermeneutics attempts to marry both the ontological project that Gadamer had in mind, and the epistemic project of critical theory. It signals particular ways to go about designing and conducting research. It represents a *bricolage* that draws widely on disciplines such as philosophy, sociology, psychology, history and economics, and on research scholarship. This of course includes phenomenology, Gadamerian hermeneutics, critical theory and many postmodern influences, such as gender studies, cultural studies, indigenous research, discourse theory, autoethnography and narrative. While this sounds like a random and eclectic mix, critical hermeneutics gets its coherence from its emphasis on analysis uncovering power and ideological influences, its focus on social justice outcomes, and the contextualised place of researcher, participants and research texts in their varied forms.

Post-Intentional Phenomenology

A final influence over the content and analysis in this book is attributable to the recent work of Vagle (2010, 2014). He has developed a critical dimension to phenomenology (2015), thus taking it beyond its descriptive/interpretive bounds, and his work adds dimensions not present in Gadamer's hermeneutics. He emphasises postmodern strategies such as journaling, and appeals to the postmodern concept of 'playing' with different approaches to disrupt customary flows of thought and action. It is especially Vagle's use of 'post-intentional phenomenology' that is worth grappling with, however. I do so as it provides some of the tools to enable a discussion of the meaningful ways in which practitioners within and across schools engage with the policy imperative to implement modern teaching and learning practice, characterised by flexible learning environments and digital technology.

Vagle (2014) described intentionality as the inseparable connectedness between subjects (people) and objects in the world (animate, inanimate, ideas). Intentionality signifies our meaningful connection to the world, *not* conscious planning to take action, or deliberate choice. Having an understanding of intentionality is central to engaging in research that has a phenomenological impetus. There are intentional relations 'that manifest and appear' (p. 27), and the researcher is attempting to grasp these, which appear to take the form of ways in which people are connected to other people, their workplaces and their work. The manifestation of these relationships may be evident in their feelings, such as hopefulness, despair, confusion, joy or resistance. The development Vagle posited, building on earlier phenomenological uses of intentionality, was to see intentionality as a meaningful connection people make to their world. In this sense, he prefers the notion of consciousness-*with*, rather than consciousness-*of*. The latter sense speaks, Vagle argued, of Western ego-centred rationality (and here we can see his postmodernism come into play). Clearly, Vagle's intent was to place "phenomenological philosophies in dialogue with aspects of post-structural philosophies" (p. 29).

The "dynamic intentional relationships that tie participants, the researcher, the produced text, and their positionalities together" (p. 30) yield understanding in the research process. For Vagle, "this positioning is only known through intentionality" (p. 30), and he thus gave significant emphasis to constant self-critique by researchers of their performance in the field, which he considered an ethical act. Vagle clearly indicated that the researcher is implicated in the findings of research, by virtue of being positioned. Just as research participants are constantly projecting forward into various relationships, so the researcher is projecting into the research relationship. Research findings are anything but final, being instead "de-centered as *multiple, partial and endlessly deferred*" (p. 31. Emphasis in the original).

The concept of intentionality is one I now attempt to integrate into my research, particularly in regard to making sense of ways my participants make sense of their lived experience and describe their meaningful connection to their lifeworld. Vagle's post-intentional approach is liberating insofar as it de-emphasises the notion of deriving universal or defined essences of meaning and understanding. Apart from recognising my own place in the research process, there is an opportunity to share and develop mutual understandings with my participants. Vagle furthermore suggested constant self-reflection, fundamental to which is the awareness researchers have of their own position.

A Personal Note

There are several influences that intersect with, and overlap, the concerns, themes, ideas and topics presented in this book. The obvious concerns relate to a question about what is happening to teachers' work in the midst of rapid changes. Change is, surely, one of life's constants, so I want to be careful from the outset not to create the impression that I think teachers and school leaders find themselves caught up in some kind of 'revolution', or that decades of idyll have been suddenly and rudely interrupted.

Like countless other teachers before (and many still today), I practiced my work in cellular rooms with fixed, uniform furniture. Indeed, some of my early teaching was carried out in classrooms not unlike the ones in which I spent my school years, replete with rows of the solid wooden desk/seat and hinged top and inkwell! More modern furniture allowed a little more flexibility, the overhead projector and slide projector (if you were a really progressive sort) may have been replaced with the data projector and interactive whiteboard, but, by and large, the single-cell room, with the teacher the focus of attention at the front, has remained largely unchanged.

In the past five years or so, in New Zealand, and in schools elsewhere in the world (in parts of Australia, in some Scandinavian, English and American contexts, for example), this picture has been undergoing considerable change, however. Contemporary architectural and furniture design has been implemented in the building of new schools and other educational institutions, and in the renovation of exiting buildings. 'Eco friendly' and 'smart' design principles have been utilised, combined with the provision of technology-rich infrastructure (such as ultra fast broadband and sophisticated servers) to create places of learning that have been dubbed 'modern', 'innovative', 'flexible', 'agile' and 'new generation' to name some of the more popular terms. In these spaces, much larger than single-cell rooms, multiple classes are combined and teachers work in teams. No longer is the sole teacher at the front the focus of attention (indeed, there is no longer a discernible 'front').

Moreover, the focus in education has been shifting steadily in this century from 'knowing' to 'learning'. Teachers are becoming 'facilitators', 'learning coaches' or 'learning advisors', and 'students' are 'learners'. These changes in the physical space of learning, the changes in the way we think and speak about teaching and learning, and the tools and artefacts which support teachers' work, are all bringing about significant demands on teachers to reconceptualise they way they think and carry out their work.

As a teacher educator, I have some interest in conveying to my students an understanding of what underlies these changes. I also have an interest in supporting them to develop some of the strategies they will find invaluable once they step into the classroom, particularly if it is to be a shared, collaborative space. Universities can work with, and support schools in their work. Research work with schools falls into this category, and as Freire said, as a researcher I have a responsibility to "communicate and proclaim what I discover" (1998, p. 35). Schools have a vested interest in the external perspectives researchers can provide on the nature and processes of their work.

Division of Content

In the following chapter, I will introduce readers to the specifics of the research process that has generated the findings on which the book's content reflects. To challenge the oft-heard comment that "there is no research" to support the shifts towards flexibility in architecture and pedagogy and digital strategies, Chapter 3 will consider a review of relevant literature informing the field on which my research inquiries into flexible, modern environments and pedagogy is based. Chapters 4–8 will present and discuss the findings, with reference to impacts on teachers' work, reflective practice and responses to the policy drive to implement '21st-century learning'. The book concludes with a chapter of 'take home lessons'.

References

Biesta, G. (2007). Why 'what works' won't work: Evidence–based practice and the democratic deficit in educational research. *Educational Theory, 57*(1), 1–22. doi:10.1111/j.1741-5446.2006.00241.x

Bohman, J. (2005). Critical theory. *Stanford Encyclopedia of Philosophy*. Retrieved from http://plato.stanford.edu/entries/critical-theory/

Denzin, N., & Lincoln, Y. (2005). The discipline and practice of qualitative research. In N. Denzin & Y. Lincoln (Eds.), *The SAGE handbook of qualitative research* (3rd ed., pp. 1–32). Thousand Oaks, CA: SAGE.

Farganis, J. (Ed.). (2011). *Readings in social theory: The classic tradition to post-modernism* (6th ed.). New York, NY: McGraw Hill.

Freire, P. (1998). *Pedagogy of freedom: Ethics, democracy and civic courage*. Lanham, MD: Rowman and Littlefield.

Gadamer, H.-G., Dutt, C., Most, G. W., Grieder, A., & von Westernhagen, D. (2001). *Gadamer in conversation: Reflections and commentary* (R. E. Palmer, Ed. and Trans.). New Haven, CT: Yale University Press.

Geuss, R. (1981). *The idea of a critical theory: Habermas and the Frankfurt School*. Cambridge, United Kingdom: Cambridge University Press.

Horkheimer, M. (2004). *Eclipse of reason* (revised ed.). London, United Kingdom/New York, NY: Continuum.

Kinsella, E. (2006). Hermeneutics and critical hermeneutics: Exploring possibilities within the art of interpretation. *Forum Qualitative Sozialforschung/Forum: Qualitative Social Research, 7*(3), Art. 19. Retrieved March 29, 2016 from http://www.qualitative-research.net/index.php/fqs/article/view/145/319

Mantzavinos, C. (2016). Hermeneutics. In E. N. Zalta (Ed.), *The Stanford encyclopaedia of philosophy* (Fall ed.). Retrieved from http://plato.stanford.edu/archives/fall2016/entries/hermeneutics/

Marcuse, H. (1998). Some social implications of modern technology. In D. Kellner (Ed.), *Technology, war and fascism: Collected papers of Herbert Marcuse* (Vol. 1, pp. 39–65). London, United Kingdom/New York, NY: Routledge (Original published in 1941).

Nair, P. (2011). The classroom is obsolete: It's time for something new. Retrieved from http://www.edweek.org/ew/articles/2011/07/29/37nair.h30.html

Ramberg, B., & Gjesdal, K. (2009). Hermeneutics. In E. N. Zalta (Ed.), *The Stanford encyclopaedia of philosophy* (Summer ed.). Retrieved from http://plato.stanford.edu/archives/sum2009/entries/hermeneutics/

Roberge, J. (2011). What is critical hermeneutics? *Thesis Eleven, 106*(1), 5–22. doi:10.1177/0725513611411682.

Saavedra, A. R., & Opfer, V. D. (2012). Learning 21st-century skills requires 21st-century teaching. *The Phi Delta Kappan, 94*(2), 8–13. Retrieved from http://www.jstor.org/stable/41763587

Steinberg, S., & Kincheloe, J. (2010). Power, emancipation, and complexity: Employing critical theory. *Power and Education, 2*, 140–151. doi:10.2304/power.2010.2.2.140

Steinberg, S., & Kincheloe, J. (2012). Employing the bricolage as critical research in science education. In B. J. Fraser, K. Tobin & C. J. McRobbie (Eds.), *Second international handbook of science education* [Springer international handbooks of education] (pp. 1485–1500). Dordrecht, The Netherlands: Springer. Retrieved from http://link.springer.com.ezproxy.aut.ac.nz/book/10.1007/978-1-4020-9041-7/page/1

Vagle, M. D. (2010). Re–framing Schön's call for a phenomenology of practice: a post–intentional approach. *Reflective Practice: International and Multidisciplinary Perspectives, 11*(3), 393–407. doi:10.1080/14623943.2010.487375.

Vagle, M. D. (2014). *Crafting phenomenological research*. Walnut Creek, CA: Left Coast Press.
Vagle, M. D. (2015). Curriculum as post-intentional phenomenological text: Working along the edges and margins of phenomenology using post-structuralist ideas. *Journal of Curriculum Studies, 47*(5), 594–612. doi:10.1080/00220272.2015.1051118.

Chapter 2
Presenting the Research

Good qualitative purpose statements contain information about the central phenomenon explored in the study, the participants in the study, and the research site. [They] also convey an emerging design and [use]...the language of qualitative inquiry... (Schwandt, 2007, cited in Creswell 2014, p. 124)

Introduction

My intention in writing this book is not simply to describe teaching and learning in the second decade of the 21st century. The two studies on which it is based, '21st-Century Learning' and 'Being a Teacher in the 21st Century', provided an opportunity to gain deeper insight to the rich tapestry forming the backdrop to teachers' work as it has been evolving in this, the second decade of the 21st century.

Around 2011, I began to pay attention to the strident and zealous clamour around the concept of '21st-century learning'. I was somewhat sceptical (mainly because missionary zeal tends to cloud and conflate multiple concepts and sweeps up adherents in an uncritical maelstrom). I began drilling into this concept philosophically, presenting a conference paper in 2011 that was eventually published in 2015 (Benade 2015a). The links between 21st-century learning and *The New Zealand Curriculum* (Ministry of Education 2007) can be seen in its general vision for schooling of "young people...who will seize the opportunities offered by new knowledge and technologies to secure a sustainable social, cultural, economic, and environmental future for our country...[and]... who will be confident, connected, actively involved, and lifelong learners." (p. 8). Further, one of the values to be encouraged in New Zealand schooling is "innovation, inquiry, and curiosity, [encouraged] by thinking critically, creatively, and reflectively" (p. 10). Among the 'key competencies' are included 'thinking', 'understanding language, symbols and texts' and 'managing self'. Within these, the following stand out: students will be "problem-solvers [who] actively seek, use and create knowledge"; who will "confidently use ICT...to access and provide information and to communicate with others"; and who will be "enterprising, resourceful, reliable, and resilient...[able to]... establish personal goals, make plans, [and] manage

© Springer Nature Singapore Pte Ltd. 2017
L. Benade, *Being a Teacher in the 21st Century*,
DOI 10.1007/978-981-10-3782-5_2

projects" (p. 12). A striking feature of this curriculum document is its limited reference to teachers and teaching, though there is reference to 'teaching as inquiry', which "requires that teachers inquire into the impact of their teaching on their students." (p. 35). In support of this aim, a three-step model is provided, and serves as a tool of reflective practice.

Furthering a personal interest in, and a critical focus on, teachers and teachers' work, with financial support from the Faculty of Culture and Society of the Auckland University of Technology, I framed a study in 2013, guided by this question: **What is the influence of the concept of '21st-century learning' on reflective practice, pedagogy and leadership in a selection of New Zealand schools?** My funding proposal drew attention to the features of the concept of '21st-century learning' in New Zealand schools including the use of digital technologies and the emerging development of flexible teaching and learning spaces. There was some evidence in research literature for a claim that new pedagogies are required to support the widening and deepening use of technologies, which, in turn, would require teachers to take up an increasingly critical (self-reflective) orientation (Wright 2010). There was an associated likelihood of students becoming more motivated, engaged and able to engage in critical and collaborative learning (2010). The intention of the project at this stage (2013/4) was to critically appraise the claim that the introduction of digital tools and working in flexible spaces brings about changed pedagogy, and, in particular, critical practitioner reflection. To achieve this purpose, the lived professional experiences of teachers and school leaders in a small number of case study schools were considered (see Benade et al. 2014; Benade 2015b, c). Data was gathered in the field by interviewing 23 participants selected from six schools. In addition, a focus group was held, consisting of a further four participants not associated with the six participant schools.

In 2015, the study focus developed, with this guiding question: **What is it to be a teacher in the twenty-first century?** This study (with further university financial support) continued to focus on the work of teachers and the strategic actions of leaders at a selection of New Zealand schools. As in the earlier study, this was a qualitative study. It sought to explore, interpret and develop greater understanding of modern teaching and learning practices, and the transitions teachers and school leaders make as they grapple with the challenge of 21st-century learning, the development of flexible learning spaces and the rapidly changing nature of knowledge and learning in a digital age. Teachers and leaders were selected from among the participant schools to the earlier study. Data was gathered through interviews, focus groups and observations of teachers working in flexible spaces and/or implementing BYOD (Bring Your Own Device) and/or e-Learning. The intent was to continue to encourage these participants to explore and reflect on their lived professional experiences in the context of 21st-century learning, but now with the focus being on their evolving understanding and experience of leading and managing their transition to modern teaching and learning practices. It was also important to understand the challenges and obstacles they were encountering in this transition process, and how they were sustaining fundamental pedagogical change.

Design and Participants

The '21st-century Learning' study was designed as a multiple case study, due to the likelihood (as will be seen shortly) of what Yin (2003) had identified as complex and highly contextualised research settings, with multiple uncontrollable variables. Of particular interest was the view of Ary et al. (2006), who saw in case study designs the opportunity to understand how and why individuals respond to changes in their environment. Stake (2006) advised against single researchers working on multiple case studies, given their complexity. In this study, I enlisted the support of a colleague (Andrew Gibbons), who helped with interviews and data analysis, and subsequently contracted the support of two others (Michele Gardener and Christoph Teschers) who undertook literature review work.

A purposive selection (choice of specific participants who display specific characteristics) was made to ensure there were six participating schools that represented a range of deciles[1] (SES) and sectors (primary and secondary). Additionally, school orientation was taken into account: the schools were either:

(a) overtly future-oriented[2];
(b) shifting from traditional cellular spaces and pedagogies to flexible spaces and pedagogies influenced by e-Learning and future-focused concepts, or
(c) retaining the use of traditional spaces and more conventional pedagogies (which could range from teacher-centred to learner-centred).

The selected mix of schools in orientation, deciles and sectors was segmented as follows:

(a) was represented by two high–decile (affluent neighbourhoods) state schools, one of which was a primary (elementary) school, one of which a secondary (high) school;
(b) was represented by two schools, one mid–high decile state-integrated primary,[3] one low-decile state primary; and
(c) was represented by two schools, one mid–low-decile state primary and one mid-decile state secondary school.

---

[1]The 'decile' rating system has been used in New Zealand as a way of allocating funding equitably. Based on a number of measures, schools are rated 'low' in areas of greatest socio-economic deprivation; 'high' in affluent areas. Per capita funding is greatest to low-decile schools. The system is being reviewed at the present time, and is slated for imminent replacement.

[2]While the New Zealand Curriculum refers to 'future focussed' concepts such as sustainability, citizenship, enterprise and globalisation (2007, p. 39), the term used here indicates a school established with clear focus on the principles of 21st-century learning in an innovative context.

[3]New Zealand schools that were previously private (notably, but not solely, Catholic schools), which are integrated into the state system, thus attracting state support (particularly teachers' pay, but also decile funding). These schools continue to have the right to advance their 'special character'.

Table 2.1 Participant schools by sector and classification: 21st-century learning study

School	Sector	Classification
School A1	Primary	'Futures oriented', built by modern learning environment (MLE) design
School A2	Primary	Blends single-cell classes and MLE
School A3	Primary	Single-cell classes; limited ICT use across curriculum
School B1	Secondary	'Futures oriented', built by modern learning environment (MLE) design
School B2	Secondary	Overt BYOD approach across curriculum
School B3	Secondary	Single-cell classes; limited ICT use across curriculum

Table 2.1 below captures this information in a different format.

The design allowed for the 'School 2' case to be either a school upgrading single-cell rooms to flexible learning spaces, or be a school that had recently introduced BYOD. This was so in case B2. In either kind of school, significant pedagogical shifts by teachers would be required.

Individual participants were also purposively selected, specifically the principal of each school, the head of ICT or e-Learning, one long-serving teacher and one recently appointed teacher (1–2 years of service) from each school. The reasoning here related to questions of strategic leadership and management of change; the demands of ICT and/or e-Learning on staff; and gaining the perspectives of teachers from opposite ends of the experience continuum.

Data was gathered from one-hour interviews, conducted with the participants. Although the original design allowed for focus groups to be formed from 12 invited participants made up of two teachers from each of the six schools, this did not materialise. On reflection, Stake (2006) was correct in suggesting that a multiple case study is not practicable for one person. Nevertheless, somewhat serendipitously, a group of individuals not linked to the six schools, but with an interest in the project, agreed to participate in a focus group. A further participant agreed to an individual interview (see Table 2.2).

The interviews and the focus group were audio-recorded and transcribed by a contracted transcriber. Themes emerged in the process of interviewing and as transcripts were analysed. The first stage of this analysis utilised NVivo software. At this stage, I did not seriously make use of field notes, and was not yet keeping any kind of journal.

The 'Being a Teacher in the 21st Century' study reflects a methodological shift from focussing on finding patterns and differences among a number of participant schools to evaluating and understanding how individual participants across the schools find themselves in relationship with 21st-century learning. This evaluation takes into account 21st-century learning as an exemplar of macro-level, global governance (specifically the OECD), and as a national education policy commitment at the meso or national level. In the New Zealand context, this means considering the commitment of the New Zealand Ministry of Education to introduce flexible learning spaces (or, Innovative Learning Environments [ILE]) to all New

Table 2.2 Individual participants not linked to case study schools: 21st-century learning study

Role	Comments
Ex-principal	Was a recent leader of a futures oriented secondary school
Consultant to schools	Engages with schools on e-Learning
Consultant to schools	Engages with schools on e-Learning
Principal	Leads a traditional low-decile regional primary school

Zealand schools by 2021 (MOE 2011). In addition, and in line with the promotion of ICT in The New Zealand Curriculum, is the stated intent that schools adopt digital technology and teachers acquire e-Learning expertise. An evaluative focus at the micro-level of the classroom and school allows for description and judgement of actual practices, including making some judgments about school policy intent as expressed in documentary evidence and the voices of participants. This evaluation of practice was therefore considered through the lenses of pedagogical principles that can be considered essential to the development of '21st century skills', such as: personalisation, interdisciplinary and project-based inquiry, student direction or agency and collaborative practices (Nair 2011; Pearlman 2010).

The participant schools to the 'Being a Teacher' study were Schools A1, A2, B1 and B2 (see Table 2.1), as these are schools committed to engaging the policy impetus that schools develop modern, technologically rich, pedagogies.[4] My focus, influenced by my reading of Vagle (2014), was not to describe or explain teacher (and school) practices as much as to establish the intentional relationships of the participants towards each other, their schools, to the policy imperatives, to digital technology, to flexible learning spaces and even to me, the researcher. How do they find themselves where they are, and how do they make sense of what they *are* or are *becoming*? I wanted to examine how these participants respond to, and make sense of, the commitment to 21st-century learning, to the process of transition from more conventional and traditional approaches to teaching and learning, and to the suggestion they re-fashion themselves as teachers for the 21st century.

As in the earlier phase of study, School B2 was again approached as it was in the early phase of BYOD implementation. It was likely that its teachers were living through the experience of implementing a significant new strategy, which, as suggested above, would be placing demands on their pedagogy and sense of professional identity.

Teachers at all four schools were approached, with the support of the principals, to participate in the research, which in this second phase, involved several observations across the second term of 2015. In addition, teachers were asked to commit to informal debriefing discussions. The teachers at all four schools were invited to a focus group at each school as well. These were run at the conclusion of the observation phase. The principals also agreed to be interviewed.

---

[4]My use of 'pedagogy' refers to teachers *thinking* about their work and their actual *classroom-related work*.

Data was gathered from 31 observations across the four school sites, ranging from 45–100 min each. In addition, 16 debriefing interviews, of 5 min–1 h were conducted with a range of teachers. In later chapters, these are denoted as 'DB'. All four principals were interviewed, and these are denoted as 'IV' in later chapters. Where data is used from the 2013 interviews, these are denoted as 'IV 2013'. Four staff focus groups (one at each school) of an hour were held, and these are denoted as 'FG'. In the case of School B2, I ran focus group sessions of between 45 min and an hour with a group of Year 9 and Year 10 students, and one with a selection of parents. Although not originally planned, a student survey was run at School B2. Once again, the overall task was considerable, and I thus once more invited my colleague, Andrew Gibbons, to assist at one of the school sites with observations, a principal interview and the staff focus group. Some literature review work was contracted to one of my Ph.D. students, Alastair Wells, and I contracted a transcriber. Table 2.3 below summarises this data gathering.

The interviews, informal debriefing discussions and the focus groups were audio-recorded and transcribed by a contracted transcriber. Again, I used NVivo, and consciously tried to develop the idea of whole-part-whole analysis advocated by Vagle (2014). Once more, as in the previous study, themes emerged inductively, or through the multiple processes of observation, discussion, interviewing and as transcripts were analysed. A further addition to the design was my intention to create field notes. Towards the end of the '21st-Century Learning' study, I had begun to experiment with a journal in the form of electronic notes that followed the suggestion of Hughes (2006). I voice recorded personal reflections—field notes after observations and discussions during the 'Being a Teacher' study, and framed these according to the categories suggested by Hughes (2006). In these reflections, I was aware of Vagle's perspective on self-reflexive 'bridling' in which the researcher's intentionality is held in rein, allowing the researcher to be open to the intentional relationships that always already exist in the lives of the participants. These voice recordings were also transcribed, and thus became evidence on record to be utilised in the analysis.

The participants included some of those involved in the first phase of the research. In an earlier iteration of this book, and in published articles elsewhere, I attempted to humanise and personalise the participants by assigning them pseudonyms. In response to reviews of this book, and the possibility of participants potentially being identified by readers who correctly guess which schools participated, I have resorted to de-identification of the teachers. It is not possible to completely de-identify all participants, as some are identified by virtue of their roles. All participants have, however, had the opportunity to review Chaps. 4–8.

A final point about design: one of the fundamental difficulties of this design (and a weakness, some will doubtless point out) is the inclusion of a traditional single-cell school among the schools with flexible learning environments. Indeed, when I told a colleague about the various schools, he thought that, in fact, there were two studies—one that was evaluating BYOD at the traditional school, and one that was evaluating flexible learning spaces at the other three. While I can see why he would think along those lines, to do so misses the point, which I will make here,

Table 2.3 Field data summary: being a teacher study

School	Sector	Classification	Data gathering
School A1	Primary	'Futures oriented', built by modern learning environment (MLE) design	3 teacher interviews 2 principal interviews 6 observations 1 staff focus group
School A2	Primary	Blends single-cell classes and MLE	1 teacher interview 2 principal interviews 6 observations 1 staff focus group
School B1	Secondary	'Futures oriented', built by modern learning environment (MLE) design	2 teacher interviews 2 principal interviews 8 observations 1 staff focus group
School B2	Secondary	Overt BYOD approach across curriculum	3 teacher interviews 1 principal interview 11 observations 1 staff focus group 2 student focus groups 1 parent focus group

by repeating my purpose: this study sought to explore, interpret and develop greater understanding of modern teaching and learning practices, and the transitions teachers and school leaders make as they grapple with the challenge of 21st-century learning, the development of flexible learning spaces and the rapidly changing nature of knowledge and learning in a digital age. The implementation of a BYOD policy and the development of associated e-Learning pedagogies by teachers is as much part of what it means to be a teacher today, as I write in 2016, as is the implementation of flexible learning spaces and the development of pedagogies now associated with those spaces. I will now say something about ethics, and then introduce the four sites of investigation.

Ethics

The two phases of research, namely the '21st-Century Learning' and 'Being a Teacher', each required separate applications to the Auckland University of Technology Ethics Committee (AUTEC). Challenges included the likelihood of my knowing the principals, and the recruitment of a purposive sample (see Table 2.1) of participants in specific people job roles, thus requiring some kind of privileged access (through the principal), and an 'all or nothing' approach (all four participants at each school were required to complete the research).

A challenge in the second phase related to School B2, where classes are typically cohort classes of around 30 taught in a single cell by one teacher. The research focus here was on the delivery of BYOD in Years 9 and 10, thus the principal's support was required as the invitation would be delivered to a particular group of teachers rather than the whole staff, as was the case at Schools A1, A2 and B1. In those schools, the informational material and invitation was made available to all the teachers, who could self-select whether to be involved.

A more significant problem, requiring much negotiation with both schools and more specifically AUTEC, was around the prospect of my engaging with underage students during my observations. As a registered New Zealand teacher, my presence in the classroom does not a pose a legal problem; but do students become incidental participants (there by necessity)? What is the status of any informal conversations I might have with them? My copious parental consent and student assent documentation, was in my view, forbidding. As part of my commitment to a robust ethics process, I nevertheless engaged the staff of all four schools in looking at my various ethics documents and my observational protocol. Of some interest was the attitude of the schools—especially the three with flexible spaces, which had the view that students are so accustomed to visitors, and talking with visitors, they could see no value in asking for these permissions. Indeed, their view was that such permissions would *raise* concerns, not quell them. Several teachers suggested the research could be tainted or corrupted by students assuming a different orientation towards me as the documentation could imply something intriguing or 'dangerous' in what I was doing.

Further discussion with AUTEC clarified this matter, and we agreed that I was not in the schools to focus on the students, but on the teachers. I could, however, be 'chatting casually' with students without voice recording. As it transpired, whenever I initiated these 'chats', I always first asked if I could do so, and if I could write my impressions after we had talked—so, there was no recording of data in the face-to-face situation with students, and field notes were written subsequently. The focus groups at Holyoake, not part of the original design, are covered by an amendment to my original ethics application.

The Four Schools

In Tables 2.1 and 2.3, I have referred to these sites as School A1, A2, B1 and B2. Subsequently, in other publications, and in the earlier iteration of this book, I gave the schools fictitious names. Despite my decision to de-identify (and thereby, depersonalise) my participants, I have decided to hold fast to the names of the schools. These institutions, like the people who work and learn in them, are living entities. The notion of materiality is one I will refer to in Chapters Three and Six, to illustrate the idea that we should not think of physical artefacts in the world as somehow passive and waiting for human intervention. To some extent, physical artefacts, like buildings, have agency, and have a way of acting on their inhabitants; thus, the schools will have names!

Innovation Primary

Innovation Primary (School A1) is a Year 1–8 state primary school, established in 2013, and designed according to innovative educational design principles. It is located in a rapidly growing suburban area.

Angelus School

Angelus School (School A2) is a Year 1–6 state-integrated special character school, established in 2010. It is located in a rapidly growing suburban area. Angelus School has a blend of traditional single-cell rooms (one class, one teacher), and two flexible spaces accommodating three classes and three teachers in each.

Millennial College

Millennial College (School B1) is a state secondary college, located in a rapidly growing suburban area, established in 2014. In 2015, when the 'Being a Teacher' study took place, its roll was made up of only Year 9 and 10 classes. The roll will continue to grow as the foundation cohort moves through senior secondary, eventually to Year 13.

Holyoake College

Holyoake College (School B2) is a Year 9 to Year 13 state co-educational school, established in 1970. Its current, multi-ethnic enrolment is 1755 students and it has a staff of 105 teachers. It is located in a long-established suburban area.

Conclusion

The critical development of new knowledge is urgently required in the area of current developments around learning environments in New Zealand, where the subject is somewhat under-researched and beset by negative media commentary and ill-informed anecdotal opinion amongst many teachers and parents. In the area of initial teacher education, fresh and informed perspectives will support the preparation of student teachers faced with quickly changing working contexts. This chapter has, by way of introduction to the later content of this book, given a sense of the initial studies that have provided the data on which this book is based. Still with the objective in mind of challenging the notion that 'there is no research', the following chapter provides a literature review. The review also serves the purpose of highlighting specific themes on which to base provocations and raise areas of further interest to researchers, particularly once various findings are considered in the framework of critical discussion.

References

Ary, D., Jacobs, L., Razavieh, A., & Sorensen, C. (2006). *Introduction to research in education* (7th ed.). Belmont, CA: Thomson Wadsworth.
Benade, L. (2015a). Bits, bytes and dinosaurs: Using Levinas and Freire to address the concept of 'twenty-first century learning'. *Educational Philosophy and Theory, 47*(9), 935–948.
Benade, L. (2015b). Teachers' critical reflective practice in the context of twenty-first century learning. *Open Review of Educational Research, 2*(1), 42–54. doi:10.1080/23265507.2014.998159
Benade, L. (2015c). Teaching as inquiry: Well intentioned, but fundamentally flawed. *New Zealand Journal of Educational Studies, 50*(1), 107–120. doi:10.1007/s40841-015-0005-0
Benade, L., Gardner, M., Teschers, C., & Gibbons, A. (2014). 21st Century learning in New Zealand: Leadership insights and perspectives. *New Zealand Journal of Educational Leadership, Policy and Practice, 29*(2), 47–60.
Creswell, J. (2014). *Research design: Qualitative, quantitative, and mixed methods approaches* (4th ed.). Los Angeles, CA: SAGE.
Hughes, C. (2006). *Developing reflexivity in research*. Retrieved April 16, 2017 from http://www2.warwick.ac.uk/fac/soc/sociology/staff/hughes/researchprocess/
Ministry of Education. (2007). *The New Zealand curriculum*. Wellington, New Zealand: Learning Media Limited. Available from http://nzcurriculum.tki.org.nz/The-New-Zealand-Curriculum
Ministry of Education. (2011). *The New Zealand school property strategy 2011–2021*. Retrieved from http://www.education.govt.nz/assets/Documents/Primary-Secondary/Property/SchoolPropertyStrategy201121.pdf

References

Nair, P. (2011). The classroom is obsolete: It's time for something new. Retrieved from http://www.edweek.org/ew/articles/2011/07/29/37nair.h30.html

Pearlman, B. (2010). Designing new learning environments to support 21st century skills. In J. Bellanca & R. Brandt (Eds.), *21st century skills: Rethinking how students learn* (pp. 117–148). Bloomington, IN: Solution Tree Press.

Stake, R. E. (2006). *Multiple case study analysis*. New York, NY/London, United Kingdom: The Guilford Press.

Vagle, M. D. (2014). *Crafting phenomenological research*. Walnut Creek, CA: Left Coast Press.

Wright, N. (2010). e-Learning and Implications for New Zealand Schools: A Literature Review. Report to the Ministry of Education. Waikato, New Zealand: The University of Waikato. Retrieved from https://www.educationcounts.govt.nz/publications/e-Learning/e-learning-and-implications-for-new-zealand-schools-a-literature-review/background.

Yin, R. K. (2003). *Case study research: Design and methods* (Vol. 5). Thousand Oaks, CA: Sage Publications.

Chapter 3
The Future Is Now: What '21st-Century Learning' Means for Teaching

…students learn best when they are engaged…students can now do most of the work…21st century knowledge and skills not only build upon core content knowledge, but also include information and communication skills, thinking and problem-solving skills, interpersonal and self-directional skills, and the skills to utilize 21st century tools, such as information and communication technologies (Pearlman 2010, p. 119).

Introduction

Reviewing and contextualising the terminology of 21st-century learning is a process I began to engage with in some earlier work (Benade 2015a, b, c; Benade et al. 2014). The selection of literature in this chapter attempts to provide a fuller understanding of the wider context for considering learning environments, including a consideration of practices that are emerging in relation to the evolution of learning environments, particularly in New Zealand.

What follows here then is a narrative of an educational discourse strongly influenced by emerging notions of an unknowable future, located in a rapidly moving period of digitisation. It is a narrative that attempts to capture the flavour of the notion of '21st-century learning', and what this might mean for pedagogy. Two key manifestations of the phenomenon of 21st-century learning are the penetration of digital devices into schools, and the changing face of school building design. Both manifestations challenge pedagogy in specific ways. They challenge teachers to be more reflective in their practice and also challenge school leaders to address some important change-related issues.

Futures Discourse and the Status of Knowledge

A radically and dramatically altered world landscape has aided the development of various 'futures' discourses, which unsettle previously held views of knowledge and its status in ordinary life. Challenging issues, such as climate change, global threats to peace and stability, advancing and rapidly changing digital technology, now influence every aspect of daily life. Traditional hierarchies are radically undermined in a world shifting from massive economies of scale to economies emphasising the personal and in which individuals potentially have the capability and the capacity to create their own content, services and experiences. (Miller et al. 2008). In this decentred world, personalisation is the key characteristic of a digital age, in which each person is a content-creator, social networker and designer of uniquely tailored 'walls' and 'feeds'.

University-level knowledge and content is available to anyone with a reliable Internet connection and a mobile device. As a result, argue Beetham and Sharpe (2013), disciplinary knowledge has been displaced by provisional, and culturally constructed, 'knowledge' that meets the interests of its users. Unsurprisingly, then, notions of knowledge are evolving, and knowledge is differently conceived: There is "the '20th century' idea of knowledge as content or 'stuff', and the 21st century view of it as something that *does* stuff" (Bolstad and Gilbert 2012, p. 31. Emphasis in the original). In this context, the 'immensely successful' (Miller et al. 2008, p. 9) learning institutions of the industrial age find their traditional authority and control over the definition and certification of knowledge is significantly challenged. Nevertheless, schools and universities continue to treat knowledge as a sealed system, rather than as reflective of the multiplicity and plurality characteristic of 21st century life (O'Brien et al. 2013).

The views of knowledge associated with futures discourses emerge from strong arguments questioning the very assumptions with which we view education and its place in society and role in economic development (Bolstad and Gilbert 2012; O'Brien et al. 2013). These assumptions may be related to the persistence of traditional notions of schools as factories (for example, Bolstad and Gilbert 2012), producing docile wageworkers unable to think creatively or critically. This assessment-driven model emphasises "standardization, learning outcomes, and performance indicators" (O'Brien et al. 2013, p. 50). As a result, individuals emerge from the system able only to conform to change, rather than self-initiate change, a requirement (it is argued) of living in a digital age.

In sharp contrast with these views are 'social realist' arguments favouring strong disciplinary boundaries, and regarding the integration of knowledge areas as weakening those boundaries (for example, see McPhail 2016; McPhail and Rata 2015; Rata 2012; Young 2008, 2012, 2013; Young and Muller 2010). These theorists prioritise epistemic or disciplinary knowledge over social knowledge. Social realist theory seeks to reveal how power relationships influence epistemic knowledge. Consequently, social realists reject curriculum reform premised on futures discourse and knowledge economy discourses which seek to dilute epistemic knowledge with key competencies, skills and statements of values (Benade 2014).

The social realist perspective may seem to be an echo of entrenched educational practices that bedevil educational reform, including the conservatism inherent in traditional building infrastructure and practices such as written examinations (Leicester et al. 2009). This critique fails to take account of the nuances of the social realist perspective in education, however. It is not a perspective that seeks a return to Victorian conceptions of education (Rata 2012), but is one calling for a recognition that children come to school to learn what they do not already know, rather than building on knowledge developed in the home, church or tribe (Rata 2012; Young 2012). Furthermore, the social realist perspective is motivated by a concern for social justice, specifically the idea that the steady dilution of epistemic knowledge advocated by futurists and constructivists denies the socially and economically marginalised access to 'powerful knowledge' (Young 2012). It is not as clear, however, that competing curriculum discourses emphasising social and networked knowledge, underpinned by competencies, are as decisive regarding social inequalities (Benade 2014). What is clear, though, is that futures discourse does not reject knowledge *per se*, but rather its pursuit for intrinsic reasons, preferring that knowledge connects with the extrinsic purposes of its users.

Character of the Digital Age

On reflection, there may be said to be few other developments that have had the impact on all facets of education, in the past half century at least, of advances in digital technology. In this context of fast change, terms such as 'digital revolution', 'Net Gen' and 'digital natives' are touted in relation to education and technology. It is important, however, to place these terms (and others) in perspective, rather than fall into what Bennett and Maton (2010) term a 'certainty-complacency spiral', whereby the glib use of these terms is passed off as fact, when they are no more than conventional wisdom. In what follows, I want briefly to consider two dimensions in particular, namely the charge of technological determinism, and the notion of digital natives.

Technological Determinism

The danger associated with the terms suggested above, is to greatly exaggerate their potential effect or the influence of digital technology on education. Jones (2011) made this point when suggesting that policymakers are wont to take up into policy the perceived effects of technology on social (or educational) change, if they believe there is a linear relationship between these. Jones questioned whether the link is that simple. Talk of a 'revolution' encourages a 'moral panic', leading to policy imperatives that put current pedagogical practices into a state of upheaval (Bennett and Maton 2010; Helsper and Eynon 2010; Jones 2011). One such example is the shift to notions of 'collaborative learning' (discussed later), which is aided by the collaborative 'sharing' characteristic of social media. Jones makes the point that collaborative learning and participatory teaching are not the preserve of the digital age, but existed well before this period. His critical point, however, is that technological determinism is evident in the crude suggestion that collaborative learning arises from the affordances of digital media, or that rapid changes brought on by technology demand flexibility in planning and in developing relationships across teaching teams, with students and with the wider community.

The notion of 'affordances' provides a context in which to think more carefully about the possibility of technological determinism. James Gibson coined affordance theory in 1979, in his book, *The Ecological Approach to Visual Perception*. He theorised a world of many objects, devices and tools, which can be used by people to get things done, to make life easier, to perform tasks and so on, but only so long as the user perceives the object in that way. Thus direct perception is critical. So, objects represent affordances if we recognise them as such, and have use for them. Some objects have multiple uses, such as a chair, which can be used for standing on, or for defence against an intruder (Dant 2005). Affordances can also be understood to be the inherent qualities of material items that lie dormant until used to their potential. Therefore, it may be possible to argue, as Dant (2005) does, that material objects in the world of users have the potential to shape the way people act and behave. What he rejected, though, is the idea that this agency of material artefacts is anything more than limited, as artefacts fail to "demonstrate sufficient autonomous intention or reflective awareness to be equivalent to human agency" (p. 60).

Digital Natives

Possibly 'digital native' is an over-used concept (Green et al. 2005). Coined by Prensky (2011), who seemingly contrasted the younger generation of 'natives' with the older generation of 'digital immigrants', he has latterly (2011) defended his position, claiming only that there exists a new generation of young people more at ease with technology than the older generation (such as teachers). He further defended himself by rejecting the suggestion that being a 'digital immigrant' is a proxy for making no effort to learn; or being a 'native' means having ready-packaged digital knowledge and competence. Still, the damage seems to have been done, and this simple bifurcation persists.

It was thus argued by Helsper and Eynon (2010), that it is an error to crudely link digital expertise to age or generation, and that instead, "breadth of use, experience, self-efficacy and education are just as, if not more, important than age in explaining how people become digital natives" (p. 504). The consequences of persisting with a deterministic deployment of crude analyses for education are problematic, as teachers may assume greater digital knowledge on the part of their students than is warranted by this evidence.

The quality of student digital use is also of concern. While access to technology by young people has increased, their deep-level engagement with technology use beyond communication and social networking is not as widespread as some may argue (Bennett and Maton 2010). To some extent, this is reflected in the findings of the OECD *Students on Line* report of the 2009 Programme for International Student Assessment (PISA) results (2011). Thus, there remains a valid role for schools and teachers to contribute to student learning in this area. Moreover, the notion of what learning might look like in the 21st century should consider more than just digital technology.

21st-Century Learning

Skills Students Need for the 21st Century

Research conducted by the Organisation for Economic Cooperation and Development (OECD 2003) went some way to defining a broad range of competencies (dispositions and skills). The so-called 'DeSeCo' research envisaged three groups of 'key competencies': using tools interactively; interacting in heterogeneous groups; and acting autonomously. Thinking was (appropriately) at the centre of this framework. A dominant argument was that higher order thinking and processing skills were becoming essential as international economies and workplaces evolved away from industrial manufacture to knowledge-based activities (Dumont and Istance 2010). Underpinning the DeSeCo research was the realisation that such changes demanded flexible and adaptable adults, and the obvious place to begin was the school system. Within three years of the publication of DeSeCo, the revised New Zealand Curriculum detailed 'key competencies', namely thinking, understanding language, symbols and texts, managing self, participating and contributing and relating to others (Ministry of Education [MOE] 2007). On closer analysis, the strong links between this statement of key competencies and that outlined in the DeSeCo report are plainly evident. While these remain (for now) beyond the reach of formal assessment regimes, their significance is unequivocally stated: "The key competencies take account of the vast changes in society, work, knowledge, and technology that have occurred since education systems were established" (MOE 2014, "Why do key competencies matter?").

The interest in developing '21st-century skills' now has considerable international reach. Ananiadou and Claro (2009) reported on a 2009 questionnaire of 17 OECD member states that asked specific questions concerning 21st century skills. An 'overwhelming majority' (p. 12) of the respondent countries indicated specific coverage of these skills, either in terms of formal, regulatory documents, guidelines or specific intent to formalise such coverage. Among the responses to this particular survey were those that distinguished generic skills and competencies from specific ICT skills.

Referring to the Asia-Pacific region, Anderson (2010) suggested: "Learning and innovation skills are what separate students who are prepared for increasingly complex life and work environments in the 21st century and those who are not" (p. 25). Related to these skills are the commonly mentioned ones of creativity, critical thinking, communication and collaboration. Given the ubiquity of digital devices and the pervasive presence of the Internet in daily life in the 21st century (notably in the developed world, it should be added), it comes as no surprise that several skills and competencies relate to media and information literacy—also referred to as 'digital literacy'.

In the New Zealand context, definitive statements concerning the nature of skills for the 21st century appear in several state documents, notably The New Zealand Curriculum (MOE 2007), where the Foreword by Karen Sewell, then Secretary for Education, commended the curriculum as "a framework designed to ensure that all young New Zealanders are equipped with the knowledge, competencies, and values they will need to be successful citizens in the twenty-first century." (p. 4). This document envisions young New Zealanders as "confident, connected, actively involved, and lifelong learners" (p. 8), who reflect the competencies mentioned above, namely thinking, using language, symbols and texts, managing self, relating to others and participating and contributing (in communities, for example). In particular, references to self-management in the curriculum allude to instances of student agency, where agentic behaviour includes students being able to "set and monitor personal goals, manage time frames, arrange activities, and reflect on and respond to ideas they encounter" (p. 38).

More recently, statements about the ideal 21st century learner have emanated from reference groups convened by Nikki Kaye, the Associate Minister of Education under the current National-led government. These were the *Inquiry Into 21st century Learning Environments and Digital Literacy* (New Zealand Parliament 2012) and the independent *Future-Focused Learning in Connected Communities* (21st Century Learning Reference Group 2014). These two documents, narrowly focused on the digital dimension of learning, nevertheless reveal a clear policy intent. In the former case, the Education and Science Committee took 21st-century learning "to mean the changes to teaching and learning in schools that result from digital technology" (New Zealand Parliament 2012, p. 9). In the latter, a successful 21st century citizen was proposed to be one equipped to deal with "a lifetime of new technology and change…[a]…competent digital learner…[who can]…deal proactively with a changing world…[possessing]…digital…and media literacy… [and]…the social competence to practise safe, legal, and ethical behaviours" (21st Century Learning Reference Group 2014, p. 9). A common element amongst the various documents reviewed here is lifelong learning.

Lifelong Learning

Learning does not cease at adulthood, nor is it confined to the formal setting of the classroom, but can happen in non-formal and informal settings (Dumont and Istance 2010). Learning, it is argued, must continue throughout life, ensuring adults are well prepared for rapid socio-economic changes. For example, the European Commission claimed *"lifelong learning must accompany a successful transition to a knowledge-based economy and society"* (Commission of the European Communities 2000, p. 3. Emphasis in the original). Europe's leaders, at the outset of the twenty-first century, thus linked an employable and adaptable workforce to European economic competitiveness. For its part, the New Zealand Ministry of Education has firmly committed itself to ensuring that schools achieve the aim of The New Zealand Curriculum: "Young people who will be confident, connected, actively involved, lifelong learners" (2007, p. 7).

The knowledge economy requires schools and universities to shift their emphasis from presenting finite and defined courses of study that have clear end-points (such as school-leaving certificates or graduation) to providing 'learners' with the skills and competencies that empower them to be 'lifelong' learners. The key competencies and development of various soft skills and dispositions are thus integral to developing lifelong learners and their passion for ongoing learning.

The trend to lifelong learning is accompanied by shifting responsibility from society to the individual. Knowledge becomes capital in the hands of individuals who are now more or less desirable by virtue of their knowledge, adaptability, flexibility and portable skills. This support for human capital theory, popularised in the 1960s, suggests a link between personal investment in education and earning power, an idea appealing to politicians and policymakers (Brown et al. 2011): "Everyone could become a capitalist, whether or not people knew it (or liked it), by investing in themselves through learning" (p. 17). These authors have, however, roundly critiqued the link between 'learning and earning', demonstrating that the empirical evidence merely upholds the idea that the rich get richer. In the global auction for talent, an aristocracy persists, and appeals to rising average wages make a poor argument for increasing levels of education (2011).

Learning at the Centre

Dumont and Istance (2010) link the centring of 'the learner' to such developments as the increasing ubiquity of a digital and electronic culture, with its attendant influence on creating non-hierarchical and personalised experiences of the world, and the development of the 'knowledge society', a trend that began to be evident in the late 1990s. Referring to the centring of the learner in educational discourse, Biesta (2014) has coined the term, 'learnification'. He noted:

'Learnification' refers to a fairly recent development in which the language of education has been taken over by a language of learning. As a result, the emphasis in the discussion has shifted from questions about the content of education to questions about process, for example, in the now ubiquitous idea of 'learning to learn' or in the influence that so-called '21st [century] skills' are having on curricula in many countries... (p. 1)

Dumont and Istance (2010) further identified the centring of 'the learner' and 'learning' in formal education, with the focus of policymakers and political leaders on data and measurement (2010). Aside from the debates that swirl around 'basics', 'standards', citizenship and 'soft skills' (2010), there is considerable contention over the invasive influence of the OECD PISA testing programme. A key question, for example, is whether PISA is simply a vehicle relentlessly driving global education systems towards standardised education (Meyer and Benavot 2013), which is somewhat ironic in the context of a simultaneous demand for personalised 21st century education that steers away from 'one size fits all' solutions (Bolstad and Gilbert 2012).

Nevertheless, agencies such as the New Zealand Ministry of Education (and many like it across the world) are convinced of the merits of finding evidence to support the case for making a difference to student learning outcomes (or pointing out schools failing to make a difference). An important tension exists, however, as noted earlier, between the desire for measurable outcomes (perhaps possible when assessing academic progress) and the desire for education systems to better prepare young people with '21st century' soft skills and competencies, that are perhaps not so easily measured.

21st-Century Learning and Modern Learning Practices

The idea of '21st-century learning' is shorthand for several teaching and learning practices that may be considered to provide educational experiences more closely aligned to the evolving demands of 21st century living. In what follows, the terms 'modern (teaching and) learning practices', 'innovative teaching practices' and 'future-oriented teaching and learning' will be used interchangeably. The specific features or characteristics of these approaches include personalisation (which coheres with young peoples' digital experiences); culturally responsive pedagogy as a subset of personalisation; anchoring learning in activities that have a 'real world' relevance, often achieved through projects or problems; the role of innovation, collaboration and flexible approaches to grouping students and scheduling their day. These approaches to learning are supported in flexible learning spaces. Although technology integration is central to developing modern teaching and learning practice, it will be considered later, in relation to ICT and Bring Your Own Device (BYOD).

Personalised Learning

Personalisation may refer to the ways people make their spaces comfortable, and consistent with their own personal tastes. Pedagogically, the term has more to do with providing opportunities for individuals to follow their interests and preferences, though it also relates to the quality of in-class relationships, including teacher responsiveness to cultural identity (Blackmore et al. 2011). The education system conforming to the learner, rather than the other way around, is how Green et al. (2005) defined personalised learning. The shift to student-orientation, self-directed learning and student agency may be supported by the rising popularity of socio-constructivist theories of learning, noted by Vieluf et al. (2012). Green et al. (2005) identified four goals of personalisation: providing students the opportunities to make informed choices; recognising diversity in skills and knowledge; creating diverse learning environments; and developing assessment and feedback attuned to learners, rather than the system.

Associated changes to teacher practice in support of attaining these goals are collaborative, reflective and deprivatised teaching approaches. It may be argued, as do Davidson and Goldberg (2010), that these shifts in classroom pedagogy are evidence of education responding to the challenge presented by the self-learning and user content generation made possible by the Internet. Digital technology thus plays a key role in developing personalised approaches in the classroom, as various forms of digital technology and Internet developments are strongly oriented to personalised and customised use. The personal lives of students in the 21st century are intimately connected with the retrieval and sharing of relevant information, and peer-to-peer communication (Davidson and Goldberg 2010; Green et al. 2005), hence students coming into educational settings do so with a greater expectation of being able to self-determine features of their learning, however, school life can fail to acknowledge this digital dimension of student life (Green et al. 2005). Furthermore, school life is notoriously able to neglect or disregard the important cultural dimension of student life.

Culturally Responsive Pedagogy

Culturally responsive pedagogy may be regarded as a subset of personalised learning, the reason for which will become clear. The notion of drawing on personal life experience to bridge to new learning is not new to effective teachers. It is nevertheless this act that potentially places teachers in contact with the culture of their students, and will enhance their success. This view stands on the premise that culture, emotion and motivation are linked (Bishop 2011; Wlodkowski and Ginsberg 1995). As mismatches in the classroom are likely due to the differences between the student's experience and that of the teacher, it is the teacher who must make the necessary cognitive adjustment to allow the student to engage with learning (Bishop 2011). This is one sense in which there is a link with personalised learning.

Traditional classrooms—teacher talk dominating, students speaking only when spoken to, closed questioning—all contribute to silencing cultural groups and minorities (Gay 2002). Instead, the classroom must become a meeting place where community can be built, so that effective cross-cultural communication can be built (2002), and one way to achieve this, Bishop (2011) argued, is for students to be engaged with their teachers in making decisions about curriculum planning, as this will bring cultural values to the fore. (In this context, Bishop (2011) clarified, 'culture' is not iconography or rituals, but sense-making processes). Here too is a clear link to personalisation.

The problem with traditional classrooms, however, is that teachers maintain power by controlling the design of classroom curriculum and teaching content. In these classrooms, teachers are seen as the active source of knowledge; students are seen, in contrast, as the passive receivers of knowledge. Freire (1970/1996, 1998) famously referred to this model as 'banking education'. Furthermore, traditional classroom spatial designs privilege teacher space, with the teacher front-of-room, and students in ordered arrangements to facilitate control and surveillance by the teacher (Bishop 2011).

What then might precisely constitute culturally responsive teaching, or, more broadly, pedagogy? Reacting to the 'carrot and stick' notion of extrinsic motivation in traditional schooling, Wlodkowski and Ginsberg (1995) suggested a model emphasising the creation of a classroom atmosphere of respect and personal connection, personal relevance and choice, experiences that were inclusive of student perspectives and values, and developing student confidence in their own abilities. Gay (2002) meanwhile believed culturally responsive teachers to be knowledgeable of students' culture, to have expert knowledge and understanding of all forms of curriculum (overt and covert), with the ability to respond appropriately to these. Such teachers make effective use of their students' cultural knowledge to develop reciprocal and caring classrooms, in which high expectations of student success is the norm. Gay emphasised holistic and integrated teaching in such classrooms that develop as cross-cultural, communicative communities. In this regard, teachers must seek to connect with culturally appropriate ways of communicating.

Bishop has done much to drive home the relevance of these international views to the New Zealand situation, particularly as it applies to the skewed academic performance of Māori in mainstream schooling. Expert teachers, based on his research with effective Māori-medium teachers, have a strong and secure philosophy of teaching, secure content pedagogical knowledge, and deep cultural knowledge. They have high expectations of their students, and are critically self-reflective. These teachers use non-confrontational methods of dealing with behaviour issues. They incorporate students' prior learning, and use materials related to the students' world. Cultural identities are strongly affirmed and validated by such teachers (2011).

Relatedly, and following on from the point regarding behaviour, it has been argued by Macfarlane et al. (2007) that the creation of culturally safe schools—creating the "freedom to be who (individually) and what (collectively) we are" (p. 69)—is complemented by the development of restorative justice practices. These approaches to dealing with challenging student behaviour eschew Western models of justice, favouring instead the creation of opportunities to rebuild the dignity of victim and wrongdoer through constructive engagement with the affected community. Thus an adversarial cycle of accusation, blame, trial and punishment are replaced with practices that connect all affected parties to discuss an offence, its effects and aftermath, and to jointly decide on an outcome. These practices encourage offenders to take responsibility for their offences, provide redress to victims, and promote the reintegration of both back into the community, as both are damaged by offences, and both experience stigma (Van Ness and Strong 2010). This approach is consistent with the development of relational classrooms called for by advocates of culturally responsive pedagogy, such as Russell Bishop in New Zealand.

On the strength of his research, Bishop proposed an Effective Teaching Profile for teachers working with Māori students, though it is now a widely accepted dictum in New Zealand education that what works for Māori will work for all students. Bishop's proposed profile operationalises what he termed a 'Culturally Responsive Pedagogy of Relations' (2011), thus placing relationships at the centre of his pedagogical concept. In summary, a teacher conforming to this profile has a deep sense of care and respect for students as they come (in Māori terms, this is a respect for self-identity); has high expectations of student achievement, no matter their individual circumstances; is well prepared and creates "a secure, well-managed learning environment" (p. 64); provides for learner autonomy and self-direction with minimal teacher interference; creates a dialogical climate in which teachers are learners and learners can be teachers; and enables students to be independently self-monitoring.

Authentic Learning

One of the critiques of 'industrial age', 20th century education is its lack of relevance of the content of schooling to the 'real world' of students. It must also be recognised that this increasingly diffuse world is a networked one, providing possibilities for learning and connection—possibilities often not recognised by a traditional school system that sees knowledge and expertise only in terms of the curriculum, teacher and confines of the classroom (Green et al. 2005) and that replicates a "bureaucratic–hierarchical" (Nair 2014, p. 16) model of education. Yet, beyond the classroom, lie opportunities for students to connect with, and seek the support of, relevant experts, a process that will deepen student knowledge and skill (Green et al. 2005).

A feature of authentic learning is to present students with (or allow them to formulate) problems that have concrete relevance in the 'real world' (OECD 2013), or to work on projects that can play out in the community, such as running a vegetable stall, selling produce grown by the students. This kind of 'rich task' matters because it is performed as a culminating event for a real audience, thus leading to higher performance levels by students (2013).

Project-Based, Problem-Based and Design-Based Approaches to Learning

These are approaches to learning drawing on one or a combination of approaches relating to projects, problems or designs (for learning). The ideas underpinning these approaches lend themselves to collaborative spaces, where students come together to discuss and analyse a project, then move away in smaller groups to work on the project, to later return to a larger group (Lippman 2015). Project and problem-based approaches provide students 'real-life' problems to solve, often by following an inquiry model including such processes as hypothesis generation, research and reflection (OECD 2013).

In problem-based learning (PBL) courses, students work collaboratively, solving real-world problems. Along the way, they develop content knowledge and a range of skills, which help to motivate students. For Wilkerson and Gijselaers (1996, pp. 101–102, cited by the Center for Teaching and Learning 2001, p. 1), PBL teachers are "facilitators rather than disseminators", and open-ended (or 'ill-structured') problems "serve as the initial stimulus and framework for learning". PBL therefore supports a student-centred approach, where process learning is more important than content recall. Collaborative group work helps students to become self-directed learners, and peer feedback and personal reflection are important dimensions. The end-point of learning is to complete a 'rich task', which can be defined as "having variety, scope and depth…requiring academic rigour; and… being multidisciplinary" (Matters 2006, p. 18). The successful completion of rich, authentic, tasks depends on having adequate blocks of time for conceptualisation and execution, however.

Time

Flexible approaches to time create possibilities for collaboration and integrated, project-based work (Nair 2014), while simultaneously allowing for deeper learning (OECD 2013). The rigid periodisation of the day that assumes learning occurs in abbreviated bursts of time, and on cue is an obstacle, however. The model of six or seven daily periods, punctuated by bells and associated mass movement around school is inefficient and wasteful (Heppell 2016), with time lost each time a class rises to move to a different classroom. This leads some (such as Robinson 2010) to the view that traditional schooling bears little relation to almost any adult life activity (apart from incarceration), underscoring its irrelevance. Some of this critique is rhetorical, however, as the need for the regulation of time and movement underpins many daily activities; nevertheless, learning to cope with flexible time is an important skill too.

Flexible time enhances personalised learning, enabling students to autonomously structure their workday within the context of the day's routines. Thus, multiple students work on different tasks at the same time (OECD 2013). The CERI researchers noted in the schools they studied, however, that this autonomy is, in fact, underpinned by a highly structured set of routines demanding careful student accounting of activities undertaken and completed.

Significant amendments to the physical dimensions and shape of learning space will suggest changes in scheduling (Blackmore et al. 2011). Considerations of physical space are reviewed shortly, though arguably, flexible timetabling does not depend on physical space. Nor should the way students are grouped across classes and schools require particular spatial configurations.

'Stage, Not Age'

Traditional schooling groups students by age, a phenomenon unlikely to be replicated outside school (Robinson 2010). A conference of the Specialist Schools and Academies Trust in England suggested organising students by stage of learning and not by their age as a key to supporting personalised learning (Marley 2007). This shift in practice, it was suggested almost ten years ago now (Paton 2008), would allow students to learn at their own pace. Notwithstanding criticism of the examination orientation of the English education system, a 'stage not age' arrangement means students can be examined when scholastically ready, rather than being at the required examination age. These considerations are, however, incongruously out of step with the intent of futures-focussed learning, which is less focussed on assessment and more on skill and dispositional development.

The CERI research of innovative learning environments found flexibility in regard to age cohorts, with preference given to grouping by stage of learning instead (2013). The advantages mentioned by the researchers included mentoring of younger by older students, and encouraging social mixing across ages (2013). In the New Zealand context, this principle of the older 'expert' child guiding a younger, is widely accepted in education, and is referred to by the Māori term, *tuakana–teina*. Also noted by the CERI research team was greater flexibility in arranging the day, thus it may be provisionally concluded that personalised, culturally responsive pedagogy, making use of authentic, problem or project-based learning will benefit by flexible timetabling and avoiding the conceptualisation of learning being linked to age. Such approaches to education require innovative approaches, in order to shift away from traditional practices.

Innovation

The term 'innovation' is associated with novelty and newness. This label must be used with care, however. The Centre for Educational Research and Innovation (CERI) of the OECD has made this case: "innovation…is not necessarily to be judged by practices that can be judged as 'new' or unique but rather how the different practices and approaches are put together into the whole" (OECD 2013, p. 27). It may be asked, for example, what the useful life of newness and novelty might be. Furthermore, as Leicester et al. (2009) have suggested, innovation does not necessitate significant change, as innovation may be deployed to sustain and maximise the performance of the status quo. In an organisational context, Peter Senge's, seminal work, *The Fifth Discipline* (1992), noted that inventions only become innovations when they can be widely replicated. Thus there may be critical issues surrounding the possibility of systematising 'innovation'.

The notion of innovation is not limited to the systemic level, but applies to learning and teaching too. Students will develop skills and abilities to be employable in an uncertain future by reaching beyond the confines of the conventional classroom (Green et al. 2005). Teachers too, are called upon now to be far more creative and innovative in their approaches to their work, indeed to attempt to surpass the attractions of interactive technologies (MacBeath 2012) readily available to their students. Teachers are thus caught between the demand to be innovative in endorsing and supporting the social knowledge of students on one hand, and their commitment to their store of knowledge and experience, on the other (2012). A further innovation affecting the lives of teachers is collaborative practice.

Collaborative Teaching

While learners and learning have shifted to the centre, a critical element of modern learning practice is modern *teaching* practice. The imaginary of the office-less workplace, and the emphasis on collaborative teamwork in future (and present) work environments, allows collaboration among teachers to take on new meaning. The concept moves beyond teachers merely preparing together, or discussing issues of mutual professional concern, to teachers team-teaching. Stephen Heppell, currently Professor of New Media Environments of Bournemouth University, in England, is well known as an innovative educator. His 'Rule of Three', is applied to learning design, pedagogy, and BYOD (2016). In reference to pedagogy, two of his rules specify collaboration: 'ask three then me' encourages peer learning and collaboration; 'three heads better than one' refers to the benefits of collaborative team teaching, for both students and teachers. These include, for teachers, shared practice, shared responsibility, shared workload and raised motivation, while for students there is variety and multiple sources of knowledge and support (2016).

Greater efficiencies become possible when multiple teachers work together in a space, while permutations include one teacher working with a large group just as another is working with smaller groups (OECD 2013). Nair (2014) argued that breaking away from the isolated teaching encouraged by single-cell rooms provides opportunities for the development of a "professional learning community" (p. 13). The CERI researchers discovered flexible spaces create possibilities for collaborative planning, sharing ideas and learning together with colleagues (OECD 2013). Working in deprivatised and public settings is, however, challenging to a generation of teachers accustomed to individual work, and largely private practice behind closed doors (2013). Working in this way is increasingly unlikely as learning environments evolve away from the single-cell model. Developing an understanding of space and the material is thus the following area of focus.

Learning Environments

While the area of learning environments research is in an emergent phase in New Zealand, this should not be taken to mean there is 'no research' (an oft-heard phrase in relation to the advance of changes in education, such as the development of learning environments and digital pedagogy, for example). Blackmore et al. (2011) have pointed out that much available learning environment research has tended to focus on building and technical specifications and performance, neglecting what occurs within, and around, buildings. Indeed, there are significant veins of research to draw on that go beyond the narrow boundaries of physical property. New learning spaces and considerations of how to work in them and their educational impact has become the subject of increasing scrutiny and professional activity in New Zealand (for example, Bradbeer 2015; McPhail 2016; Osborne 2016; Page 2016; Smardon et al. 2015), Australia (for example, Blackmore et al. 2011; Cleveland and Fisher 2014; Imms and Byers 2016), and in Europe (for example, Dumont and Istance 2010; Woolner et al. 2012).

Education and education systems have experienced significant reform pressures at least since the 1980s. Critiques of teaching, education and school systems have included the spaces in which teaching and learning has traditionally occurred, suggesting that the working environment of schools is conservative and out-dated. Spatial design for learning requires significant redirection if learning is to become authentic, personalised and lifelong, and be experienced in collaborative and social groups, as a context for working on complex problems and developing critical thought (Nair 2014; Oblinger 2005).

Nair, a prominent schools' building designer, has boldly claimed that the (traditional) classroom is obsolete (2011, 2014). Embedded in this claim is the idea that schools are not geared to the 'real' world of work; and of building design being outmoded. Nair's claim draws attention to the artefacts and technologies within education spaces, the practices occurring in these spaces, and the relationship of these spaces to the rest of the world, suggesting that traditional school 'cells-and-bells' architecture resemble factories which no longer exist (2014). Such schools fall woefully short if teachers and students are to engage in practices that are preparation for a 21st century world of work and life.

To more fully understand the significance of learning environments to education and the drive to design learning environments for the 21st century, several intersecting and overlapping influences will be considered in what follows. These include the notion that the physical world of work as it is emerging in the 21st century is a model for education; the role of designers; and global reform influence. Teaching and learning for the 21st century presupposes certain design principles, though this in turn raises questions concerning the proper relationship between environmental design and the process and outcomes of teaching and learning.

The Imperative of Workspaces

Gensler (2016a), an international architectural and design firm, identified 18 trends in the workplace of the future. Two, overarching trends, are the revolutionisation of workplaces by younger workers and the innovative economy, and second, changes to 'the old economic order' that led to the demand for a 'connected and agile' workforce (2016b, "The future of workplace"). Among the 18 identified trends, relevant indicators include:

- the need for places where people can collaborate, converse and communicate using multiple media and in multiple contexts;
- creating informality for 'next-gen' workers;
- developing 'smart' environments that emphasise community and co-working;
- shifting from conventional and traditional means of movement around and within buildings;
- integrating spaces to cross over traditional boundaries and siloes;
- consequently, leading to greater interdisciplinarity in working teams, and team-based workspaces replacing conventional offices;
- mastery of media and digital technology in all its forms, requiring workplaces to have high levels of connectivity, as much as users who are connected; and
- bespoke, small-scale manufacture of innovative and niche products, greatly accelerated by 3D printing (2016b, "The future of workplace").

The influence of the workplace on its occupants has received scholarly attention. For example, Fabbri and Charue-Duboc (2013) attempted to show that connected and mobile workers no longer require fixed, conventional offices, while open plan offices encourage collaboration, creativity, innovation and learning. Although questioning the link between office design and creativity, Fabbri and Charue-Duboc (2013) did argue that open plan designs influence human interactions within that space, including creating a climate that encourages motivation. This view may be contested, however, as indicated by Ruismäki et al. (2015). Their evaluation of the occupancy experiences of lecturers and students at the University of Helsinki found that students, while generally taking greater responsibility over their own learning, in some cases, actually preferred passive learning, and would engage in social networking (such as Facebook) rather than in their assigned collaborative work.

Also challenging the imaginary of the 21st century workplace as a place of excitement, creativity and productivity, is the research of Morrison and Macky (2017), for example. They report the demands of working in shared office spaces, open plan offices and with other flexible arrangements, such as hot-desking, to be associated with distractions (such as overhearing unwanted conversations), unco-operative behaviours and feelings of distrust that undermine notions of collegiality and teamwork, and negativity arising from the absence of personal, private space and territory in shared spaces. Furthermore, despite indications in the research literature they investigated, their empirical study found reduced levels of friendship in open plan offices. Of interest to schools with flexible learning environments, in which multiple teachers work with multiple students on multiple tasks, Morrison and Macky discovered (also in contradiction to their research literature) that open plan offices are associated with lower levels of supervisory support. Nevertheless, they did find support in their data for positive indications in relation to collaborative work, *when workers were working on projects or achieving common goals*. Merely putting people together in a shared space will not lead to collaboration.

The notion of 'next-gen' workers may be considered in a similar light as the 'Net Generation' referred to earlier, that is, it may be too crude to assume that all new workers aged in their 20s will, by default, have specific characteristics. There may be increasing waves of 'next-gen' workers entering the workforce who will be accustomed to working in open environments, if they have been 'schooled' in flexible learning environments, or be habituated to the experience of self-directed learning. These are an open questions requiring further inquiry over the coming years. It seems, however, on the basis of the research of Morrison and Macky (2017), the appeal to the workplace as a guide to the design of schools requires some caution.

Design Initiative

It is appropriate to consider whether designers are (or should be) leading the changes in thinking about educational space, or whether educators are. Moore and Lackney (1993) and Nair et al. (2013), writing from an architectural design perspective, questioned the torpidity in educational facility design, yet acknowledged there is a body of education research and a public education discourse that both suggest amending educational practices:

> Despite the fact that the educational establishment itself has embraced a number of innovative approaches over the years, architects often hear educators speak with a vocabulary reminiscent of their own childhood experiences in school buildings designed for a different time (Nair et al. 2013, p. 13)

These authors posited the view that school designers and planners can give form to emerging educational concepts, while Moore and Lackney (1993) suggested two possibilities as the impetus for altering facility design, namely, translations of empirical research or extrapolations from educational reform ideas in combination with the practical experience of educators. In later work, Nair et al. (2013) asked whether designers ought to be influenced by 'external factors', such as national curriculum changes.

The empirical research Moore and Lackney (1993) thought to 'translate' is that which relates the effects of school building design on educational performance. They believed it possible to devise ideal-type designs by engaging in what amounts to a meta-analysis of extant design research in order to establish design guidelines, patterns, or principles, to be implemented when building or renovating schools. The second option would be to consult 'reflective educators' on their educational reform ideas, providing an architectural form to these ideas. In this sense, their question may be to ask how building design could support the reformist ideas. Given, however, the view of Nair et al. (2013) that 'external forces' (and here I assume reform ideas are included) are better disregarded due to varying political influences and election cycles, the first option must then be preferable, at least to this group of designers. Not surprisingly then, the 'patterns' referred to by Moore and Lackney (1993) are a central feature of *The Language of School Design: Design Patterns for 21st Century Schools* (Nair et al. 2013), co-authored by Lackney. These patterns are regarded as models for schools that will outlive political changes.

The Place of Learning

Apart from the influence of the changing workplace in the 21st century, and the motivations of designers to dramatically alter educational space, global policy-makers, have created an influential role for themselves. The OECD, for example, has "…ratcheted up the stakes for the schooling sector by questioning the relevance and role of its current institutional form for the new demands that are made on it for the development of a knowledge-based economy" (Robertson 2005, p. 153). The OECD Centre for Educational Research and Innovation (CERI) extends the significant global governance role of the OECD, influencing education policies across its member states with its 'Innovative Learning Environments (ILE)' research (2013).

The homogenising effects of the influence of OECD thinking are apparent in the motivation of CERI "to positively influence the contemporary education reform agenda with forward-looking insights about learning and innovation" (2013, p. 3). The CERI research set out to define learning (Dumont et al. 2010) then examined specific contextual instances of innovative learning environments in practice, to develop learning principles underpinning ILE (OECD 2013). Flowing from this research base, CERI is currently considering wider, system-level measures to implement from a macro perspective. It may be suggested that the CERI research has already made a significant impact on the thinking of the New Zealand Ministry of Education, which altered its labelling of its new school building structures from 'Modern Learning Environments' (MLE) to 'Innovative Learning Environments' (MOE 2016; "Talking Terminology", nd.) in response to the OECD research.

It pays to develop an understanding of what is meant by terms such a 'modern/innovative/flexible learning environments' by considering the ways these terms are used. The New Zealand Ministry of Education defines an innovative learning environment as "the complete physical, social and pedagogical context in which learning is intended to occur" (2016). For its part, CERI regarded 'learning environments' as "an organic, holistic concept—an eco-system that includes the activity and the outcomes of the learning" (OECD 2013, p. 11). More important for CERI is that the organisation of learning be the starting-point, not educational institutions, or physical buildings. These buildings ought to be part of the learning process, not separate from it.

This definition, arguably wider than the one proposed by the New Zealand Ministry of Education, enables a view of 'learning' as occurring in multiple locations. Thus, not all learning needs to occur in the formal classroom (Dumont and Istance 2010). A learning environment concerns the relationship between learners, teachers and other learning professionals, content and facilities and technologies (2010). Green et al. (2005) took a similar line, some years earlier, when they suggested that the learning environment is a confluence of factors, people, technology and resources. Learning must be possible beyond the confines of the physical school if it is to be genuinely personalised (2005), and because knowledge can no longer be considered either the preserve of teachers alone, or possible for any one person to retain, experts outside the school are key ingredients in the learning environment. It is for the school to act in ways that will facilitate these important connections (2005).

The principles of learning in ILE as advocated by CERI research are derived from its earlier review of research (Dumont et al. 2010). The CERI researchers indicated the following principles are to be in place and met, if places of learning are going to be innovative:

- place learners and learning at the centre;
- emphasise collaborative learning; ensure that priority is given to motivation and emotional maintenance;
- prioritise sensitivity to individual difference and prior knowledge;
- advocate the maintenance of high, but reasonable, expectations of students;
- call for relevant assessments, with formative feedback playing a key role; and
- seek curriculum integration, which includes extending learning to the outside world.

Learning Space Design Principles

Notwithstanding the broadly defined concept of the place of learning as beyond the confines of a rigid classroom, architectural designers have sought to develop spaces that coincidentally bring about some of the principles indicated by CERI, such as de-centring the teacher, and emphasising personalised learning (Blackmore et al. 2011). Beginning from the perspective of the teaching and learning principles, curriculum strands and domains, and key pedagogical approaches of the curriculum of the Australian state of Victoria, Kenn Fisher[1] determined that

> pedagogical activities require specific spatial qualities to be effective. Each principle requires specific pedagogical approaches to support that principle, and these pedagogies are applied through the five core activities or modes. These modes have direct implications for learning settings design (2005a, Slide 2.01).

The 'activities' or 'modes' Fisher deduced from his reading of the Victorian curriculum were: delivering; applying; creating; communicating; decision-making (2005a). From these modes, he was able to extrapolate various spatial configurations appropriate to putting these modes into practice. Of these, only 'delivering' (most like teacher-directed activity) is suited to single-cell classrooms, while the remaining modes suggested configurations the single cell is likely to rule out (or at least limit to a greater or lesser extent).

Following Fisher, it may be suggested that teacher-centred approaches to teaching will therefore persist, as long as schools are designed on a 'cells-and-bells' model, a view Nair (2014) concurred with. His approach to educational architecture is that purpose-built physical settings will enable student-centred learning that endorses personalisation, collaboration, authenticity, and innovation. Such designs will also permit flexibility in regard to class composition and time (2014). Nair described an agile learning environment as a "learning building…that supports student learning in a cutting-edge way (a building for learning) and a building that can be adapted…as…needs evolve (the building itself 'learns')" (p. 6).[2]

Nair (2014) outlined four design principles for schools:

- Schools should be welcoming places where students will feel nurtured and safe, contributing to developing positive habits of citizenship.

---

[1] Associate Professor in Learning Environments at the University of Melbourne and consultant to the OECD. See https://msd.unimelb.edu.au/people/kenn-fisher.

[2] Notwithstanding the desirability of buildings that are innovative in design and that incorporate technical advances (in regard to acoustics and lighting, for example), a question that should be at the heart of any investigation of educational facility design is the link between conceptualisation, the physical setting and the practices occurring in and around the setting. From the perspective of Fisher and Nair, appropriate design will powerfully influence practice. This question will continue to be raised, suffice for now to indicate caution in relation to the possible linearity implied in what Fisher, and particularly Nair, have indicated.

- Agile buildings are sufficiently versatile to be adapted to multiple learning requirements.
- Thus, schools ought to have multiple use zones, such as learning commons, theatres and gardens.
- Finally, a school must communicate positive messages about appropriate behaviour and personal identity within the space, achieved in part by replacing traditional monolithic school design with buildings offering opportunities for small communities to flourish.

In reference to learning space, Stephen Heppell's 'Rule of Three' is:

- no more than three walls, so that space is flexible, and neither enclosed nor fully open;
- no fewer than three points of focus, so as to eliminate 'stand and deliver approaches', thus enabling varied approaches (which also then demands a new approach to furniture); and,
- create space large enough to accommodate three teachers, three activities and three 'classes' (2016).

The New Zealand Ministry of Education suggests ("Core elements for property", nd.) eight elements as essential ingredients in the design of new, innovative, learning spaces:

- accessib[ility];
- air quality;
- heating;
- [be] healthy and safe;
- lighting;
- insulation;
- sustainab[ility]; and
- acoustics.

Ensuring these elements are present is more easily attained with its new buildings, whereas retrofitting existing buildings is more challenging. In these cases, typical changes will include the removal of internal walls, opening up or incorporating corridors, creating breakout spaces (often using existing 'dead space'), adding skylights, and creating attractive outdoor spaces closely adjacent to learning areas.

It is notable that the design principles important to the New Zealand Ministry of Education are more overtly focussed on technical features. This may be an indication of the suggestion that research into learning environments tends to focus on these elements, rather than the practices associated with differently conceived space (Blackmore et al. 2011). Nevertheless, some commonalities are evident across these various articulations of design principles. The principle of flexibility (agility) underlies the others, and is specifically indicated in the shift from confined space to large space, and indeed, to the incorporation of multiple and varied space. This shift in design is important if the multiple modalities of learning, beyond traditional 'stand and deliver' from the front, as suggested by Fisher (2005a), are to be encouraged and developed. Further common features (also encouraged by multiple and varied spatial design) are the possibilities for group size to vary, and for spaces to be differently furnished.

Furniture

The deployment of well-designed and non-traditional educational furniture contributes to the visual impact of flexible learning environments. Some early metaphorical ideas expressed by futurist, David Thornburg, are relevant to personalised learning, and have been transported into furniture design. Specifically, he referred to the 'campfire', 'watering hole', 'cave' and 'life' (2007). The campfire is the place where the entire community meets to hear expert narratives. While this continues to be an important metaphor in education, Thornburg's position was that it over-dominates classrooms. The watering hole is a place where small pockets of people come together for common cause, and use the opportunity to share, discuss and problem solve. The cave is a place of quiet contemplation, in private. Life is the world of experience and application, namely experiential learning.

Thornburg applied these metaphors to technology, arguing that these metaphors can apply equally to our exchanges through digital media (2007). Thus, for example, the shared reflections in online communities of learning can be instances of campfires. Returning, however, to furniture—it is possible to arrange furniture in ways that emulate these metaphors of learning, as Davis and Kappler-Hewitt (2013) found when they toured a selection of Australian schools. Arguably, although progressive teachers have been utilising small groupings to replace rows for decades, they will have been restricted by the limitations of conventional thinking not only in regards to space but also to furniture.

Such limitations are an enduring feature of the traditional, industrial model classroom, with its rigid, uniform furniture, and the principle of 'one student, one seat'. Personalised, authentic and project-based learning requires collaboration, easy transition from one activity to a different activity, and the rapid dissolution of groups and reformation of new groups. Therefore, educational furniture must contribute to learning spaces in support of this shift in pedagogical activity. Furniture design literature focuses on ways "to facilitate multimodal pedagogies that accommodate individual learner's needs, and personalisation of space" (Blackmore et al. 2011, p. 8).

The 'one size for all' of regular classroom furniture (Sullivan 2012) not only fails to recognise differences in body position and posture, but also disallows the kind of movement just described. As Kuuskorpi and Cabellos González (2011) discovered in their European study, the traditional single-cell classroom is perceived as passive and an obstacle to flexibility. For their respondents, flexibility was associated with larger space and mobile furniture. Flexible, or mobile, furniture can be configured to accommodate a mixture of direct instruction, large and small group work, and individual work (Hassell 2011). Similarly, in an earlier New Zealand study by Nielsen, into the role played by the physical environment in achieving learning outcomes, respondents identified the desirable role of flexible furniture (2004).

Furniture development has been encouraged by the shift from desktop computing to mobile computing. Huang et al. (2009) noted the marked influence of such changes and additional advances in technology. These allow the integration of digital tools and furniture, such as the creation of interactive tabletops. Thus, furniture becomes a 'communication hub' (2009). Ultimately, educational furniture that coheres with the overall concept of flexible learning environments must, of course be flexible, durable and agile, with the additional merit of being resistant to damage (Nielsen 2004; Kuuskorpi and Cabellos González 2011).

Influence of Environment on Teaching and Learning

The importance of the relationship between design, setting and practice (and with it, the danger of suggesting a linear relationship between these) was flagged earlier in this chapter (see footnote 2). That question may be taken up in more detail now, as it is, arguably, a driver motivating the notion that traditional educational buildings must change. This call emanates (as already seen) from multiple sources, including global trendsetters (such as the OECD), education reformers, whose ideas may be taken up by designers, or designers themselves acting independently of educators. Collectively, these sources have influence over policymakers.

Furthermore, as previously indicated too, it could be argued that schools should resemble workplaces, in preparation for the workplace. Educational sociologists have long regarded schools to both mirror society, and be preparation for it. Indeed, those who are critical of 'industrial age' schooling make the very point that traditional school design and practices resemble factories and, in that form, fail to take account of the dramatically changed modern workplace, nature of work and types of jobs available. Despite the continued existence of manufacturing (though in decline) and the continuation of many traditional job roles, technological advance has imposed pressure to work role definition and work practices. So steady and widespread is this process that it has become conventional wisdom to contend that redesigning teaching and learning is critical to the adequate preparation of forthcoming generations. Suggestions for redesign include schools developing flexible time arrangements, re-conceptualising groupings of students, and creating new possibilities for personalised, authentic learning and collaborative teaching (for example, Bolstad and Gilbert 2008; Nair 2014; Pearlman 2010; Robinson 2010).

The argument supporting the redesign of educational buildings coheres with these various education redesign suggestions, which is not to say that education reformers are united in their views regarding curriculum, knowledge, skills, competencies and the context for teaching and learning. Nevertheless, it is a relevant question to consider whether building design changes will bring about the realisation of desired changes to the process and content of the education experience.

It is, however, evident that research into significant spatial change is failing to take adequate account of pedagogy (Blackmore et al. 2011; Cleveland and Fisher 2014; Moore and Lackney 1993). An early review indicated that published studies of the relationship between environment and learning are more likely to emphasise environmental considerations, such as light, ventilation and air quality (Higgins et al. 2005). Similarly, Blackmore et al. (2011) stated some years later: "Much of the literature focuses on the quality of conditions or perceptions and not educational practices or how space is used and to what effect" (p. 5). Blackmore et al. (2011), Cleveland and Fisher (2014), and Fisher (2005b) noted these technical aspects of building performance are usually developed as quantitative measures that often relegate pedagogical concerns to a handful of coincidental questions. Alternately, some qualitative measures, also seeking to adopt an 'evidence-based' approach, establish a range of key performance indicators against which building performance is evaluated. Such approaches are frequently driven by the need to justify financial outlay. There are, however, many aspects of building design that are more significant, at least to educators.

In their review of literature, Blackmore et al. (2011) found claims arguing for the influence of design on the attitudes of students and staff, particularly when buildings may inspire or present a desirable physical appearance. The quality of the school environs are a reflection of the level of care or concern a school organisation has for its members. Moore and Lackney (1993) had found high density conditions to encourage anti-social tendencies, leading them to the view that large schools are less able to provide a full range of participatory activities, which might otherwise contribute positively to character development and socialisation. "Conversely, students in smaller and medium-sized schools take more part in extra-curricular activities, there is more overlapping of roles, they are more satisfied with the participation, and overall they have more positive self concepts" (p. 105). This view led to their design notion of creating small learning centres within classrooms, to combat noise and reduce distractions for students.

Educators would be encouraged by evidence of enhanced citizenship and positive behaviour amongst their students, and would, no doubt, prefer to work in modern, well-designed facilities. The question remains, however: can redesigned space influence learning? While it may seem obvious to ask what kind of influence altering the spaces of learning might have over actual student achievement, this question seems to have been less significant in much of the research into flexible learning environments, according to Blackmore et al. (2011). The question of the link between space and learning is not new, however, as Moore and Lackney (1993) sought to make some connection between the built environment and student outcomes. They continued to puzzle over the problem of the role of 'mediating variables' that seemed to insert themselves between the space and the outcomes. These variables are the 'prosocial' (or 'soft') skills they believed are developed when teachers and students occupy spaces that are safe, clean, well-ventilated, well-lit with an abundance of natural light, and that are acoustically superior to traditional classrooms. Thus the question may be more complex: do the prosocial skills contribute to enhanced academic performance, or is it the building that enhances academic performance?

This conundrum was highlighted by Blackmore et al. (2011) who acknowledged a range of tangible variables, such as air, light and spatial density, and intangible variables, such as the development of integrated curriculum approaches, better management of scheduling, varying traditional approaches to the organisation of students, and team teaching. School culture and leadership also have their part to play in student learning, as do teacher–student relationships. Byers (2016) recently developed and used novel quantitative measures to carefully assess the influence of changes in the learning environment to teaching and learning (measured by student achievement in mathematics). His conclusions reinforced the view that teacher actions are a more likely determinant of student outcomes. Arguably, however, those actions are modified (or are possible to modify) *because of* changes to the place of learning. These actions may not necessarily be positive, however, as Chapman et al. (2014) have demonstrated.

Reporting on an ethnographic study of flexible learning environments in a New South Wales primary setting, Chapman et al. (2014) suggested significant challenges for teachers and students working in dynamic, open and shared learning spaces. Their teacher participants were concerned that the personalised choices made by students allowed some to hive off into various spaces, where they could appear to be engaged, yet may simply be 'coasting' (p. 42). Arguably too, the innovative approaches to personalised learning made possible (or required) by large, flexible spaces leads to an over-reliance by teachers on student self-monitoring, so that they are able to actively engage passive students and those who are struggling (2014).

This study highlighted noise as a further obstacle to achieving learning outcomes in flexible learning spaces. Some teacher participants regarded noise to be a significant factor requiring various strategies (such as 'zoning out'), while the researchers observed some students "retreating behind boards, under tables, or into cupboards in order to find a quiet place to read or do their work" (p. 44). A report in Melbourne's *The Age* (Cook 2015) suggested flexible learning spaces had noise and distraction as an unintended consequence of learning in these spaces. In the research on which *The Age* article was based, Mealings et al. (2015) argued that "converting to these open plan learning spaces [is] compromising acoustic privacy, hence potentially hindering educational development" (p. 96). While acknowledging the possibilities for alternative teaching methodologies, such as student-directed activity, they concluded that modified flexible learning spaces are preferable, to allow for greater opportunities to close off spaces, for example, with concertina doors, and that no space ought to accommodate more than 90 students, though even this was too many, in their view.

On the balance of what is presented here, the purpose of arguments for educational reform to better equip future generations for the 21st century world, may be in danger of being lost to technical considerations. A focus on the technical design features and performance of buildings may over-influence thinking about redesigned spaces, whereas considerations should focus on whether pedagogical practices and learning experiences are significantly enhanced by building redesign. There must be more to redesigned space than the potentially positive effect of desirable building facilities on school culture or mood. It is thus well to remain open to the question of the links between redesigned space, teaching practices and student learning. Also missing from much of the current extant research on learning environments is a deeper philosophical critique.

Critical Perspectives on the Technology of Space

Apart from research literature on changing learning environments emphasising the technical features of the emerging technology of space, it is also radically under-theorised. It is noteworthy, however, that some writers do acknowledge their indebtedness to critical, theoretic perspectives, and in particular, Blackmore et al. (2011), Chapman et al. (2014), Cleveland and Fisher (2014), and McGregor (2004) recognise the work of Lefebvre (1991). There is generally little evidence, however, of these theoretical perspectives having any exercise in the open. In the context of the zealous uptake by some, and the dismissive attitudes of others, in relation to the changes in the technologies affecting teachers' daily life and work, it is important to canvass some critical theoretic perspectives here. In particular, are some thoughts about materiality and Lefebvre's notion of space.

Materiality

Materiality is fundamental to human existence (Miller 2005). It is possible to think of space as a container to be filled with material artefacts; then, by extension, to imagine that an analysis of what occurs in that space refers to the ways the people in that space interact with the material artefacts, such as ICT, furniture, pin boards or open boundaries. One reason to transcend such common-sense notions of space and the material is that these notions lead to the idea of a world of passive objects that require human subjects to activate (Pickering 2013). As already suggested, however, space, and more specifically, the materiality of space, can have a *prefiguring* effect (Reh et al. 2011) by providing opportunities for (dis)placements of the teachers(s), thus de-centring the traditional front-of-room focal point. These opportunities are afforded by the introduction of mobile plasma screens, multiple and varied seating options, and, of course, greatly enlarged space, which may be differently configured than a traditional cellular box. In turn, these changes invite—and prompt—changes to the teaching and learning process.

Pickering argued that the material and the human interact in a world of performance, thus, space is not simply passive: "…at the level of performance, we are constitutively engaged with our environment: we do consequential things to it, and it does things back to us…" (2013, p. 26). Following Foucault, Pickering argued against the dualist conception of the individual 'subject' as a rational and autonomous chooser enacting upon a passive built environment. The built environment is, however, apparent and inescapable (Reh and Temel 2014). From their perspective, the built space or environment does not plan, intend or reflect. Still, recognising the built environment as active opens up the possibility of recognising when this space works and when it does not—for example when visitors or pedestrians are confused by the layout (2014). The frustration arising from working in the single cell is, by definition, its fixed, cellular and cramped nature. Reh and Temel (2014) were led by their insight to the view that ethnographic researchers ought to suspend their observations of people and what they are doing in space, in order to spend some time observing what space and the environment does to people —thus calling for an analysis of materiality as an important dimension of spatiality, the complete environment occupied by people.

There is much to be said for technological advances that improve the human quality of life (which includes, of course, the quality of what is possible in any educational or schooling situation). In this sense, technology adds to human materiality. The ironic problem, Dant (2005) pointed out, is that some technological advances simultaneously disengage humans from their immateriality "that no machine can substitute for—imagination, creativity, ideas, passion, love" (p. 34). Machines, while transforming lives, also affect the embodied material relationship of humans to the world, such that their social relationships are affected. Project forward one decade on from Dant's words, and consider that individuals or groups of people at leisure in cafés, restaurants and malls, or commuting from place to place, are more attentive to 'checking the phone' than to cultivating their social relationships or observing the passing scene.

Questions may therefore be raised regarding whether modern teaching and learning approaches incorporate technologies of space and/or media, or if they are driven by these technologies. Evidently, flexible space is interfaced with flexible furniture; so do advances in furniture design help push the boundaries of spatial design or do they respond to legitimate educational and health concerns? ICT developments have seemingly spawned an industry of providers and technicians, without whose support schools' daily business may be significantly hampered. The rapidity and frequency of upgraded hardware and software keep users in permanent thrall to technicians and also have the effect of imposing an undue sense of urgency on school administrators, leaders and teachers, who fear they and their schools will 'miss out' if the latest developments are not accommodated, added or utilised. It is in the realm of ICT that not only are some of the greatest changes to the education process noted, but also a material reality having a marked effect on teacher attitudes and practices.

Lefebvre

Henri Lefebvre developed a critically insightful analysis of space, human interactions in space and lived human relationships with material objects within space, in his classic, *The Production of Space* (1991). His project was to reconcile what he saw as the gulf between the notion of space as a mental construct, and the space of real life. This gulf was akin to the Cartesian bifurcation of mind and body. As a Marxian thinker, Lefebvre was certain that capitalism influences the practical dimension of space, seen in buildings and investment in buildings. Furthermore, Lefebvre associated capitalism with hegemony, a concept which extends beyond influence or even the permanent use of force. It applies to ideas, culture and knowledge. Lefebvre sought a 'unitary theory' connecting the physical, mental and social fields. For his purposes, the physical related to nature and the Cosmos; the mental to abstract thought; and the social to the world of practice. Lefebvre's epistemological project is conveyed by a number of such tripartite conceptualisations, the most well known being his notion of *representations of space*; *representational space*; and *spatial practice*.

For Henri Lefebvre, 'representations of space' refers to the "conceptualized space, the space of scientists, planners, urbanists, technocratic subdividers and social engineers…all of whom identify what is lived and what is perceived with what is conceived" (1991, p. 38). The space of lived experience is 'representational space', and Lefebvre noted that space so understood will "tend towards more or less coherent systems of non-verbal symbols and signs" (p. 39), and includes the "discursive practices [and] symbolic codings of the space" (Reh et al. 2011, p. 95). What Lefebvre termed, 'spatial practice', is articulated through the discourse of society: the "spatial practice of a society is revealed through the deciphering of its space" (p. 38). Members of society, and the society as a whole, come to a mastery of spatial practice, which presupposes a level of competence. There is a corporate social sense, in other words, that this particular building is designated as a place of learning, or this a place or worship, or that a repository of social memory, or that this is consecrated space of the deceased. Along with this sense, is an understanding of the kinds of practices to be associated with such spaces, and so a particular discourse (language and behaviour) arises in relation to such spaces.

The application of Lefebvre's triadic understanding of space supports an understanding of the modern, flexible and innovative learning spaces, by providing three interrelated, yet distinctive, perspectives on space. For example, it may be suggested the flexible and collaborative spaces have their own 'hidden curriculum', conveying messages about these spaces. Lefebvre's insights prompt thought regarding the particular purposes and form of space. Spaces are places where appropriate practices and protocols governing behaviour and conduct in such spaces may prevail. Spatial practice provides clarity concerning the way space influences, shapes and directs the work of educators, and the messages it conveys regarding what counts as worthwhile education for students in the 21st century. These critical insights will be further developed in Chap. 5.

ICT in Schools/BYOD

The core theme of this book is a concern with the becoming of teaching in the 21st century. What has been revealed from a sampling of literature is that there is a tide of discourse that has swept across the face of teaching, education, and school systems for at least two decades now. This discourse has been essentially critical, expressing itself in futuristic terms, encapsulated by the idea that schools and the education system must be realigned to focus on learning (not teaching), on skills and dispositions (not disciplinary knowledge), and on preparing young people to engage in a lifelong pursuit of learning as they navigate their way through an uncertain and unknowable future. This future is one that (at least for now) has digital technology as an overriding characteristic. Workers work in spaces (however defined or diffuse), generally with people, with raw materials (intellectual or material) and products (intellectual or material) in stages of manufacture or completion, and with tools of all kinds. The focus now shifts to considering some key themes in relation to the influence on teachers' work that has been brought about by the steady introduction to the school workplace of information and communication technologies (ICT).

'Digital Revolution'

References to a 'digital revolution' may typically include comments about the rise of technology spelling the fall of well-known and well-established companies like Kodak, Polaroid and Blockbuster (Nair 2014). Others may draw attention to the inroads into traditional business made by businesses operating in the non-traditional digital terrain—for example, Netflix, with 75 million subscribers (Netflix 2015) challenging conventional television subscription channels, and more lately, the cinema industry (Lang 2015) with its digital (Internet) streaming service. Similar challenges come from Uber (https://www.uber.com), a smartphone application enabling customers to network with independent drivers willing to provide a fetch and ride service, often undercutting taxi operators; and Airbnb (https://www.airbnb.com), an online peer to peer accommodation provider connecting travellers with private individuals willing to let accommodation on a short term.

This 'revolution' is pertinent to schools due to similar challenges made by the Internet and various software applications to traditional modes of conveying knowledge and information (Beetham and Sharpe 2013). Other ways technology engages students in new ways include blogging, video blogging, gaming and video creation.

Student Access

In consideration of student access to ICT in schools, or education more generally, it is not enough to focus only on questions of access to devices and Internet at school, but also at home, and to consider what lies in-between. A Microsoft Partners in Learning project identified critical gaps between the home world and the education world; between the skills being learned at school and those actually required in later life; and between the educational haves and have-nots (Shear et al. 2011). These are all matters of access, and refer to broader issues than simply the notion of the 'digital divide'.

The digital divide does, nevertheless, draw attention to the reality that some students have greater digital and ICT exposure than others. While many students may have access to digital technology at school, they do not have access at home. Nor do all students have access to home Internet, while differential broadband capabilities point to a further divide (Anderson 2010). Apart from divisions arising from differential access to digital technology and the Internet, there is also a discrepancy found in the quality of use even when accessing these tools (OECD 2011). Shapley et al. (2009), in their study of technology immersion in Texan schools over 2004–2008, found that relevant (i.e. task-focussed) use of laptops at home by students is significant "in promoting ubiquitous learning and in equalising the out-of-school learning opportunities for students in disadvantaged family and school situations" (p. vii). Still, lack of access to the Internet robs students of many freely available opportunities for formal and informal learning (OECD 2015).

Infrastructure

Access to ICT at school reveals (or masks) more complex issues, one of these being infrastructure (Cowie et al. 2011; Shear et al. 2011). While somewhat dated now, the Cowie et al. (2011) investigation of the Laptops for Teachers scheme in New Zealand from 2003–2005, revealed infrastructure and technical support to be significant constraints on teachers' use of ICT. Infrastructure provision, pre-BYOD, would extend to the provision of hardware for students, and Shear et al. (2011) reported that, for their teacher participants, of "the biggest barriers to using ICT in their teaching, the lack of student access in classrooms was the runaway leader" (p. 23). School-wide and systemic shifts are required if technology integration is to make a difference to the quality of the innovative schooling experience. These shifts include providing strong leadership support and targeted professional development, and saturating the entire school environment with technology, so that all daily practices occur in contact with technology (Cowie et al. 2011; Groff 2013).

Staff PD/L

The successful preparation of teachers for change, and their ongoing learning and development in the area of change, are a priority for schools and systems implementing new strategies (such as BYOD). An additional challenge is that initial teacher education (teacher training programmes) may be falling short in providing quality teachers who understand and can practice digital pedagogy (Hipkins et al. 2015). Brečko et al. (2014) placed staff professional learning at the top of their list of ten recommendations for the successful integration of ICT-enabled learning. Change may be linked to innovation, Shear et al. (2011) concluding from the findings of their study of 159 schools across seven nations, that strong and continuous teacher professional learning was important in supporting innovative teaching (specifically involving ICT). The best examples (from the perspective of the teachers) was learning that involved practical work, such as physically attempting new methods. This was preferred over learning the technical aspects of ICT (2011), a finding echoed in New Zealand amongst teachers, who preferred contextualised professional learning support over generic PD sessions (Cowie et al. 2011).

The conventional approach of providing 'staff training' (and calling it 'professional development' or 'professional learning') is perhaps an out-dated model, and fails to address one of the objectives of 21st-century learning, namely needs-based and personalised learning. Rather, a strong partnership model, such as that in evidence in the 'Manaiakalani Education Trust', a cluster of Auckland schools that brings a radical digital programme and provision to its working-class community, may be an option. In seeking to address the lack of knowledge and skill in relation to digital pedagogy, this cluster of schools has forged a successful school–university partnership that delivers a practice-based early career development model, embracing experienced mentor teacher partnerships with newly graduated teachers. Within this model, academic study and digital skills training are combined with the mentoring to create a three-pronged strategy (Hipkins et al. 2015). The costs associated with devising such a strategy may, however, prove too prohibitive to most schools, which are likely to default to traditional PD/L options.

Integrating ICT in Schools

While modern or innovative teaching and learning practices do not specifically require a designer-built environment, it is difficult to imagine how these practices could be possible without the support of ICT (Green et al. 2005). Although an imbalance between the in school and out of school ICT lives of students exists (Green et al. 2005; OECD 2011; Shear et al. 2011), the integration of ICT into daily schooling life may enable innovative teaching and learning (2011) in a way that analogue, paper-based methods do not. Furthermore, the integration of technology in schools may be associated with efforts to focus on lifelong learning and the development of appropriate skills for the 21st century (Groff 2013; Hipkins et al. 2015), including the increased possibilities for between-teacher collaboration (Cowie et al. 2011; Hipkins et al. 2015).

Change resistance from teachers is, however, a factor from the outset of any change. While evolutionary change may be the least disruptive, it will be ponderous, and may be domesticated into the status quo (Groff 2013; Leicester et al. 2009). On the other hand, when a school is fully immersed in technology, there is the likelihood of faster uptake by teachers, whose own learning and pertinent use of ICT will progress more rapidly than for those teachers in schools that implement ICT piecemeal or more gradually (Cowie et al. 2011; Shapley et al. 2009). Whatever the pace of change, however, it may be that the coordination and re-design of the entire school infrastructure is required (Cowie et al. 2011; Groff 2013). In light of what has been stated already, this may include modernisation of the physical learning space, re-conceptualising the physical organisational arrangement of students, the approaches to curriculum and assessment, and the structuring of the school day.

Digital Pedagogy

The steady addition of new technologies, first with the arrival of television and video, and then, increasingly since the mid to late 1990s, digital devices, has required (or spawned) an 'e-Learning' industry. This industry cannot, arguably, thrive if its key message is that technology is merely a 'tool' (like an overhead projector). Anderson (2010), for example, found the integration of ICT in the classroom to shift teachers' roles from directed teaching to facilitation. Indeed, Brečko et al. (2014) argued that teachers should focus on pedagogy, rather than subject knowledge, suggesting that skills (particularly in ICT and innovating learning) are more important than disciplinary knowledge. These messages serve to liberate technology from its label as a 'tool' or 'electronic pencil'.

While the first stage of the development of the World Wide Web created a relatively static world accessed using the Internet, with key functions being browsing, messaging and information retrieval, the development since 2004 of the interactive Web 2.0 has created opportunities for content creation, manipulation and curating, shifting the emphasis away from machines and software. With this development too, has arisen the notion that 'everyone is an author', which has strengthened the hold of relativist epistemologies in schools and social life. Now, more than ever, 'knowledge' is whatever is trending that day on social media.

These challenges are also opportunities that have significant implications for education, and of course, for teachers. Yet, as Tambouris et al. (2012) suggest, teachers who fail to distinguish between Web 2.0 as a range of technologies (e.g., blogs, podcasts, wikis) and Web 2.0 as particular practices (e.g., blogging, podcasting, writing collaboratively) will continue to employ conservative approaches to teaching. By contrast, proactive and positive engagement with these media create opportunities for children to develop writing and reading skills, for example, as seen in the experience of the Manaiakalani Education Trust cluster of schools (Hipkins et al. 2015; Jesson et al. 2016). In these schools, the 'learn, create, share' model scaffolds initial learning, enabling this to be converted by an appropriate activity to a new product that a student shares more widely (by blogging, for instance).

ICT and Student Learning

Digital technology is reshaping the way people live and work, providing rapid access to knowledge and information. Accordingly, 'connectivism' is suggested as a new theory of learning (Siemens 2005) to supplant behaviourism, cognitivism and constructivism. These traditional theories reflect the slow pace of information development in an Industrial-Age model of schooling. Siemens argued the standard theories of learning are based on stable epistemologies that privilege the individual mind and do not provide for significant external technological manipulation and storage by digital technology. Digital technology developments have led to a situation where information and knowledge is available at unprecedented levels, and is added to and manipulated in ways that prioritise the ability to quickly evaluate, analyse and synthesise.

Instead of imagining that it is possible to learn established content, or seek to make meaning through social processes, it has become important to realise that meaning exists, but is hidden in the complexity and chaos that now presents itself. Knowledge (and understanding) arises from recognising hidden meanings, making connections and developing networks (Bolstad and Gilbert 2012; Siemens 2005). Thus the emerging picture of successful learners in a digital age is that of people able to be self-organised, discerning and proactive lifelong learners who seek to establish networks with others, in order to understand the patterns lying hidden beneath the apparent chaos and complexity of 21st century knowledge societies. Now the individual learner is required to discern what is important and to seek to make the connections among the myriad options, both human and digital (Siemens 2005).

Whether connectivism is a viable alternative learning theory or merely an offshoot of constructivism (Kop and Hill 2008) remains to be seen. Nevertheless, Siemens has brought attention to the implications for learning of an ICT-saturated world. Yet, conventional education systems still fail to fully grasp this new, complex and chaotic reality. As earlier noted, even where ICT has entered education, as Shear et al. (2011) discovered, content consumption by students continues to be prioritised over problem-solving, innovation and content creation. Yet, those who argue that school ought to prepare young people for life in the 21st century would prioritise students' collaborating, creating and curating content, and manipulating data. In the context of digital pedagogy in New Zealand, this concern is frequently captured in appeals to the 'SAMR model'.

The Substitution, Augmentation, Modification and Redefinition (SAMR) model identifies the level of complexity at which ICT is being integrated with teaching and learning (Puentedura 2013), and the demands e-Learning is making of students' engagement with ICT and associated software and applications. Converting a teacher-made document from paper form to electronic form is mere substitution, and results in nothing more than an electronic worksheet, posing few cognitive challenges. In contrast, creating new content moves students into the realm of redefinition, and depending on the complexity and uniqueness of the task, may represent that which was previously unimaginable without current digital technology. The SAMR model implies, therefore, not only that student learning can be greatly enhanced by technology, but also that teachers are required to extend their own digital capabilities to ensure they structure and facilitate activities to encourage redefinition.

Implementing SAMR does not avoid the question raised by sceptics of whether the integration of ICT into schools actually contributes to student learning. Sceptics may thus be pleased (or grimly satisfied) that some research findings report mixed results in this regard (Groff 2013; Jesson et al. 2016; OECD 2015). Evaluative research conducted in the state of Maine (Silvernail and Gritter 2007, in Groff, 2013, p. 15) indicated less than satisfactory effects on student learning in areas such as reading. Yet other studies have indicated positive results, such as Shapley et al. (2009), who reported students developing thinking skills and undertaking deeper, more complex inquiries, than students in regular classrooms. Groff was led to claim, "conflicting results [such as these] leave researchers timid to wholeheartedly endorse large investments in ICT in education" (2013, p. 15).

Despite the mixed results, Groff maintained that ICT integration benefits students' levels of engagement and motivation, providing opportunities for flexible, inquiry-driven personalised learning and collaboration. The Texan study mentioned above echoed this perspective, at least partly, as Shapley et al. (2009) found that technology immersion had positive effects on student collaboration, but, surprisingly, seemed to have little effect on student self-directed learning. And while there were some gains (based on the specific testing parameters of their study) for students in both reading and mathematics, the results were not statistically significant. Similarly, Jesson et al. (2016) did note increasing incidences in observed classes in the Auckland Manaiakalani cluster schools, of collaborative student learning. On the other hand, there continued to be relatively high incidences of independent work confined to single text analysis and worksheet completion.

As noted earlier, the quality of usage of ICT and the Internet may suggest a second 'digital divide', and in support of this contention is the general finding of the 2012 PISA round, that 88% of students reported Internet browsing as their most common leisure activity when using computers (OECD 2015), closely followed by social networking, downloading music and gaming. "Only 31% of students use computers at least once a week to upload their own content, such as music, poetry, videos or computer programs" (p. 42). A key finding suggested that the "impact [of

ICT] on student performance is mixed, at best", with the results of PISA "show[ing] no appreciable improvements in student achievement in reading, mathematics or science in the countries that had invested heavily in ICT for education" (p. 15). This observation lends weight to the idea (such as expressed by Green et al. 2005), that the provision of, or access to, ICT will not, alone, guarantee successful student learning or academic outcomes. A limitation of the OECD PISA test in this case (apart from any other critiques of it) was its reliance on self-reporting (2015).

Teachers' Reflective Practice

The demands made by 21st-century learning, and associated pedagogical shifts required to operationalise a personalised, authentic pedagogy in technology-rich flexible learning environments, conceivably require teachers to become intensely reflective about their work. The idea that teachers be reflective about their work is, however, not new, nor unusual. A simple Google search on the term, 'teachers' reflection' yields 39.5 million results; the question, "what does it mean to be a reflective teacher?" narrows the search to just 620,000 results; although the term, 'teachers' reflective practice' yields 3.5 million results.

In the New Zealand context, the professional act of teachers reflecting on their own work and performance is given added weight by the inclusion in The New Zealand Curriculum (MOE 2007) of 'teaching as inquiry', a suggested model to support teacher reflection. In addition, the last of twelve 'practising teacher criteria' indicates behaviours consistent with using "critical inquiry and problem-solving effectively in...professional practice" (Education Council New Zealand, nd.). In what follows, I will scope out some definitional boundaries around the act of reflective practice, suggest what it means to *become* reflective as well as to *be* reflective, and conclude with some comments about the implications for teachers' practice of their being critically reflective.

Definition

Argyris and Schön (1974) did much to embed the idea of professionals responding to their work by reflecting on its content, process and implications, and doing so in the professional company of peers and colleagues. Reflective thought is the search for grounds or evidence for beliefs. Dewey (1910) termed reflective thought the process whereby "the ground or basis for a belief is deliberately sought and its adequacy to support the belief examined...[this process]...is truly educative in value" (pp. 1–2). So, an understanding of reflective practice may begin with practitioners searching for good grounds and evidence to support their beliefs about their practice. This alone is not enough, however, as reflective thought, for Dewey, had to be deliberate and organised, with thoughts being logically and sequentially connected. There remains one more dimension to the picture Dewey built, namely habit: "*Active, persistent, and careful consideration of any belief or supposed form of knowledge in the light of the grounds that support it, and the further conclusions to which it tends,* constitutes reflective thought" (p. 6. Emphasis in the original).

Becoming Reflective

The stresses and demands of teaching in the 21st century include, as the subject of this book contends, the ability to work creatively and productively with digital media, to develop personalised learning approaches and to work collaboratively in large, flexible spaces. These may be added to those Larrivee (2000) referred to, such as child neglect, abuse and hunger, not to mention rapidly diversifying classrooms. Thus, teachers cannot move into their occupational roles to take up hermetically sealed positions; rather, they must develop the capacity to look beyond the technical requirements of their roles.

Being Reflective

Following Dewey (1910), being reflective would, at some point, require evidence gathering. Dewey regarded evidence to be crucial as the reflective process is prompted when thoughts about evidence suggest other possibilities. By probing those possibilities, a practitioner is being reflective. Therefore, simply thinking, is not an instance of 'being reflective'. Dewey was then asking for "something else which stands as witness, evidence, proof, voucher, warrant; that is, as *ground of belief*" (p. 8. Emphasis in original). Simply believing without hard evidence leads the believer to make groundless assumptions about practice.

The examination of personal assumptions is central to reflective practice (Brookfield 1995; Larrivee 2000). Getting to these assumptions requires practitioners to engage in penetrating self-reflection on their beliefs and values, which, Larrivee (2000) suggested, play out in the daily practice of teachers. Inquiring critically requires deeper consideration by teachers of the moral dimension of their practice, coupled to recognition of broader ethical issues and their impact on the classroom. It is the combination of personal self-reflection and critical inquiry that constitute reflective practice. By seeing teaching in terms of a broader moral purpose, underpinned by ethical actions, Larrivee was following Freire, both rejecting a notion of teaching as a technical matter (Freire 1998; Larrivee 2000), and both thus at odds with the steady reprofessionalisation of teachers by education reform. As Codd (2005) scathingly said of the post-1984 neoliberal reforms, "the culture of professionalism has been largely surrendered to a narrow and reductionist instrumentalism" (p. 194).

Freire has been criticised by some for his approach to developing criticality (for example, Lather (1998). See Roberts (2000) for a comprehensive discussion of these critiques). While he did not intend the approach he took (named 'conscientisation' by many, but not by Freire) to be taken up in a linear manner, he did nevertheless see developing criticality as a lifelong process of moving from states of 'ingenuous curiosity' to 'critical curiosity' (1998). Relatedly, he argued that teaching must develop from 'spontaneous teaching' to 'critical pedagogy' (1998). The defining feature of making this transition is critical reflection on practice (1998).

Larrivee (2000) outlined three essential practices for reflective practitioners: making time for solitary reflection, becoming a perpetual problem-solver and questioning the status quo. Examples of ways practitioners can self-reflect include reflecting alone, taking time to dwell on themselves and their practice, writing a journal entry, composing a blog or making notes on the plan for the lesson that did not go to plan. Larrivee regarded journal writing as a 'safe haven' and historical record (2000). For Brookfield (1995), this written self-examination, while difficult, is less stressful than having a colleague to critique one's practice. Recording of this kind was called 'describing' by Smyth (1992).

It is when practitioners realise that something is not as it ought to be, or is out of the ordinary, that they become sufficiently puzzled to reflect—a point emphasised by Argyris and Schön (1974). Teachers as professionals are people who must work within multiple contingencies presented by their daily work. Facing up to what is going on in the classroom, or in Larrivee's terms, problem-solving, is, for Smyth (1992), informing one's practice. Brookfield (1995) suggested a role here for theoretical literature, which can give teachers the vocabulary they require to name their practice. Once teachers can identify and name the problems or puzzles in classroom practice, according to Larrivee (2000), they may begin to recognise their own assumptions and, presumably, the brakes these place on their practice. This is challenging, and so Smyth quite rightly termed this 'confronting' (1992). Taking this examination of personal assumptions a step further, Smyth argued that teachers ought to recognise their personal belief and value system to be a product of wider "entrenched cultural norms" (p. 298), located "in a broader cultural, social and political context" (p. 299). Here again, Brookfield's (1995) suggestion of referring to theoretical literature can help to place practice in a wider context.

Lifting their gaze higher and over the parapet, teachers ought to question the status quo, suggested Larrivee (2000), though this is 'risky business' (p. 298). Just as individual teachers must probe their own assumptions, so they must "remain open to examining the [taken-for-granted] assumptions that underlie classroom practices" (p. 297). This may begin by looking critically at the policies governing school life, for example (2000). Smyth (1992) called this 'reconstructing', which entails, in part, challenging views that see teaching, teachers and education as somehow broken and deficient.

Echoing some of what has gone before, Reid (2004) motivated the view that teachers have to inquire into their professional practice because 20th century rationality and certainty have been replaced by 21st century complexities and uncertainties. This therefore calls on teachers to question their routine practices and assumptions and, most importantly, be capable of investigating the effects of their teaching on student learning. The school system, he argued, should prioritise inquiry and research, which will enhance the agency and capacity of teachers as professionals.

Seemingly, the New Zealand school system has been one that has sought to rise to this challenge, with the 'teaching as inquiry' (TAI) model, presented in The New Zealand Curriculum (MOE 2007). TAI is one of the 'teacher actions promoting student learning', and these actions are the basis of 'effective pedagogy' (p. 34). One important action is to "inquire into the teaching–learning relationship" (p. 34). The model suggests three inquiring questions: What is important (and therefore worth spending time on), given where my students are at? ('focusing inquiry'); What strategies (evidence-based) are most likely to help my students learn this? ('teaching inquiry'); What happened as a result of the teaching, and what are the implications for future teaching? ('learning inquiry') (p. 35). Using all available and relevant data and information (including collegial support), teachers ought to address these questions, with the answers pointing the way to improved practice that will enhance student achievement.

The TAI model has some deficiencies, not least that it is a model, which implies a formulaic approach to reflective practice. Furthermore, an unreflective approach to TAI will limit teachers' inquiries to just the questions posed by the model. The questions themselves are narrowly focussed on curriculum implementation in the context of individual lessons, despite teacher–student interactions occurring across a far broader range of activities. Although the designers of the model, Sinnema and Aitken (2011), argued that TAI does have a social justice orientation, it is difficult to tease out legitimate ethical concerns or social justice perspectives from the suggested questions. Countering the objections here, it can be argued that the high-profile presence of TAI in The New Zealand Curriculum at least provides teachers a tool and purpose to engage more reflectively with their work.

Implications for Practice

Those who attempt to reflect deeply on their own practice, in particular, the assumptions underpinning their practice, will find the process confronting, painful and perplexing (Dewey 1910; Larrivee 2000). An example closely related to developing the idea of modern teaching and learning practice, is the belief that the teacher must be in control to be effective. Challenging this idea can lead to uncertainty and vulnerability, but a critically reflective practitioner will be required "to act with integrity, openness, and commitment rather than compromise, defensiveness, or fear" (Larrivee 2000, p. 295). One implication for practice then is to actively seek feedback from colleagues and students (Brookfield 1995; Larrivee 2000).

A further implication (and also confronting) is the realisation that teaching practice is embedded in wider socio-political and economic contexts (Brookfield 1995; Freire 1998). As Freire noted, there is no neutral pedagogy, so failing to (or opting not to) take a position in relation to the status quo is, effectively, to support the status quo. This is a position accepted by Brookfield (1995) too. Curriculum policy and education policy more broadly, are underpinned by ideology and thus create contested and contestable terrain (1995). A status-quo orientation, Freire would have argued, is to accept curriculum and curriculum policy as taken-for-granted, and as unquestionably 'natural'. From such a perspective (and it *is* a perspective), no questions need to be raised. A critically reflective practitioner would, however, raise questions.

Reflective practice is evolutionary and dynamic (1995), and in this sense, Brookfield was in accord with Freire's view of teachers as unfinished (1998). Critical thinkers are always enquiring and good teaching is synonymous with self-conscious reflection (Brookfield 1995). Yet, reflection remains a deliberate act that is purposeful and not accidental (Dewey 1910), in which summative judgment and taken-for-granted assumptions must be suspended, while evidence and good grounds are sought.

Change Management

So far, a clear narrative has been built to make the case for a focus on 21st-century learning, supported by rapid advances in digital technology. These imperatives have implications for the content and manner of teachers' thinking about their work, though this process can have disruptive effects. These less perceptible changes of state are paralleled by more overt changes that have management and strategic implications for school leaders. Change is uncomfortable for many individuals and organisations, thus arguably, abrupt and poorly managed change can lead to conflict and disruption, with far reaching consequences for all those impacted by the effects, suggesting that there is merit in the view of Levin and Schrum (2012) that a managed process of collaborative reflection and discussion is required, to ensure the alignment of school mission and teacher expectations. This may therefore be a subject of ongoing professional learning and development. Thus, what follows will focus on questions around teacher stress, change management, and professional learning in relation to change.

Teacher Stress and Work Intensification

"Teacher stress may be defined as the experience by a teacher of unpleasant, negative emotions, such as anger, anxiety, tension, frustration or depression, resulting from some aspect of their work as a teacher" (Kyriacou 2001, p. 28).

The shifts now required of teachers may contribute significantly to creating stress. Stress can have unwelcome effects on health and well-being, and displaying stress can be seen as a weakness (Caulfield 2015). The research conducted by Caulfield (2015) indicated teaching multi-age and multi-ability as among the causes of teacher stress. Although their study indicated stress was prevalent among teachers, McCarthy et al. (2014) did not conclude that stress would always cause vocational concerns for teachers, apart from those who feel under-resourced.

Kyriacou (2001) detailed a number of sources of teacher stress, which included, among others, demotivated, ill-disciplined students, pressures of workload and time, and, significantly, being evaluated by others and dealings with colleagues. The reason for suggesting these latter two, is their relevance to shaping modern teaching and learning practice in environments where classroom practice is deprivatised, and working closely in small teams with colleagues. Yet, ironically, Kyriacou (2001) also found that strong collegiality, good communication and a pleasant building environment are all conducive to addressing teacher stress.

Work intensification may be related to significant changes to teachers' work heralded by managerialist reform measures such as standardised assessment, minutely detailed record-keeping for accountability purposes and rigorous teacher performance appraisal systems. At their inception, these measures created a low-trust working environment for teachers, and were strongly associated with neoliberal policy frameworks (Codd 2005; Snook 2003). Kane and Mallon (2006) identified the heavy workloads associated with reformist change in New Zealand as prompting teachers to consider departing the profession. Intensification means, for example, that teachers are required to give up more of their free time (MacBeath 2012) to deal with the business of schooling that seemingly, never ends. The ethos of the competitive market economy requires teachers to work harder and to work more demanding hours, against the demands of progressively higher stakes (2012). As is clear from what has already been said about modern teaching and learning practice, the emphasis has shifted from the teacher to the 'learner', and from a curriculum of disciplinary knowledge to a curriculum of dispositions. MacBeath (2012) noted this new social and moral teaching responsibility, simply deepening work intensification.

Change Management for Leadership

Consultants to the Scottish inspectorate of schools, Leicester et al. (2009) referred to a model of 'three horizons' of change. These horizons represent three stages of development in organisations, such as schools. Development moves from the status quo, through innovation into a disruptive space, which prefigures more radical change. In education, they suggested, the first horizon is traditional, mass schooling, the second personalised learning, while the third represents 'anywhere, anytime' open access learning.

Extending their horizons metaphor, Leicester et al. (2009) conceptualised mind-sets and variations in the concept of innovation across the three horizons. A managerialist mind-set dominates horizon one, where innovations focus on achieving efficiencies. An entrepreneurial mind-set at horizon two seeks out opportunities, while a visionary and aspirational mind-set at horizon three questions all assumptions, and strategises for a completely changed scenario. Critically, the status quo holds the power and resources, thus horizon two innovations look back at the status quo for approval, while horizon three innovations represent a clean break, but rely on these ideas taking hold across a wide front.

Drawing on lessons from the presidential life of Lincoln, Alvy and Robbins (2010), suggested that leaders should develop 'situational competence' to manage change as a complex and unpredictable process. Their notion of this concept may be summed up as having a good sense of timing, understanding and awareness of the context (or situation), and having a keen sense of the need for change (despite the potential for pain). It speaks of dissatisfaction with the past, and of a moral commitment to apply new thinking to a changing and challenging situation. Principals, say Alvy and Robbins, often deal in difficult situations, manage change that varies from mere tinkering to more fundamental change, and the resulting pain of loss associated with significant change. This change is contextual (and not necessarily universal or generalisable). In any event, managing this change process requires certain competencies (2010), including not taking for granted the impact of change on others, recognising the uniqueness of each school's culture, and having the ability to garner support from key stakeholders before commencing change. Sensitivity, empathy, visioning and modelling are critical characteristics (2010).

Staff Development and Learning

Although the adoption of modern or innovative teaching practices, including digital pedagogies, diminishes the 'teacher' in place of the 'facilitator of learning' or the 'learning coach', considerable 'pedagogic insight and skill' and 'strategic resourcefulness' is nevertheless required of teachers, to support them as they accommodate self-directed and flexible learning (MacBeath 2012, p. 91). This insight suggests new and ongoing challenges for teachers' professional development and learning. Indeed, teachers are required to be 'model learners' and must be able to mirror the ideal of the lifelong learner, adding significance to professional learning and development. But for teachers whose careers span decades, and who did not have to rely on technology, but instead on their long experience and well-developed classroom expertise (George et al. 2008), these changes are not easy to make. Developing competencies in their students while their own competencies are weak takes them beyond their existing comfort zones (Levin and Schrum 2012).

While the adoption of modern teaching and learning practices can occur in traditional, single-cell spaces, the introduction to education of flexible, digitally rich learning environments adds a significant layer of complexity to the change process.

Working in these environments comes with the expectation that teachers will work in collaborative teams, not only to plan together, but in fact to share teaching and pastoral duties, working in common, transparent surroundings with large groups of students (Bradbeer 2015). Teachers whose experience of teaching is limited to working alone behind the closed doors and walls of single-cell rooms, with perhaps no more than 30 or 35 students, are required to make considerable shifts in work and thought, which may be a bridge too far for some (2015). In their evaluation of the occupancy experiences of lecturers and students at the University of Helsinki, Ruismäki et al. (2015) found that teachers were less than keen to deprivatise their teaching. One of participants stated: "Not everyone wants to come to an aquarium-like space like this. Anyone can see what's happening…For many it is a big step to come and teach here. The smaller spaces…seem safer for some teachers…" (2015, p. 973).

The adoption of self-directed and autonomous learning is critical to the shift into flexible learning environments, as the practicalities of working in shared spaces with large groups makes demands on teachers that working with single classes in traditional classrooms does not. This change in practice is not automatic, however, and even in altered learning environments, pedagogic practice may default to the traditional (Imms and Byers 2016), or be rejected by teachers, who fear their autonomy is denied, and, ironically, their flexibility diminished (Murphy 2016). Thus, as Byers (2016) and Imms and Byers (2016) conclude, there may be an influential link between the learning environment and pedagogic practice, but not a causal one. Thus the provision of new and innovative facilities and technologies, while representing a considerable investment by governments, depend heavily on wider systemic and cultural change (Osborne 2016).

Any significant spatial reorganisation within a school must be coupled to revised "teaching and learning practices and based genuinely on the development of shared understandings of all those involved" (Woolner et al. 2012, p. 57). Realising the potential of innovative building designs and implementation of digital technology requires, therefore, that teachers be well prepared. This process ought to be inclusive and 'bottom up' rather than 'top down' (2012), and when spatial and pedagogical change is imposed, it may be associated with negativity, experienced by teachers, students and community (Murphy 2016). In the absence of adequate and effective professional development and learning, teachers default to traditional, default pedagogies (Byers 2016). There are thus ongoing implications of these insights for both professional learning developers and initial teacher educators.

Conclusion

While this book reflects on research conducted in New Zealand, in reality, the narrative is a global one. Education reform discourse is seemingly everywhere to be in evidence, and there are many common features of what I have noted in this chapter that international readers will recognise within their own national contexts.

The notion of '21st-century learning' can and does flourish thanks to the narrative of an unknowable future, greatly propelled by ubiquitous digitisation and web-saturation. Significant manifestations of this notion include the penetration of digital devices into schools, and emergent innovative building designs. These manifestations encourage, enable and demand non-traditional approaches to teaching and learning. They challenge teachers to become reflective practitioners, and school leaders to be agents of change leadership.

References

21st Century Learning Reference Group. (2014). *Future-focused learning in connected communities.* Retrieved from http://www.education.govt.nz/assets/Documents/Ministry/Initiatives/FutureFocusedLearning30May2014.pdf

Alvy, H., & Robbins, P. (2010). *Learning from Lincoln: Leadership practices for school success* [EBL version]. Retrieved from http://www.aut.eblib.com.au.ezproxy.aut.ac.nz

Ananiadou, K., & Claro, M. (2009). 21st century skills and competences for new millennium learners in OECD countries. *OECD Education Working Papers*, No. 41, OECD Publishing. doi:10.1787/218525261154

Anderson, J. (2010). *ICT transforming education: A regional guide.* Bangkok, Thailand: UNESCO. http://unesdoc.unesco.org/images/0018/001892/189216e.pdf

Argyris, C., & Schön, D. A. (1974). *Theory in practice: Increasing professional effectiveness.* San Francisco, CA: Jossey-Bass.

Beetham, H., & Sharpe, R. (Eds). (2013). An introduction to rethinking pedagogy. In H. Beetham & R. Sharpe (Eds.), *Rethinking pedagogy for a digital age: Designing for 21st century learning* (2nd ed., pp. 41–61). New York, NY/London, England: Routledge.

Benade, L. (2014). Knowledge and educational research in the context of '21st century learning'. *European Educational Research Journal, 13*(2), 338–349. doi:10.2304/eerj.2014.13.3.338

Benade, L. (2015a). Bits, bytes and dinosaurs: Using Levinas and Freire to address the concept of 'twenty-first century learning'. *Educational Philosophy and Theory, 47*(9), 935–948.

Benade, L. (2015b). Teachers' critical reflective practice in the context of twenty-first century learning. *Open Review of Educational Research, 2*(1), 42–54. doi:10.1080/23265507.2014.998159

Benade, L. (2015c). Teaching as inquiry: Well intentioned, but fundamentally flawed. *New Zealand Journal of Educational Studies, 50*(1), 107–120. doi:10.1007/s40841-015-0005-0

Benade, L., Gardner, M., Teschers, C., & Gibbons, A. (2014). 21st Century learning in New Zealand: Leadership insights and perspectives. *New Zealand Journal of Educational Leadership, Policy and Practice, 29*(2), 47–60.

Bennett, S., & Maton, K. (2010). Beyond the 'digital natives' debate: Towards a more nuanced understanding of students' technology experiences. *Journal of Computer Assisted learning, 26,* 321–331. doi:10.1111/j.1365-2729.2010.00360.x

Biesta, G. (2014). Pragmatising the curriculum: Bringing knowledge back into the curriculum conversation, but via pragmatism. *The Curriculum Journal, 25*(1), 29–49. doi:10.1080/09585176.2013.874954

Bishop, R. (2011). Freeing ourselves from neo-colonial domination in public school classrooms. In R. Bishop (Ed.), *Freeing ourselves* (pp. 31–73). Rotterdam, The Netherlands: Sense Publishers. doi:10.1007/978-94-6091-415-7_2. Retrieved from http://link.springer.com.ezproxy.aut.ac.nz

Blackmore, J., Bateman, D., Loughlin, J., O'Mara, J., & Aranda, G. (2011). *Research into the connection between built learning spaces and student outcomes.* Literature review, paper

No. 22 June. State of Victoria (Department of Education and Early Childhood Development). Retrieved from http://www.education.vic.gov.au

Bolstad, R., & Gilbert, J. (2008). *Disciplining and drafting, or 21st century learning? Rethinking the New Zealand senior secondary curriculum for the future*. Wellington, New Zealand: NZCER Press.

Bolstad, R., Gilbert, J., McDowall, S., Bull, A., Boyd, S. & Hipkins, R. (2012). *Supporting Future-Oriented Learning and Teaching: A New Zealand perspective*. Report prepared for the Ministry of Education. Wellington: New Zealand Council for Educational Research and Ministry of Education. Retrieved August 8, 2015, from http://www.educationcounts.govt.nz/publications/schooling/109306.

Bradbeer, C. (2015, August). *Finished beginnings: Finding space for time in collaborative teacher practice* [Video File]. Paper presented at Terrains 2015 Conference, E21LE, Melbourne, Australia: University of Melbourne. Retrieved from http://www.metacdn.com/r/m/vfahnolm/2i7yURX9

Brečko, B., Kampylis, P., & Punie, Y. (2014) *Mainstreaming ICT-enabled innovation in education and training in Europe: Policy actions for sustainability, scalability and impact at system level*. Luxembourg: Office of European Union, European Commission, Joint Research Centre. doi:10.2788/52088. Retrieved March 6, 2016 from http://ipts.jrc.ec.europa.eu/publications/pub.cfm?id=6361

Brookfield, S. (1995). *Becoming a critically reflective teacher*. San Francisco, CA: Jossey-Bass.

Brown, P., Lauder, H., & Ashton, D. (2011). *The global auction: The broken promises of education, jobs and incomes*. New York, NY: Oxford University Press.

Byers, T. K. (2016). *Evaluating the effects of different classroom spaces on teaching and learning* (Doctoral thesis). The University of Melbourne, Melbourne, Australia. Retrieved from http://hdl.handle.net/11343/115307

Caulfield, A. (2015). *The contribution of the practice of mindfulness to stress reduction among school teachers: A qualitative study of Irish primary teachers*. Unpublished Doctor of Education thesis, University of Lincoln, United Kingdom.

Center for Teaching and Learning (2001). *Problem-Based Learning* in Stanford University Newsletter on Teaching, 11(1), pp. 1–7. Retrieved from http://web.stanford.edu/dept/CTL/cgi-bin/docs/newsletter/problem_based_learning.pdf.

Chapman, A., Randell-Moon, H., Campbell, M., & Drew, C. (2014). Students in space: Student practices in non-traditional classrooms. *Global Studies of Childhood, 4*(1), 39–48. doi:10.2304/gsch.2014.4.1.39

Cleveland, B., & Fisher, K. (2014). The evaluation of physical learning environments: A critical review of the literature. *Learning Environments Research, 4*(17), 1–28. doi:10.1007/s10984-013-9149-3

Codd, J. (2005). Teachers as 'managed professionals' in the global education industry: The New Zealand experience. *Educational Review, 57*(2), 193–206. doi:10.1080/0013191042000308369

Commission of the European Communities. (2000). A memorandum on lifelong learning. *Commission Staff Working Paper*. http://www.bologna-berlin2003.de/pdf/MemorandumEng.pdf

Cook, H. (2015, November 23). Schools hit a wall with open-plan classrooms. *The Age*. Retrieved May 25, 2016 from http://www.theage.com.au/victoria/schools-hit-a-wall-with-openplan-classrooms-20151123-gl5vo8.html

Cowie, B., Jones, A., & Harlow, A. (2011). Laptops for teachers: Practices and possibilities. *Teacher Development, 15*(2), 241–255. doi:10.1080/13664530.2011.571513

Dant, T. (2005). *Materiality and society*. Berkshire, United Kingdom: Open University Press.

Davidson, C. N., & Goldberg, D. T. (2010). *The future of thinking: Learning institutions in a digital age*. Cambridge, MA: The MIT Press.

Davis, A. W., & Kappler-Hewitt, K. (2013, June/July). Australia's campfires, caves and watering holes. *Learning & Leading with Technology*, 24–27. International Society for Technology in Education. Retrieved from http://files.eric.ed.gov/fulltext/EJ1015175.pdf

References

Dewey, J. (1910). *How we think* (pp. 1–13). Lexington, MA: D C Heath. doi:10.1037/10903-001. Retrieved from http://ovidsp.tx.ovid.com.ezproxy.aut.ac.nz

Dumont, H., & Istance, D. (2010). Analysing and designing learning environments for the 21st century. In H. Dumont, D. Istance & F. Benavides (Eds.), *The nature of learning: Using research to inspire practice* (pp. 19–34). Paris, France: Organisation for Economic Cooperation and Development Publishing. doi:10.1787/9789264086487-3-en

Dumont, H., Istance, D., & Benavides, F. (Eds.). (2010). *The nature of learning: Using research to inspire practice*. Paris, France: OECD Publishing. doi:10.1787/9789264086487-3-en

Fabbri, J., & Charue-Duboc, F. (2013). The role of physical space in collaborative workplaces hosting entrepreneurs: The case of the 'Beehive' in Paris. In F.-X. de Vaujany & N. Mitev (Eds.), *Materiality and space: Organizations, artefacts and practices* (pp. 117–134). Basingstoke, United Kingdom: Palgrave Macmillan.

Fisher, K. (2005a). *Linking pedagogy and space* [Slide presentation]. Retrieved from http://www.education.vic.gov.au/Documents/school/principals/infrastructure/pedagogyspace.pdf

Fisher, K. (2005b). Research into identifying effective learning environments. Retrieved from http://www.oecd.org/education/innovation-education/centreforeffectivelearningenvironmentscele/37905387.pdf

Freire, P. (1970/1996). *Pedagogy of the oppressed* (M. Ramos, Trans.). London: Penguin Books.

Freire, P. (1998). *Pedagogy of freedom: Ethics, democracy and civic courage*. Lanham, MD: Rowman and Littlefield.

Gay, G. (2002). Preparing for culturally responsive teaching. *Journal of Teacher Education, 53*(2), 106–116.

Gensler. (2016a). *About Gensler*. Retrieved from http://www.gensler.com/uploads/document/355/file/About_Gensler_Fact_Sheet_160219.pdf

Gensler. (2016b). *The future of workplace*. Retrieved March 4, 2016 from http://www.gensler.com/the-future-of-workplace

Green, H., Facer, K., Rudd, T., Dillon, P., & Humphreys, P. (2005). *Personalisation and digital technologies*. Bristol, England: Futurelab. Retrieved February 6, 2016 from http://www.nfer.ac.uk/publications/FUTL59/FUTL59_home.cfm

Groff, J. (2013). Technology-rich innovative learning environments. *OECD CERI Innovative Learning Environments Project*. Retrieved from http://www.oecd.org/edu/ceri/Technology-Rich%20Innovative%20Learning%20Environments%20by%20Jennifer%20Groff.pdf

Hassell, K. (2011, October 1). Flexible classroom furniture. *American School and University*. Retrieved March 23, 2016 from http://asumag.com/Furniture/adaptable-classroom-furniture-201110

Helsper, E. J., & Eynon, R. (2010). Digital natives: where is the evidence? *British Educational Research Journal, 36*(3), 503–520. doi:10.1080/01411920902989227

Heppell, S. (2016). *Total learning*. Retrieved February 21, 2016 from http://rubble.heppell.net/three/

Higgins, S., Hall, E., Wall, K., Woolner, P., & McCaughey, C. (2005). *The impact of school environments: A literature review*. Produced for the Design Council. University of Newcastle, The Centre for Learning and Teaching School of Education, Communication and Language Science. Retrieved from http://www.ncl.ac.uk/cflat/news/DCReport.pdf

Hipkins, R., Whatman, J., & MacDonald, J. (2015). *Evaluation of the Manaiakalani Digital Teaching Academy*. Wellington: New Zealand Council for Educational Research. Retrieved from https://www.educationcounts.govt.nz/publications/e-Learning/evaluation-of-the-manaiakalani-digital-teaching-academy

Huang, J., Cherubini, M., Nova, N., & Dillenbourg, P. (2009). Introduction: Why would furniture be relevant for collaborative learning? In P. Dillenbourg, J. Huang & M. Cherubini (Eds.), *Interactive artifacts and furniture supporting collaborative work and learning* (pp. 1–13). New York, NY: Springer. doi:10.1007/978-0-387-77234-9_1

Imms, W., & Byers, T. (2016, online). Impact of classroom design on teacher pedagogy and student engagement and performance in mathematics. *Learning Environments Research*. doi:10.1007/s10984-016-9210-0

Jesson, R., McNaughton, S., Rosedale, N., Zhu, T., Meredith, M., & Kegel, A. (2016). *Manaiakalani Whānau capability building and classroom instruction*. Final Report—Executive Summary. Auckland: Auckland UniServices Limited, The University of Auckland. Retrieved from http://www.manaiakalani.org/our-story/research-evaluation/2015%20Executive%20Summary.pdf

Jones, C. (2011). Students, the net generation, and digital natives: Accounting for educational change. In M. Thomas (Ed.), *Deconstructing digital natives: Young people, technology and the new literacies* (pp. 30–45). New York, NY: Routledge Taylor & Francis e-Library.

Kane, R. G., & Mallon, M. (2006). *Perceptions of teachers and teaching*. New Zealand: Ministry of Education. Retrieved March 24, 2016 from https://www.educationcounts.govt.nz/publications/ECE/2535/5967

Kop, R., & Hill, A. (2008). Connectivism: Learning theory of the future or vestige of the past? *International Review of Research in Open and Distance Learning, 9*(3), 1–13. Retrieved March 12, 2016 from http://www.irrodl.org/index.php/irrodl/article/view/523/1137

Kuuskorpi, M., & Cabellos González, N. (2011). *The future of the physical learning environment: School facilities that support the user*. CELE Exchange, Centre for Effective Learning Environments, OECD Publishing. doi:10.1787/5kg0lkz2d9f2-en

Kyriacou, C. (2001). Teacher stress: Directions for future research. *Educational Review, 53*(1), 27–35. doi:10.1080/00131910120033628

Lang, B. (2015, January 1). Movie box office drops 5% in 2014: what's behind the fall. *Boston Herald*. Retrieved February 22, 2016 from http://www.bostonherald.com/entertainment/movies/movie_news/2015/01/movie_box_office_drops_5_in_2014_whats_behind_the_fall

Larrivee, B. (2000). Transforming teacher practice: Becoming the critically reflective teacher. *Reflective Practice, 1,* 293–307. doi:10.1080/14623940020025561

Lather, P. (1998). Critical pedagogy and its complictities: A praxis of stuck places. *Educational Theory, 48*(4), 487–497. doi:10.1111/j.1741-5446.1998.00487.x

Lefebvre, H. (1991). *The production of space* (D. Nicholson-Smith, Trans.). Malden, MA: Blackwell.

Leicester, G., Stewart, D., & Bloomer, K. (2009). *Transformative innovation in education: A playbook for pragmatic visionaries*. Axminster, England: Triarchy Press Ltd.

Levin, B. B., & Schrum, L. (2012). *Leading technology-rich schools: Award winning models for success*. New York, NY: Teachers College Press.

Lippman, P. C. (2015). Designing collaborative spaces for schools. Condensed from *T.H.E. Journal*, February 2013. Available from http://thejournal.com/articles

MacBeath, J. (2012). *Future of teaching profession*. Cambridge, England: University of Cambridge, Education International Research Institute. Retrieved from http://download.ei-ie.org/Docs/WebDepot/EI%20Study%20on%20the%20Future%20of%20Teaching%20Profession.pdf

Macfarlane, A., Glynn, T., Cavanagh, T., & Bateman, S. Creating culturally-safe schools for Maori students. *Australian Journal of Indigenous Education, 36,* 65–76. doi:10.1017/S1326011100004439. Retrieved from http://researchcommons.waikato.ac.nz/bitstream/handle/10289/3297/creating%20culturally%20safe%20school..?sequence=1

Marley, D. (2007, November 23). Stage, not age, is key to better learning, specialist schools told. *TES Newspaper*. Retrieved February 21, 2016 from https://www.tes.com/article.aspx?storycode=2466355

Matters, G. (2006, October). Good data, bad news, good policy making. *QTU Professional Magazine*, 18–24. Retrieved from http://www.qtu.asn.au/files/8713/2268/2363/vol21_matters.pdf

McCarthy, C. J., Lambert, R. G., & Reiser, J. (2014). Vocational concerns of elementary teachers: Stress, job satisfaction, and occupational commitment. *Journal of Employment Counseling, 51,* 59–74. doi:10.1002/j.2161-1920.2014.00042.x

McGregor, J. (2004). Spatiality and the place of the material in schools. *Pedagogy, Culture and Society, 12*(3), 347–372. doi:10.1080/14681360400200207

References

McPhail, G. (2016). From aspirations to practice: Curriculum challenges for a new 'twenty-first-century' secondary school. *The Curriculum Journal (online first)*. doi:10.1080/09585176.2016.1159593

McPhail, G., & Rata, E. (2015). Comparing curriculum types: 'Powerful knowledge' and '21st century learning'. *New Zealand Journal of Educational Studies (online first)*. doi:10.1007/s40841-015-0025-9

Mealings, K., Buchholz, J., Demuth, K., & Dillon, H. (2015). Investigating the acoustics of a sample of open plan and enclosed Kindergarten classrooms in Australia. *Applied Acoustics, 100*(2015), 95–105. doi:10.1016/j.apacoust.2015.07.009

Meyer, H.-D., & Benavot, A. (2013). Introduction. In H.-D. Meyer & A. Benavot. (Eds.), *PISA, power, and policy: The emergence of global educational governance* (pp. 9–26). Oxford, United Kingdom: Symposium Books.

Miller, D. (2005). Materiality: An introduction. In D. Miller (Ed.), *Materiality* (pp. 1–50). Durham, NC: Duke University Press.

Miller, R., Shapiro, H., & Hilding-Hamann, K. E. (2008). *School's over: Learning spaces in Europe in 2020: An imagining exercise on the future of learning*. Luxembourg: European Commission Joint Research Centre Institute for Prospective Technological Studies. doi:10.2791/54506

Ministry of Education. (2007). *The New Zealand curriculum*. Wellington, New Zealand: Learning Media Limited. Available from http://nzcurriculum.tki.org.nz/The-New-Zealand-Curriculum

Ministry of Education. (2014). *Key competencies*. Retrieved September 17, 2016 from http://nzcurriculum.tki.org.nz/Key-competencies

Ministry of Education. (2016). *Flexible learning spaces in schools*. Retrieved October 30, 2016 from http://www.education.govt.nz/school/property/state-schools/design-standards/flexible-learning-spaces/

Moore, G. T., & Lackney, J. A. (1993). School design: Crisis, educational performance and design applications. *Children's Environments, 10*(2), 99–112. www.jstor.org

Morrison, R. L., & Macky, K. A. (2017). The demands and resources arising from shared office spaces. *Applied Ergonomics, 60*, 103–115. doi:10.1016/j.apergo.2016.11.007

Murphy, C. (2016). *Making the shift: Perceptions and challenges of modern learning practice* (Masters thesis). The University of Waikato, Hamilton, New Zealand. Retrieved from https://researchcommons.waikato.ac.nz

Nair, P. (2011). The classroom is obsolete: It's time for something new. Retrieved from http://www.edweek.org/ew/articles/2011/07/29/37nair.h30.html

Nair, P. (2014). *Blueprint for tomorrow: Redesigning schools for student-centered learning*. Cambridge, MA: Harvard Education Press.

Nair, P., Fielding, R., & Lackney, J. (2013). *The language of school design: Design patterns for 21st century schools* (3rd ed.). Minneapolis, MN: DesignShare.

Netflix. (2015). Q4'15 Report to shareholders. Retrieved from http://files.shareholder.com/downloads/NFLX/1298564620x0x870685/C6213FF9-5498-4084-A0FF-74363CEE35A1/Q4_15_Letter_to_Shareholders_-_COMBINED.pdf

New Zealand Parliament. (2012). *Inquiry into 21st century learning environments and digital literacy: Report of the Education and Science Committee*. Retrieved October 11, 2014 from http://www.parliament.nz/en-nz/pb/sc/documents/reports/50DBSCH_SCR5695_1/inquiry-into-21st-century-learning-environments-and-digital

Nielsen, A. C. (2004). *Best practice in school design* (No. 1407454/1407463). Report Prepared For the Ministry of Education. Wellington, New Zealand: Ministry of Education.

Oblinger, D.G. 2005, 'Space as a change agent', in D.G. Oblinger (Ed.), *Learning spaces*, pp. 1.1-1.4. Educause, Boulder. Available at: http://www.educause.edu/LearningSpaces

O'Brien, K., Reams, J., Caspari, A., Dugmore, A., Faghihimani, M., Fazey, I. ... Winiwarter, V. (2013). You say you want a revolution? Transforming education and capacity building in response to global change. *Environmental Science & Policy, 28*, 48–59. doi:10.1016/j.envsci.2012.11.011

Organisation for Economic Cooperation and Development (OECD). (2003). *Definition and selection of competencies: Theoretical and conceptual foundations (DeSeCo): Summary of the final report*. Retrieved August 17, 2015 from http://www.oecd.org/education/skills-beyond-school/definitionandselectionofcompetenciesdeseco.htm

Organisation for Economic Cooperation and Development (OECD). (2011). PISA 2009 results: Students on line: Digital technologies and performance (Volume VI). 10.1787/9789264112995-en. Retrieved March 4, 2016 from http://www.oecd-ilibrary.org/education/pisa-2009-results-students-on-line_9789264112995-en

Organisation for Economic Cooperation and Development (OECD). (2013). *Innovative learning environments*. Paris, France: Educational Research and Innovation, OECD Publishing. doi:10.1787/9789264203488-en. Retrieved February 7, 2016 from http://www.oecd-ilibrary.org/education/innovative-learning-environments_9789264203488-en

Organisation for Economic Cooperation and Development (OECD). (2015). *Students, computers and learning: Making the connection*. Paris, France: PISA, OECD Publishing. doi:10.1787/9789264239555-en. Retrieved February 7, 2016 from http://www.oecd-ilibrary.org/education/students-computers-and-learning_9789264239555-en

Osborne, M. (2016). *Innovative learning environments* (Core Education White Paper). Retrieved from http://www.core-ed.org/sites/core-ed.org/files/Innovative-Learning-Environments-FINAL-web.pdf

Paton, G. (2008, May 5). Classes 'based on ability not age in five years'. *The Telegraph*. Retrieved from http://www.telegraph.co.uk/news/uknews/1929752/Classes-based-on-ability-not-age-in-five-years.html

Pearlman, B. (2010). Designing new learning environments to support 21st century skills. In J. Bellanca & R. Brandt (Eds.), *21st century skills: Rethinking how students learn* (pp. 117–148). Bloomington, IN: Solution Tree Press.

Pickering, A. (2013). Living in the material world. In F.-X. de Vaujany & N. Mitev (Eds.), *Materiality and space: Organizations, artefacts and practices* (pp. 25–40). Basingstoke, United Kingdom: Palgrave Macmillan.

Prensky, M. (2011). Digital wisdom and homo sapiens digital. In M. Thomas (Ed.), *Deconstructing digital natives: Young people, technology and the new literacies* (pp. 15–29). New York, NY: Routledge Taylor & Francis e-Library.

Puentedura, R. P. (2013, June 13). The SAMR model explained by Ruben R. Puentedura [Video file]. Retrieved from https://www.youtube.com/watch?v=_QOsz4AaZ2k

Rata, E. (2012). *The politics of knowledge in education*. New York/London: Routledge Taylor and Francis Group.

Reh, S., Rabenstein, K., & Fritzsche, B. (2011). Learning spaces without boundaries? Territories, power and how schools regulate learning. *Social and Cultural Geography, 12*(1), 83–98. doi:10.1080/14649365.2011.542482

Reh, S., & Temel, R. (2014). Observing the doings of built spaces. Attempts of an ethnography of materiality. *Historical Social Research, 39*(2), 167–180. doi:10.12759/hsr.39.2014.2.167-180

Reid, A. (2004). *Towards a culture of inquiry in DECS*. Government of South Australia, Department of Education and Children's Services. Retrieved March 25, 2016 from https://www.researchgate.net/publication/242749924_Towards_a_Culture_of_Inquiry_in_DECS

Roberts, P. (2000). *Education, literacy, and humanization: An introduction to the work of Paulo Freire*. Westport, CT: Greenwood Press.

Robertson, S. (2005). Re-imagining and rescripting the future of education: Global knowledge economy discourses and the challenge to education systems. *Comparative Education, 41*(2), 151–170. doi:10.1080/03050060500150922

Robinson, K. (2010, October). Changing education paradigms [Video file]. Retrieved from https://www.ted.com/talks/ken_robinson_changing_education_paradigms

Ruismäki, H., Salomaa, R.-L., & Ruokonen, I. (2015). Minerva plaza–A new technology-rich learning environment. *Procedia—Social and Behavioral Sciences, 171*, 968–981. doi:10.1016/j.sbspro.2015.01.216. Retrieved from http://www.sciencedirect.com/science/article/pii/S1877042815002463

References

Senge, P. (1992). *The fifth discipline: The art and practice of the learning organization*. Sydney, Australia: Random House.

Shapley, K., Sheehan, D., Sturges, K., Caranikas-Walker, F., Huntsberger, B., & Maloney, C. (2009). *Evaluation of the Texas technology immersion pilot: Final outcomes for a four-year study (2004–05 to 2007–08)*. Austin, TX: Texas Center for Educational Research. Retrieved from http://files.eric.ed.gov/fulltext/ED536296.pdf

Shear, L., Gallagher, L., & Patel, D. (2011). Innovative teaching and learning research 2011 findings: Evolving educational ecosystems. *SRI International*. Retrieved from http://www.itlresearch.com/images/stories/reports/ITL%20Research%202011%20Findings%20and%20Implications%20-%20Final.pdf

Siemens, G. (2005). Connectivism: A learning theory for the digital age. Retrieved from http://er.dut.ac.za/bitstream/handle/123456789/69/Siemens_2005_Connectivism_A_learning_theory_for_the_digital_age.pdf?sequence=1

Sinnema, C., & Aitken, G. (2011). Teaching as Inquiry in the New Zealand curriculum: Origins and implementation. In J. Parr, H. Hedges, & S. May (Eds.), *Changing trajectories of teaching and learning* (pp. 29–48). Wellington, New Zealand: NZCER Press.

Smardon, D., Charteris, J., & Nelson, E. (2015). Shifts to learning eco-systems: Principals' and teachers' perceptions of innovative learning environments. *New Zealand Journal of Teachers' Work, 12*(2), 149–171. Retrieved from https://teachworkojs.aut.ac.nz/autojs/index.php/nzjtw/article/view/31/56

Smyth, J. (1992). Teachers' work and the politics of reflection. *American Educational Research Journal, 29*(2), 267–300. Retrieved from http://www.jstor.org/stable/1163369

Snook, I. (2003). *The ethical teacher*. Palmerston North, New Zealand: Dunmore Press.

St. George, A., Brown, S., & O'Neill, J. (Eds.). (2008). *Facing the big questions in teaching: Purpose, power and learning*. Auckland, New Zealand: Cengage Learning.

Sullivan, C. C. (2012, February). Classroom furniture—The third teacher. *Buildings 106*(2), 24. Business Source Complete.

Tambouris, E., Panopoulou, E., Tarabanis, K., Ryberg, T., Buus, L., Peristeras, V. … Porwol, L. (2012). Enabling problem based learning through Web 2.0 Technologies: PBL 2.0. *Educational Technology & Society, 15*(4), 238–251.

Thornburg, D. (2007). *Campfires in cyberspace: Primordial metaphors for learning in the 21st century*. Retrieved from http://tcpd.org/Thornburg/Handouts/Campfires.pdf

Van Ness, D. W., & Strong, K. H. (2010). *Restoring justice: An introduction to restorative justice*. New Providence, N.J.: LexisNexis, Anderson Pub.

Vieluf, S., Kaplan, D., Klieme, E., & Bayer, S. (2012). *Teaching practices and pedagogical innovations: Evidence from TALIS*. Paris, France: OECD Publishing. http://www.oecd-ilibrary.org/education/teaching-practices-and-pedagogical-innovations_9789264123540-en. doi:10.1787/23129638

Wlodkowski, R. J., & Ginsberg, M. B. (1995). A framework for culturally responsive teaching. *Educational Leadership, 53*(1), 17–21.

Woolner, P., McCarter, S., Wall, K., & Higgins, S. (2012). Changed learning through changed space: When can a participatory approach to the learning environment challenge preconceptions and alter practice? *Improving Schools, 15*(1), 45–60. doi:10.1177/1365480211434796

Young, M. F. D. (2008). *Bringing knowledge back in: From social constructivism to social realism in the sociology of education*. London, England/New York, NY: Routledge.

Young, M. F. D. (2012). Can educational research be about social justice? *Opening a Debate, Pacific-Asian Education, 24*(1), 9–16.

Young, M. F. D. (2013). Overcoming the crisis in curriculum theory: A knowledge-based approach. *Journal of Curriculum Studies, 45*(2), 101–118. doi:10.1080/00220272.2013.764505

Young, M. F. D., & Muller, J. (2010). Knowledge, truth and the sociology of education. In R. Moore & K. Maton (Eds.), *Social realism, knowledge and the sociology of education: Coalitions of the mind*. London, England: Continuum Books.

Chapter 4
The Impacts on Teachers' Work: 21st-Century Learning

I started at this school two and a half years ago. I did my first three terms as a teacher in a single cell room and then I moved into the big space and have been collaboratively teaching in a sense. I think when I started teaching I…had this big idea about students taking more responsibility and learning alongside the teacher. But I think when I started out in my single cell room that looked more like me taking responsibility for making sure the kids had this learning activity, this learning, this learning, this learning and…in my mind…I thought oh yes, look they're taking responsibility, they're doing this, they're doing this, but looking back it was actually all my initiating their learning for them. (teacher Angelus School, FG).

The following chapters of this book focus primarily on the 'Being a Teacher in the 21st Century' study, undertaken in 2015, though they necessarily draw on the earlier, '21st-Century Learning' study. Over the following chapters, I will generate a critical discussion of, and reflection on, 21st-century learning, its manifestation in flexible learning spaces and digital pedagogies and will suggest how these impact on teachers' work. In particular, these impacts will be understood from the perspective of the participants who willingly gave of their time to speak with me, and who graciously permitted me to spend many hours in their places and spaces of work. These are practitioners who see themselves as leading, or, in some cases, being led towards, new ways of conceptualising their work. In the main, they recognise that education, or, more specifically, schooling, cannot simply continue as it always has. Thus it is important to have mapped some of the important routes their pedagogical transitions have taken.

In Vagle's view of the world, these people are each in an intentional relationship with their surrounding lifeworld, while from a critical perspective, it is apparent that this lifeworld is significantly shaped and altered by policy directives at a macro-, global level (specifically, but not solely, the OECD), at the meso-level (the Ministry of Education, clusters of schools) and at the micro-level (within each school, down to the level of the classroom or learning space). These matters are the subject of the penultimate chapter, where it is suggested that understanding some of the processes present in the dialectical play and movement between the micro-, meso- and macro-levels provides greater insight to the processes of change. The micro-, school level, remains nevertheless to be of most interest and relevance to this study, so there is considerable value in understanding change management and strategic shifts at that level, as these processes too have considerable impact on teachers' work.

In the current chapter, I will briefly consider the notion of modern teaching and learning from a critical perspective. This will prepare the reader for the primary content of the chapter, which is to provide insight to various elements of observed practices in three of the participant schools. The chapter will conclude with some critical reflections.

The Demands of Modern Teaching and Learning Practices: A Critical Perspective

The handy moniker '21st-century learning', vested with the idea of learning and teaching as preparation for the 21st century world, is imperfect, but then so are terms like 'modern learning', 'innovative learning' and 'modern teaching and learning practice', often heard among practitioners. An alternative to 'modern' may be 'progressive', though it too may be associated with some of the approaches dating back as far as the late nineteenth and early twentieth centuries, including the thinking of educators such as John Dewey, and the child-centred approaches popularised in the 1960s. Somewhat over-used, its value is probably limited. Whatever term is chosen, therefore, implies that some care be taken, as the term is quickly taken up into the vernacular, often losing any clearly defined meaning along the way. What follows here makes some critical points in relation to several practices associated with any of these terms, and serves as a precursor to considering the practical studies with the schools and practitioners I spent time with in 2015.

Policy-makers and politicians have serious intent in regard to both the improvement of school systems in general (through, for example, standardisation and 'back to basics' logic) and the rapid evolution of classroom practices towards a modern, innovative or future-focussed orientation. According to Kay (2010), today's students are different, and traditional learning outcomes do not focus on the future. What is now required, he argued, was to rigorously recreate appropriate learning outcomes for the very different 21st century world of work, and life, and here, he suggested, is the scope for educationists and the business community to collaborate. Once they agree on mutually valued student outcomes, then systems can be created to deliver an appropriate education. It is debateable whether there is clarity over what the '21st century skills' are and whether, or to what extent non-education specialists ought to influence the determination of the outcomes of education. Nevertheless, there is some unanimity regarding the ways to develop these skills, namely

- personalisation (linked to the habits and user-initiated behaviours emerging from digital practice);
- the significance of authentic, project- or problem-based learning;

- re-conceptualising the grouping of students and their daily schedule; and
- the development of flexible learning spaces.
- Underpinning much modern teaching and learning practice is the integration of digital technology.

Personalised learning does not imply a *laissez-faire* approach to schooling, despite personal choice and student co-construction of the curriculum being amongst its key characteristics. Skill development and growth in the discernment capabilities of students will engender their capacity for making sound choices—suggesting a significant role for teachers to provide a structured environment (Green et al. 2005). Arguably then, the fashionable reduction of the identity of the teacher to that of 'learning facilitator' or 'learning advisor' should be treated with caution. Metaphors such as 'learning coach' or 'learning manager' may be more apt, as these terms imply a greater degree of intervention by the teacher. Freire, while progressive (indeed, revolutionary), specifically saw teaching as an interventionist activity. His starting point was to see the teacher as learner, one who was knowledgeable, rigorous and critical, who regards teaching as a process of ethical formation, whose words and actions are coherent and who shows "a willingness to risk, to welcome the new" (1998, p. 41). Such a teacher condemns discrimination and embraces the raw, "historical, political, social and cultural experience of men and women" (p. 46). This type of teacher eschews traditional transmission styles of teaching in favour of dialogical 'problem-posing' education that will develop critical epistemological curiosity (1970/1996, 1998). Thus, personalised learning, while favouring the personal and cultural life stories of students, may require a definition and execution that does not assume all control is in the hands of students.

The aims of personalised learning are challenged by assessment regimes, as already suggested. In the United States, for example, the emphasis on standardised testing directly contradicts the spirit and intent of personalised learning. Similarly, in New Zealand, to suggest a different example, primary schools are required to have a near-obsessive focus on literacy and numeracy, in order to demonstrate that children are reaching (and exceeding) the National Standards in those curriculum areas. Similarly, secondary schools have a demanding focus on the achievement of National Certificate of Education Achievement (NCEA) results in Years 11–13. This focus on extrinsic, results-oriented 'education' runs counter to calls for education to be authentic.

A ready vehicle for generating personalised, 'real-world' learning is having students solve a problem, or produce a 'rich task', which has "variety, scope and depth…requiring academic rigour; and…[is]…multidisciplinary" (Matters 2006, p. 18). Such 'rich tasks' were at the centre of the short-lived 'New Basics' curriculum reform trial in Queensland, Australia, from 2000 to 2004. The process of learning towards the attainment of this rich task is authenticated by

- a high degree of student control over the choice of topic, project, issue or problem;
- direct access by the student to the required knowledge (minimal teacher input);

- intelligent and self-conscious use of material by students (they understand what they are doing and the reasons for doing so, and have a personal grasp of the content required); and
- comprehensible manipulation of the material by the individual student that replaces rote imitation (adapted from Griffin 2009).

A critical feature of rich tasks not mentioned in the definition provided by Matters is that assessment based on "some scoring algorithm [is replaced by] on-balance judgements made by teachers considering each performance from multiple perspectives" (2006, p. 18). A further feature of rich tasks not included in the definition relates to their conceptualisation as requiring innovation. The rich task concept is thus a challenging order for teachers schooled in traditional approaches to assignment-setting and assessment. They must find the balance between giving students adequate direction and sense of what to focus on, yet simultaneously take a sufficiently retiring role to allow students to 'muddle through' and, most importantly, to develop an idea that is unique to them or the team they are working in. The teacher must have adequate expertise to support multiple projects, or be able to facilitate student contact with expertise beyond the classroom. Assessment too demands versatility and flexibility by teachers.

Teachers therefore find themselves caught between the demand to be innovative in endorsing and supporting the social knowledge of students on one hand, and their commitment to their store of knowledge and experience, on the other (MacBeath 2012). Working in authentic and innovative ways draws heavily on social constructivist views of learning, but while the social knowledge of students is important, it remains simply to be *social knowledge* (see, for example, Rata 2012), and fails potentially to allow students the opportunity to invest in conceptual and disciplinary knowledge (McPhail 2016; McPhail and Rata 2015; Rata 2012; Young 2008; Young and Muller 2010). A similar challenge to teachers (and students) is the requirement to work collaboratively.

Collaboration and flexibility are the watchwords of the reconceptualisation of teaching and learning in flexible, technology-rich spaces. Not only has traditional teaching and learning been characterised by rigidly organised time schedules and curricula through which groups of students have moved across for twelve years, but it has taken place in particularly rigid spaces that provided, in many cases, literally little room to move, let alone collaborate or innovate. Traditional notions of learning have regarded as an ideal one teacher with 25 students in a box-like, 'single cell', often with desks and chairs in rows.

The transition to modern, innovative or future-focused learning (and teaching) invites the rearrangement of students in modes that may no longer resemble strict age groupings; that create the possibilities for having large groups of students working in one large space; and the rearrangement of the periodisation of the day, into large blocks of time, no longer punctuated by the ringing of bells. These changes are daunting enough to teachers who may sense and experience a loss of control over curriculum and behaviour management, with evidence of students being off-task and 'coasting' even when apparently self-regulating (Chapman et al.

2014); or experiencing a loss of control over the actual working space (Smardon et al. 2015). Perhaps more challenging than this, though, is working in deprivatised and public settings. This shift challenges a generation of teachers accustomed to individual work, and largely private practice behind closed doors, as the CERI researchers of the OECD discovered

> Enhanced visibility may not always be easy, however: the individual teacher closing the door and conducting his or her class away from the stare or scrutiny of colleagues might certainly be easier than sharing practice in a much more explicit way. This was expressed as "taking its toll" in one of the case studies. (p. 78)

New approaches to building design, suggested in Chap. 3, have, on the other hand, created the flexibility for teachers and students to engage in forms of learning that have previously been difficult to imagine or implement. These forms include personalised and authentic learning, often linked to projects or problems, requiring both innovation and collaboration. Significantly, teaching and learning are closely associated, thus innovation and collaboration have a key role to play in developing modern teaching practice.

The Practical Studies

In the following presentation and discussion of the practical studies, the focus will fall mainly on Innovation Primary, Angelus School and Millennial College as exemplars. In Chap. 1, I noted that the research on which this book is based focuses on the meaningful ways in which practitioners within and across schools engage with the policy imperative to implement modern teaching and learning practice, usually associated with flexible learning environments and digital technology. The chief focus of my attention at Holyoake College was its application of BYOD, though, in point of fact, the other three schools also have varying degrees of BYOD policy. All four schools engage in forms of digital pedagogy therefore, but unlike the other three, Holyoake College is a regular, single-cell school, offering a traditional curriculum. These factors influence the pedagogical approach of its teachers, just as the approach of the teachers at Innovation Primary, Angelus School and Millennial College is shaped and influenced by their flexible learning environments and unique approaches to curriculum.

Modern Teaching and Learning Practice

The critique of 'industrial age' schooling is aimed in part at teaching and learning approaches associated with tradition, notably teacher-led, content-driven lessons requiring students to passively absorb knowledge for later regurgitation in tests and exams. The schools studied here take unique approaches to curriculum, but have in common their commitment to personalised learning. Their non-traditional approach includes re-structuring the school day and the curriculum, which prioritises dispositional and/or values-based principles. An explicit focus on the attributes of responsible and self-managed learning grows out of this commitment.

Teachers ensure they are responsive to student needs by seeking strategies and opportunities to create learning experiences that arise from student interest. This is a far cry from approaches in which the teacher is the sole arbiter of content, and 'teaching to the middle'. The traditional uniform and lock-step approach, more typical of secondary schools, though still evident in many primary schools, is based on the notion that all students are to learn the same content, and that continued progress through this content requires all students to have grasped the content and associated concepts and skills.

Students are pivotal to developing a responsive, personalised approach (which I will discuss shortly) that attempts to differentiate content according to each student's interests and level of competence. Thus, student voice plays a central role in developing curriculum options and directions. Due to curriculum and teaching innovations, opportunities exist for students to follow individual inquiries. Relevant, contextual learning generates highly differentiated or personalised learning activities. These activities frequently start with immersion in big concepts that allow students to explore what is meaningful to them.

While direct instruction remains in use where and when necessary, a consequence of taking a radically personalised approach is a drastic minimisation of teaching from the front; indeed, the 'front' is much less obvious, and the physical presence of teachers is decentred. Team teaching, collaborative planning and deprivatised practice are the norm, particularly as teachers' work context is large teaching spaces accommodating multiple groups of students. This style of work provides opportunities for different members of the team to work to their strengths.

Approach to Curriculum

The three schools each take different, yet related approaches. Underpinning these approaches to curriculum are principles of student inquiry focussed on moving towards student understanding of big ideas, developing dispositions and academic skills. From a teacher perspective, collaborative approaches underpin the planning and executing of an integrated and connected curriculum that maps back to The New Zealand Curriculum (MOE 2007).

Innovation Primary uses a problem-based approach whereby real-world problems become the focus for working towards a rich task. The curriculum is viewed through the lenses of 'Digital Age Literacies', 'Inventive Thinking' and 'Effective Communication'. These major themes are introduced through a period of immersion. The themes create three annual blocks, thus teachers are able to allow for a full exploration of student ideas without the usual constriction imposed by a termly delineation of themes as may happen in other schools. Following a brainstorm session, there emerges a series of projects. For example, in the observed Year 6–8 group, some students were studying robotics; one was writing some code; another group established a farmer's market. At the centre of the curriculum are the learning dispositions that are linked to the key competencies of The New Zealand Curriculum (2007). These dispositions are the most important organising core of the projects.

Millennial College does not offer a siloed curriculum; instead, the curriculum is integrated and delivered through multiple options. Seven 'modules' are offered each semester (two school terms). Students will take three modules each semester in three, 80-min blocks, comprising around half the allotted teaching time in a school week. These modules combine two learning areas, and are taught in teams of two teachers. Each module is identified by a big idea, such as *'Disruption'* or *'A small world'*. Student voice is a critical feature of the development of integrated curriculum topics and themes. At Millennial College, the learning leaders, who have an overview of the entire curriculum, bring groups of students together to brainstorm ideas around the 'big idea' of the coming term, drawing together the ideas students offer in relation to what they would like to learn in response to the big idea (such as 'innovation'). These ideas are filtered and merged into ideas the teachers have.

The teaching staff incorporate student ideas when formulating the modules. Special Interest classes are offered by individual teachers, and offer the opportunity of detailed study of a specialist area. The construction of modules and special interest topics is checked by Learning Managers (akin to a head of department), who ensure that adequate curriculum coverage is provided across the modules and special interest options. Underpinning the curriculum is a learning design framework, used by all teachers, that provides an easily understood visual model of steps taken in an inquiry-led approach to learning. Running alongside the curriculum is the school's unique interpretation of the front pages of The New Zealand Curriculum (2007). The school values and a statement of learner habits are reinforced not only through the curriculum, but also at regular intervals during 'hub time' (akin to morning form class or register class meetings).

Angelus School is a curriculum-mapping school.[1] At the end of each preceding year, questions are asked as to what students would like to learn about. This process involves students, community and teachers, and these ideas are taken forward into big picture planning. A core team establishes overarching themes (such as 'strength') that are an anchor for 'concepts for learning', such as 'Well Being', out of which a single 'enduring understanding' is formulated. An important feature of this approach to curriculum is to ensure that learning is connected to real-life. The concept for learning (one per term) becomes a focus for teachers who plan collaboratively and share their planning with each other using curriculum-mapping software. As the other two schools, this school does not simply replicate the statements in The New Zealand Curriculum (2007), but provides its own statement of values and key competencies, which support an integrated approach to

---

[1] See https://www.rubicon.com.

curriculum. Although an inquiry-led approach to learning is a feature, a firm commitment is made to providing a rigorous grounding in literacy and numeracy. The special character teachings of the school underpin curriculum delivery, and these values are reflected in conjunction with the competency dispositions.

For any school taking the approach of the schools under study here, an important question remains as to how effective the curriculum is for students' learning, as measured by achievement results. In particular, there is a tension between a dispositional curriculum and one that emphasises attainment in literacy and numeracy National Standards or the achievement of credits towards the National Certificate of Educational Achievement (NCEA)[2]. In all cases of the schools under study, teachers are equally committed to their dispositional, inquiry-led curricula, and to attaining student success in national measures. The implementation of modern teaching and learning practice, in the context of non-traditional approaches to the curriculum was, particularly for Innovation Primary and Millennial College in 2015, still in its infancy. For Angelus School, which had a slightly earlier establishment, the use of curriculum mapping was introduced in 2011, though its flexible spaces were opened only in 2014, thus it too had minimal data in relation to student attainment arising from these curriculum approaches in combination with the flexible designs. I will return to assessment in further detail shortly, however, suffice to say, the performance of students in response to the curriculum approaches taken by these (and similar) schools, is a matter for future research.

Integrated Curriculum

The approach to integrated curriculum at Millennial College warrants further detailed examination, for its break with traditional secondary school approaches that offer siloed subjects. What is important from an integrated perspective, is not detailed, in-depth knowledge, but rather, "non-negotiable knowledge, concepts, skills and a bit of content from the learning areas" (Principal, Millennial College, IV). The strategy employed at the school is to develop learning objectives through rigorous use of a learning design model developed by the staff (see Fig. 4.1). The model presents several cognitive functions (such as 'evaluate', 'refine' and 'explore', with each function detailing related key words. Under 'evaluation', for instance, are such words as 'assess'; 'appraise'; 'critique' and 'reflect'). These labels can be traced back to key competency statements and learning area statements in The New Zealand Curriculum (2007). The model is used school-wide, and its use is intended to be visible in teacher planning, as well as their classroom discourse. The school's commitment to an integrated, competencies-based approach allows teachers to focus less on the "content [they've previously] ploughed [their] way through…which has required [them] to direct, to drive kids, to resource

---

[2]Both are a feature of the New Zealand schooling system.

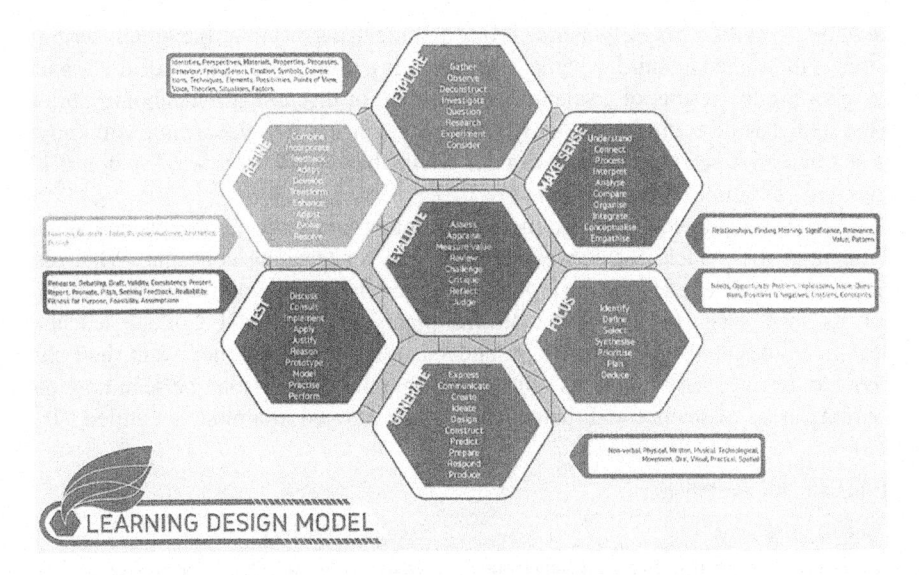

Fig. 4.1 Learning design model (with permission from Millennial College)

[themselves], which is really demanding and draining and is really disengaging for some kids" (Principal, Millennial College, IV).

Despite integrated curriculum removing the focus from content coverage, the mainstay of the disciplinary knowledge, teachers working with integrated curriculum must have secure knowledge of their learning area, in particular its central concepts. This is so particularly because "to pare back each learning area…without…losing important aspects of the curriculum…[requires teachers] to know the curriculum well." (senior leader, Millennial College, FG). This knowledge includes having a clear understanding of the various levels of achievement, and what is expected of students at those levels.

An integrated approach to curriculum in a secondary school can be liberating for some teachers, while others may find the break with disciplinary knowledge very difficult to reconcile with their previous experience. In a debriefing with one of the teaching teams, a team member enthused about being "an English teacher…a PE teacher, a science teacher and a social science teacher", while her colleague, noted, "I've had to grieve over my subject a little bit". This teacher was struggling to make the shift away from disciplinary knowledge to integrated curriculum. Now, more cheerfully, she stated her focus is "skills development and those 21st century skills around problem solving and evaluating, justifying". The visceral sense of her loss of identification with strong disciplinary boundaries seems barely assuaged by its replacement, however.

The integrated, modular approach at the College requires that teachers work and collaborate closely to plan material, ensuring that there is no needless repetition of tasks across the curriculum. Thus, paragraphing is uniform across the curriculum, which is not only less confusing to students, but minimises teacher time spent on developing skills that are generic. From a student perspective, paragraph writing follows the same structure, whether the output is a discussion of statistical variance or reporting the results of a scientific experiment or discussing a technology brief. This school-wide approach "actually reinforces things across the areas…you know, in a traditional school each department would have their own way of doing it" (teacher, Millennial College, DB).

There is nevertheless interplay between content knowledge, concepts and skills. Content is the vehicle for conveying skills and for teaching concepts. What distinguishes the integrated, dispositional curriculum is that it avoids content coverage for its own sake. In their collaborative planning, Millennial College teachers specifically focus on the knowledge, understanding and skills they want their students to acquire. An example is offered in Table 4.1. Here it may be seen how the learning areas of science and mathematics are integrated in a module entitled, *'It's*

Table 4.1 It's electrifying

Module description		Learning objectives
Exploring the concepts of electromagnetism and light and using the mathematical skills of measurement and geometry to examine sustainable energy and sustainable practices at our school		**Science**: to make sense by analysing electrical systems in the context of sustainability and to generate by constructing an environmentally electronic device **Maths**: to test by applying measurement knowledge to model and solve mathematical problems in the context of electrical systems and sustainability **Science**: To make sense by integrating battery chemistry and molecular geometry ideas into sustainable energy ideas **Maths**: to test by applying measurement and geometry knowledge to model and solve mathematical problems in the context of chemical reactions
	Science	*Maths*
Concepts	Electricity and electromagnetism; sustainable energy generation Redox reactions in batteries, possible nanotechnology	Measurement and geometry
Skills	Project planning and design; practical electronic construction Lab skills, group work, research	Taking measurements; using and rearranging formulae; calculating areas; converting measurements between S.I. units Measuring volume, identifying 3-D shapes, angles in shapes, symmetry
Curriculum focus	Physical world—physical enquiry and physics concepts	Measurement and geometry
Contexts	Sustainable energy, electronics	Sustainable energy, electricity and magnetism and light Energy in reactions

Two-term small module

electrifying'. Specific concepts are demarcated for each learning area (such as electricity in science, and measurement in mathematics), together with skills (such as group work and measuring volume). As noted earlier, the learning objectives outlined by the teachers must articulate cognitive processes detailed in the learning design, and in this case, the teachers have highlighted, 'to make sense' (which entails 'analysis' as one of its key ideas) and 'test' (which requires 'application'). The content that is expected to convey these concepts and skills, and support the learning objectives, includes 'properties and changes of matter'. This content will be encountered as the students construct an electronic device. This broad plan is a far cry from the detailed, content-based plans more traditional teachers would be accustomed to; however it is not that unusual in the context of the development of The New Zealand Curriculum.

Some participants accepted the critique that integrated teaching and learning seems to undermine disciplinary knowledge, but they argued that digital technology and access to the World Wide Web gives students access and the opportunity to acquire knowledge very quickly. This reality makes other learning a priority, such as critical discernment of the web-based content they acquire, and having the ability to critically interpret that knowledge. They realise considerably less time is devoted to teaching content, and correspondingly that their content coverage is significantly diminished, however, they also point out the overlaps across the other modules. For instance, the same learning area (such as English) may appear in two modules. Furthermore, there are overlaps across modules, which encourages the reinforcement of vocabulary and thus intellectual transfer between modules. This point made to me by a Year 10 student, Francis, who noted that the concepts he learned in a module incorporating Social Studies was supporting the English essay he was writing for a different module.

Nevertheless, the teachers face challenges arising from trying to integrate subjects that may not inherently belong together, such as Social Studies and Mathematics. Many of the observations I conducted revealed an amalgam of integrated activities (such as finding the algebraic formulae underpinning traditional Māori artistic panels) and block classes that were divided between two specific subject areas. Arguably, this latter solution denies genuine integration, though the pressure of preparing students for the NCEA must continue to weigh heavily on these teachers.

Personalised Learning

The idea of personalised learning is one that clearly sets classroom approaches in the three cases apart from many other mainstream schools. Some may suggest that what teachers are doing in their flexible spaces simply reflects what 'good' teachers have done for years, namely to differentiate. Clearly, however, at Innovation, Angelus and Millennial, 'personalising' does not equate to providing different activities related to the same topic that everyone is learning, but rather to the provision of opportunities for individual students to engage in learning that flows from working with material directly related to their interest.

Those interests are activated in different ways across the three schools. Innovation Primary uses a problem-based approach to guide much of the learning, usually channelled through a project that groups may be working on. At Angelus School, the overarching themes, previously informed by student voice, create a structure within which learning is planned to give students opportunities to take responsibility for their pace of progress. Millennial College, although constrained by having to ensure adequate curriculum exposure to enable its students to participate in national qualifications, nevertheless provides scope for students to assemble their own unique learning pathway, thus avoiding the lock-step, 'one size for all' approach of many traditional secondary schools.

The two primary schools take similar approaches to organising their classes for personalised learning, remembering, however, that Angelus School has a mixed model, thus the findings here pertain only to the observed classes that occur in flexible learning spaces. At Innovation Primary, the students set goals (one dispositional, one literacy and one numeracy) for the week that will help them achieve their project outcomes (Fig. 4.2). The teachers provide a skeleton timetable that serves as a framework for each week. At the start of the week, each student completes a timetable template with their choices, based on their goals. The

Fig. 4.2 Personal goal-setting prompts

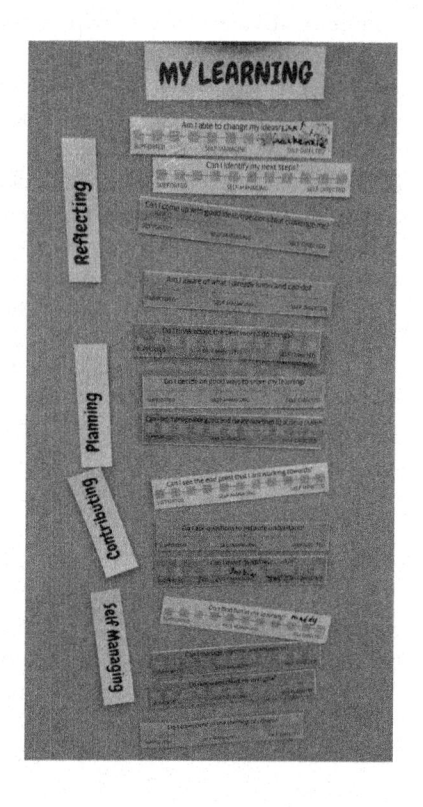

teachers have defined a series of 'must do' activities, in addition to some 'can do' activities.

Angelus School follows a similar routine, though here greater teacher direction is evident, as teachers set learning objectives for the students each week, though it is for the students to monitor their progress against these objectives. There is a fixed daily routine (for example, literacy in the morning block, and numeracy in the block after morning break), yet allowing students flexibility to range across different tasks within the block. Here too, the students have 'must dos' to be completed by Friday (for examples, see Table 4.2). Once these are completed, they can move to their 'can dos'. As at Innovation, here the students have a skeleton timetable to complete each week. In both schools, teachers monitor the timetables, to ensure that the students are managing their choice of activities appropriately. Arguably, in the 'real world' of work, these kinds of choices are not necessarily available, however, these teachers will be responding to the view that the 21st century workplace requires independent workers, rather than those who only act when told to. They will be able to justify their pedagogical decisions in relation to personalised learning against not only the context of changing work patterns, but also against the context of competency-based national curriculum statements.

For both schools, where classes in the Year 1 and Year 2 range were observed, student choice in activating personalised learning is challenging, and in each case, teachers had strategies in place, though these differed. The teachers at Innovation Primary have created a visual and tactile 'ribbon-on-felt' grid that provides a pictorial reference to various points around the learning space. The children's names, laminated, with a Velcro backing strip, are arranged on the felt area outside the grid. Children place their names in grid boxes pertaining to the area where they intend to

Table 4.2 Self managed and independents 'must do' for one week, to be completed by Friday

Task	Success criteria You have…
Update weekly timetable	1. Updated with links to all work
Daily reading	1. Read everyday with each task recorded in reading log 2. At least 3 entries from reading at school
Mathletics	1. Scored 3000 points this week 2. 15 min daily practice
Reading comprehension workshop	1. Completed the vocab follow up sheet
Writing workshop	1. Completed your first writing draft 2. Proofread your first draft 3. Asked a friend to proofread 4. Written a second draft after steps 2 and 3
Typing	1. Completed all assignments from lesson 1–9. Attempt more than 15 wpm for each assignment 2. Recorded your result in your checkpoint

work. The teachers at Angelus School use a different method, hanging lanyards from the necks of the children. These lanyards reflect two activities per session, from which the children choose. Examples during a reading session included, 'listening post', 'word work' and 'poetry'.

In both cases, 'back planning' by teachers ensures that the week is carefully planned to enable students to make relevant selections. In particular, the teachers must be aware of where students are at, so as to know what to focus on in the current week. In this regard, the division of students into groupings of supported, self-managing and independent learners informs teachers as they think about personalising learning. That being said, while this 'big picture' planning is arranged in advance, the teachers at Innovation Primary and Angelus School are discouraged from detailed long-term plans, as this implies that teachers know where students are going with their learning. What ought to drive planning "is what I did today and what the outcome was and what that means for tomorrow" (Principal, Innovation Primary, IV).

It was earlier noted how students at Millennial College select three modules and three special interest classes. The modules are taken over two terms, while a special interest class is offered anew each term. The modules have appealing titles, such as '*It's a small world*', combining two learning areas, in this case, design (technology) and science (see Fig. 4.3). In contrast, the specialised offerings delve into one learning area. The special interests have catchy titles too, such as '*Playing with*

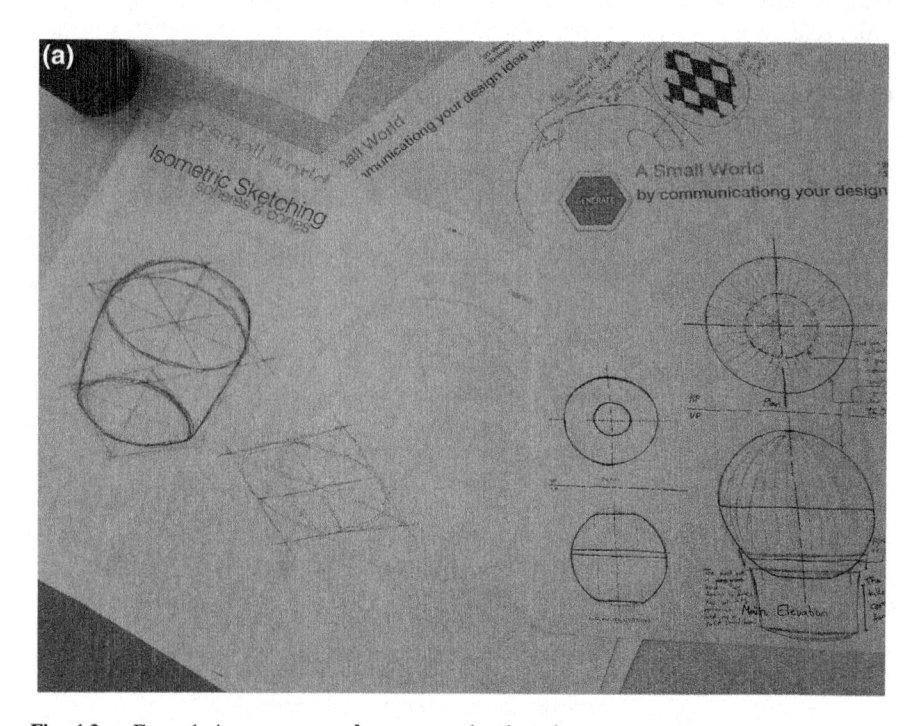

Fig. 4.3 a From design concept…, **b** …to completed product

Fig. 4.3 (continued)

Physics', 'Coding' and *'Carbon'*. Each student is a member of a Community, divided into hubs of about 12 students, assigned to a learning advisor or coach. The advisor plays several roles, an important one of which being to monitor and support the individual learning pathway of each student. Once students make their selection, their Learning Coach ensures that each student has access to all the learning areas in The New Zealand Curriculum within this selection.

Teachers ensure students have differentiated activities to choose from, or have differentiated choice within a single activity. Thus, for example, in a social justice inquiry that related to the Treaty of Waitangi, students, working in groups, were able to select from among six issues. Conversely, where students worked on a single task, such as designing and producing a terrarium, the expectation was for each student to produce a unique product. Furthermore, school-wide use is made of the SOLO taxonomy,[3] which is adapted for use in each class. Thus, students select from among smaller tasks that have been geared to working at specific SOLO levels. These are:

- Unistructural (simple identification)
- Multi-structural (accurate identification and description)
- Relational (explanation, with detail; making linkages)
- Extended abstract (explanation that reflects deep insight and an understanding of viewpoints)

---

[3]**S**tructure of the **O**bserved **L**earning **O**utcome. See Biggs (nd).

| My Treaty Issue is. | |

Complete ONE task from each column using the research you have collected about your chosen Treaty issue.

THE TREATY ISSUE	ACTION & PURPOSE	PERSPECTIVES identify 3 different people	CONSEQUENCES/ OUTCOMES	SIGNIFICANCE & SUCCESS YR 11 ONLY
Generate a pictorial timeline of all the different events and/ or injustice surrounding your issue - use facts and dates in your work - have detailed labels.	Generate a song/poem that identified and describes what actions were taken to highlight, change and address the issue.	Generate a values continuum - For the action verses Against the action. Place groups on the continuum and describe what they think and explain why they think this.	Generate a list of at least 5 different outcomes / consequences of the social action under the headings of 'social, economic and environmental'.	Write paragraphs that identify 2 consequences and explain the significance of these for NZ Society - describe these using the concept of community. Write as either an essay or report.
Generate a cartoon strip that describes what the this issue about and why it's an concern or problem for people. Have a range of characters in your cartoon.	Generate an A3 sized poster / advertisement promoting ONE major action taken to address this issue. The poster must convey a description of the what, when, where, how and intended purpose (why) of the action.	Generate 3 different blog or vlog posts written from the perspective of each person identified. Describe what "you" think of the action and why you think this way. You need to refer to roles, responsibility, rights, justice in the post.	Use Kahoot quiz or crossword maker to generate a 'resource' that educates people about the outcome of the action. There needs to be a range of facts and details and should also convey the idea	Image you are a lawyer - Generate a 'closing argument' to convince a 'jury' that the action met its intended purpose and was a success. You need to have a range of justified points with factual info to support your ideas.
Generate a 200 word newspaper article to describe the treaty issue - Identify the who, what, when, where and why in the article. Give quotes and perspectives on the issue from 2 different groups of people.	Generate a 2 min movie script for a scene that reenacts the 'action' taken to address this issue. In the scene have the who, what, when, where and WHY (ie convey what the group wants to achieve). Use the concept of 'rights' in your script.	Audio record two 1 minute "arguments" between 2 people with different opinions on your action - one recording is "emotional and heated" the other is 'factual'. You need to convey how different people feel and why they feel this way.	Generate a detailed FISHBONE diagram to identify and describe four main consequences of the action that was taken. Link the consequences with the direct action.	

Fig. 4.4 SOLO taxonomy (with permission from Millennial College)

The example in Fig. 4.4, used with a class of Year 10 students, shows tasks were mainly pitched at the multi-structural and relational levels. Students are required to indicate the level at which they are working. Casual observation and discussion with students working on this task revealed a high level of self-understanding of the difference among these tasks and why the individuals I spoke with were working at those levels. Apart from use in the course of their curriculum learning, students develop their knowledge and understanding of the use of SOLO during 'hub time', where time is variously spent focussing on their personal well being, being with others, and on their individual learning journeys.

Tracking and Reporting

Teachers in all three schools were observed actively moving about among the students and evaluating by observation and their supportive interactions with their students. At Innovation Primary, the Year 4–6 students were observed maintaining self-check documentation that includes links to evidence of work done. This documentation could be displayed to teachers on request, who actively monitored it. The Year 5–6 class at Angelus School had a similar process in place. The links can point to documents, slide shows or videos. The teachers at Innovation Primary and

Angelus School were seen to ask students at random to produce their planning for inspection to ensure students had correctly assigned themselves to work sessions.

At Innovation, weekly 'LA' (Learning Advisor) times are scheduled, allowing class teachers to support their students' learning journey. A termly Individual Education Meeting (IEM) occurs with individual students, and this forms part of feedback to parents. A variety of formative assessment and observation supports a triangulation of tracking data. Weekly 'checkpoints' at Angelus School are focussed on the supported learners, while the self-managed and independent learners ensure they are maintaining their Excel spread sheet, with its links. The teachers check these in their own time and provide electronic feedback.

Students at Millennial College are arranged in small groups of around fifteen students (in 2015). The groups are assigned a 'learning coach', and who meet in 'hubs'. These replace the conventional 'form class', and while serving similar purposes, are able to serve several purposes beyond a typical form class. These groups meet for three 90-min periods of time each week, (representing half as much time as students will spend in their small learning modules), in which time the coaches focus on academic and pastoral progress. Students in the hub meet one-on-one three times each term with the coach to discuss their progress.

Wall-sized graphic organisers at both Innovation and Angelus visually track student progress against a range of measures, intentions, objectives and other factors, such as project milestones. Each Angelus student has a blog, maintained in *e-blogger*, a Google application. The blog is used as a platform for students to reflect on their learning journey. This process of personal reflection, coupled with peer feedback, was evident at both Innovation and Millennial.

Assessment

An innovative and flexible approach to teaching and learning requires assessment to be treated differently too. The teachers at all three schools attempt to put into place assessment strategies and approaches that are better able to reflect a futures focus. The Angelus staff focus group were interested to see if their students could transfer knowledge and apply solutions in new ways. School reporting structures require more development, however, according to these participants, as its current structure is not geared to capturing advances in personalised learning. This issue resonates with comments made by teachers and leaders at Innovation and Millennial, regarding the difficulty of capturing advances in dispositional learning. While some students may be graded 'Below' (in literacy or numeracy standards), teachers are aware of significant strides their students make in their dispositional knowledge and expertise, yet these advances cannot be captured in the current reporting system, which is significantly channelled by the National Standards system: "There is a richness in what this child has grown in, yet the report…[indicates]…this child… [is]…well below. Everything in between that…is so important and more valuable is missed and the parent will only see…[her]…child is still below the standard" (teacher, Angelus School, FG).

After a year of students attending class in a flexible learning environment in 2014, "a significant number of children [went] from working at to working above the national standard in those rooms" (Principal, Angelus School, IV). Despite this positive National Standards assessment data, she did remark, however, that the progress of 'passive learners' is a school-wide concern, as this category of students does not make the same progress.

Formative assessment can serve the purpose of better aligning individual students to targeted support. Such evidence is garnered when teachers ask students to brainstorm all they know about a topic or concept on a page. In the shared learning spaces, observation data is critical, providing teachers with informally gathered data that informs summative judgements, without the need to put students through specific assessment tasks.

The principal of Innovation Primary was struggling to discern patterns in assessment data, as his school roll was in a rapid growth phase in 2015; however, like the staff at Angelus, he too was unhappy that reports are unable to capture dispositional development, the essence of personalised learning. His challenge was to find 'smart ways' of capturing his students' "ability to be self-managing learners who know what they know and know what they don't know and know where to go for their learning" (Principal, Innovation Primary, IV).

The principles of formative assessment are in play at Millennial College too, such as setting a 'pretest' and 'post-test' at the beginning and at the end of a particular theme or concept. There was not complete unanimity among all the participant teachers, however, some still being committed to conventional assessment. The school had not yet begun to fully broach the challenge of dealing with the requirements of the national examination system, with one teacher stating, "that direction has to come from" the learning leaders. This teacher remained uncertain of how she was going to implement summative assessment.

My discussion some months later with the principal revealed, however, that the learning leaders were, indeed, well on the way to guiding the school into the challenging phase of national qualifications. He acknowledged the narrowing influence of the NCEA system, but argued this to be a consequence of the general inability of schools to grasp "the flexibility around the NCEA" (Principal, Millennial College, IV). As the college staff prepared to move their first Year 10 cohort into Year 11, the learning leaders had established certain assessment principles in accord with a future focus

- low stress assessment;
- seeking naturally occurring links;
- maintain personalised learning;
- rigour;
- best practice for each learning area (which entails that the principles be applied flexibly on a case-by-case basis).

Millennial College staff decided in 2015 that the school would not follow the practice of most secondary schools, namely to make the attainment of NCEA Level 1 a focus of Year 11. Instead, Millennial College Year 11 students would begin their two-year journey towards a quality NCEA Level 2, with the intention that students would achieve between 20 and 40 Level 1 or Level 2 credits in Year 11[4].

Classroom Management

All three schools run large blocks of time, of between 90 min and 2 h. Classes at Millennial College typically begin with about 10–15 min of orientation to the content and process of the session, including some instruction, followed by an hour of student self-directed activity, actively monitored by the teachers, leaving around 15 min to wrap up the class.

Many of the sessions observed at Innovation Primary began with a 'campfire' that brings the whole class together. These campfire sessions often focus on the dispositional curriculum or reflect on some aspect of the process of self-managed learning. There will also be some discussion or reminder of what will take place in the coming session. Days at Angelus School can be punctuated by different activities to those seen in the other two schools, as it is a Special Character school. Thus, for example, the 9 am–11 am slot begins with a focus on spiritual learning, so that the scholastic part of the day begins at 9.30 am. It was noted at Angelus School that students move directly to begin their work, without any preliminary whole-class discussion, and the period of around 80 min is regularly punctuated by activity changeovers, signalled by a tiny hand bell rung by the teacher leading the session. This is unlike practice at Innovation, but may have to do with the far greater numbers at Angelus, and the need to share devices and fixed computers among the students, as Angelus was not fully BYOD at the time.

It is apparent that one teacher takes the lead in each session at each of three schools; indeed, at Angelus School, this teacher is designated as 'director' for specific sessions, a role that rotates. While one teacher is communicating with the whole class, the other(s) may be taking the roll, performing an administrative task, or contributing to the discussion. Once the student activity is underway at Angelus School, the second teacher will be actively monitoring the floor, moving among students, while the director and the third teacher will variously offer 'workshops'—teacher instruction on a topic or concept to a small group of perhaps ten students—though the director will also have one to one discussions and actively monitor other groups. At Innovation School, where the teachers were working in teams of two at

---

[4]To attain NCEA Level 1, a student is required to attain 80 credits at any level, including literacy and numeracy credits. At Level 2, students must attain 80 credits, comprised of 20 Level 1 and 60 from Level 2 or higher. A Level 3 also requires 80 credits, comprised of 20 from Level 2 and 60 from Level 3 or higher (NZQA, nd). Conventionally, students take each qualification step in each of Years 11–13.

the time of the study, the roles of director and workshop facilitator role was evident, though the director was also the person actively working the floor.

The teachers at Millennial worked in pairs, generally in a similar pattern to that of the primaries, though during a particular observation session, the whole class was divided in two, and the two teachers worked separately with each group, instructing, explaining, modelling and then moving around the group as students attended to the set tasks. This seemed to differ little from a conventional secondary classroom approach, apart from the much larger, flexible working area.

Of some interest was to note the relief teacher arrangements. As New Zealand primary schools are required to allocate Classroom Release Time to their teachers, regular part-time staff members are employed at Innovation and Angelus to provide this cover. These relievers seemed much like fixed members of the teaching team, thus were able to play any of the roles described above. When, however, an occasional relief teacher was present in any of the settings observed, the teachers seemed to absorb the load of their missing colleague. In such cases, additional care is required to ensure that the plan for the day is executed with minimal disruption. Three of the observations at Millennial College coincided with the absence of regular team members. In only one of these was a relief teacher present, who did little more than wander about among the students. In all of these situations, it was evident that the teacher present took responsibility for the whole class, and while this meant that this teacher was providing the initial instruction and explanation, in addition to floor management, active on-going instruction and one-to-one supervision, the clear advantage was no loss of learning time due to a teacher's absence, as is often the case in traditional school settings when relief teachers are present.

It is part of the routine at the two primaries that some children move off to parallel classes or events. For example, the Year 1 and 2 class at Innovation Primary were divided among several specialist teachers for an hour each Thursday morning. During a particular observation, the Year 3 and 4 class at Innovation had an hour of physical activity with external contractors, while at Angelus, a group of the Year 5 and 6 students left partway through their session to attend a book fair.

Student Agency and Engagement

Fundamental to each of the schools is the role of individualised programming and selection of activities, within a framework provided by the school and teachers. Students at Millennial College, as previously noted, select from among a range of thematic modules that integrate two learning areas of the curriculum, each offered over half a year. Students also select a required number of specialised options focussed on intensive study within one learning area, offered for one term each.

At Innovation Primary and Angelus School, the choices made by individual students are a critical feature of any day. Students map out their goals for the week, and maintain a planner to reflect their personal 'timetable' for the day and the week, rather than following, as an entire class, a uniform set and sequence of activities determined by the teacher. These choices are not, in reality, 'free' choices, but 'strategic' choices, reflecting the areas teachers believe are important for the students, given their current learning journey (Principal, Innovation Primary, IV). A similar sense of covert control was evident at Angelus School, where recent arrivals to the Year 1/Year 2 class are given close support by teacher aides, giving them the first few days to understand the system of student self-selection of activities.

Differentiated group work is the norm. For example, at Angelus School, in an observation of the Year 1 and Year 2 combined class, seven discernible and different groups were engaged in a variety of mathematics tasks while the remainder were generally working in small groups of three or so, working with mobile devices, all without teachers. They were working directly with selected small groups. Similarly, during an observation of the Year 5 and Year 6 combined class, in a group of three boys, one worked on a laptop (completing a Mathletics challenge), one read a science book (as he had selected reading for the current block of time), and one worked in an exercise book (completing some 'must do' work). At Innovation Primary, I observed two groups of approximately ten each, taking part in an editing workshop with each of the teachers in two different areas, while two groups of four worked on an art project, and a range of pairs and individuals were arranged throughout the space pursuing the various other activities they have programmed (such as narrative writing or project work).

A noticeable action is that of students taking responsibility for moving into place quickly. Without the benefit of bells at Innovation and Millennial, students move from activity to activity and place to place with minimal teacher direction. While there seems more teacher direction at Angelus School, the students, upon entering their flexible learning space after morning break, move directly and purposefully to continue their individual programmes, without comment by the teachers.

While these recorded observations do reflect student agency, it is important to highlight some specific instances and patterns of engagement and agency. A feature of agentic action is the evidence of students collaborating to develop and enhance a shared understanding, without any direction from the teacher or teacher's presence. A good example at Innovation Primary was a group of Year 2–4 students, seated by a whiteboard, practicing the fractions they had learnt in a workshop. They demonstrated basic fractions to each other using a pizza metaphor. Groups were observed in all three schools, purposefully engaged without teacher support. Systems are in place for 'learning buddies', who support each other, and in all three cases, teachers were heard to remind their students of the importance of seeking help and support from peers before reverting to the teacher (think here of Heppell's 'ask three then me'). These practices are institutionalised and given credibility at Angelus School in the categorisation of self-initiators as 'self-managed' (the other two being 'independent' and 'supported').

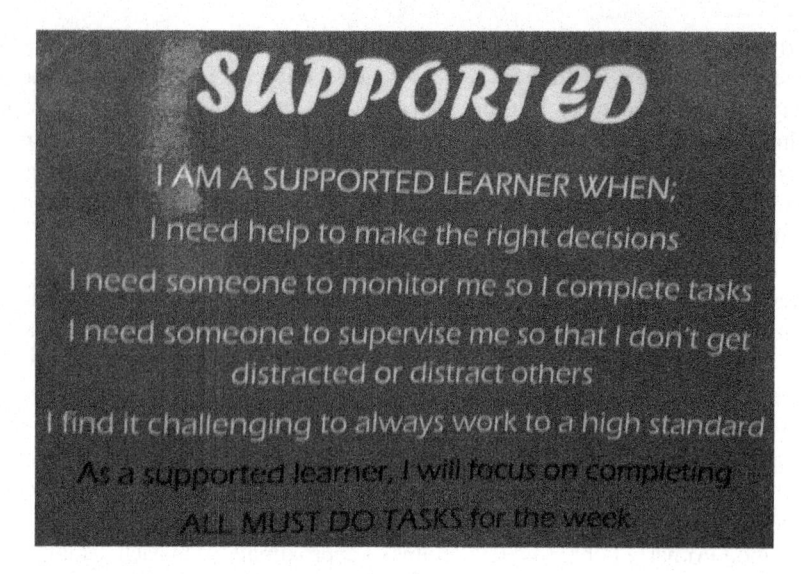

> **SUPPORTED**
>
> I AM A SUPPORTED LEARNER WHEN:
> I need help to make the right decisions
> I need someone to monitor me so I complete tasks
> I need someone to supervise me so that I don't get distracted or distract others
> I find it challenging to always work to a high standard
> As a supported learner, I will focus on completing ALL MUST DO TASKS for the week.

Fig. 4.5 Wall chart defining 'supported learners'

Each of these have success criteria descriptors. One of these for 'self-managers' is 'I can help others learn', thus self-managers are empowered to run workshops and actively support the learning of their peers. An overt sign of this empowerment are the 'smarty beads', a simple necklace sometimes worn by the self-managed learners to identify their role. In contrast, 'supported learners' are identified as those who would, in traditional settings, be identified as 'problem students'. In the discourse of modern teaching and learning practice, however, such externalised identification would amount to negative labelling; instead, it is up to the child to self-recognise and self-identify, in language that is apparently value-free. This self-recognition by students of their limitations is central to the discourse of 'self-management' and is central to the construction of student agency in this discourse. Figure 4.5 defines, for 'supported learners' the signs of their need for support, rather than being signals for disapprobation (Fig. 4.5).

The principal of Innovation Primary links positive student engagement to understanding why student behavioural issues are not a concern at his school. The starting point is the development of strong relationships between teachers and students, so that students come to realise "instead of learning being done to them it's done with them and alongside them". For her part, the principal of Angelus School identified the greater freedom of movement and ability to make choices over where to work and what to be working on in the flexible spaces as (ironically) a factor in reducing student behavioural issues. In single-cell class spaces, with one teacher and 25 or 30 students, there are fewer spatial opportunities to redirect students who have become disengaged.

Also reflecting on the ways that an amended school structure can support student agency, the principal of Millennial College had noticed the powerful difference on the attitudes and levels of engagement of Māori and Pacific Island students made by innovations such as 100 min periods in a high school, which enable students to fully pursue areas of interest and personal passion. That being said, it is also important that teachers, especially those working with older age groups, ensure they are themselves fully engaged with the various activities taking place in the large spaces, as some students are "very good at going into corners" (teacher, Millennial College, DB). Not all teachers at Millennial thought the long periods suited all students, and my observations in some spaces at Millennial College confirmed that some students were unable to sustain engaged activity for more than 80 min.

Maximum engagement by all students at all times, even in the context of personalised learning, is unlikely, as some of my observation notes remind me, such as this extract, written whilst at Innovation Primary

> There's about 10 working on art, about 10 with [teacher 1] doing editing, about 10 with [teacher 2] in a breakout space doing editing. So what about the other 10 or so? One boy aimlessly walking around, another sitting on the sofa doing no work at all. There's about 6 children on devices, and I'm not sure if they're doing the keywords or writing their narrative.

Yet, in a previous observation in the same space, which occurred in the final session of the day, I recorded as follows:

> 2.45. The students are mainly in small groups of 3-4. Virtually all are engaged in some class task or another. Only 3/19 I can see who appear to be off-task.

That day, my field notes, recorded on my way home, referred to this observation

> But by-and-large children were left…to get on with it and get on with it they did…near the end of the lesson…I counted only three out of nineteen were not really focused on doing some work. Sixteen out of nineteen were working…that's like 2:40 in the afternoon. Quite something. So, once again, there has to be a strong argument for self-direction.

And in my field notes, dated June 2, 2015, I recalled

> Apart from now and again…it looked like some students were perhaps less engaged, if by that we mean focused on the task that they're supposed to be busy with…generally I thought—there were thirty or so of them—they got on with it. So it's really interesting just to see how students quite easily fit into this way of doing things. I certainly get a sense that there's a very high level of independence being shown and developed. Clearly there are some children who are not able to work independently, work alone, and they get more individual attention from the teacher.

Student Attitudes and Opinions

The attitude of the students towards their schools in general, towards the pedagogies in use, and towards the flexible learning arrangements were overwhelmingly positive, though some expressed reservations. Tessa, a self-reported highly gifted Year 10 Millennial College student, appreciated the school's inclusive practices. She indicated that the single-cell environment and associated traditional teaching did not suit her learning style at all, and that at this school she was not marginalised for seeming 'weird'.

Also at Millennial, two Year Tens, Lester and Matiu, reflecting on their previous intermediate schools, believed those to be much stricter. One of the benefits here, according to Lester, was the more lenient uniform regulation. It should also be noted that at Innovation and Millennial (but not Angelus), the students are permitted to refer to teachers by their first names (indeed, teachers are 'advisors' and 'coaches'). The relationships at Angelus, while friendly, focussed and respectful, do not extend to breaking down all traditional barriers, thus while students at Innovation and Millennial may refer to their teachers (and principals) by their first names, and may enter staff room areas, these elements will not be seen at Angelus School, which may be attributed to its status as a Special Character school.

Not all student views were openly enthusiastic. In regard to the emphasis on self-direction, a Year 10 student in Lester's class, and who was newly arrived from a prestigious boys' school, affirmed that he was now required to be responsible for ensuring he completes tasks. It seemed, however, that he preferred the teacher to take charge. His sense was that in the teacher-directed environment of his previous school, more purposeful learning took place. While he recognised the mantra of self-direction, he remained unconvinced, and said he doubted he would amount to much in his future if he continued in this fashion, a comment reacted to with some surprise and jocularity by his friends at the group.

The fact that students are able to choose their own learning programme or to make choices within a lesson period over what to focus on gives them an empowered sense of control over their learning. Their comments indicated that they had attained a level of meta-cognitive reflection, one of the aims of modern teaching and learning practice. Students I spoke with often referred to personalised teaching and learning. They realised their programme was less teacher-driven, For example, Ben, new to Angelus School, having shifted from a traditional primary school, said he often felt frustrated in the single-cell environment, with one teacher. He used the example of learning a new maths concept in his new school—by Tuesday, if he had mastered the concept, he could move on to other work, whereas at his last school, the same concept would have been taught the whole week, until everyone in the class had understood the concept. Francis, a Year 10 student new to Millennial College, provided a similar example, stating that in Physics at his previous school, he would be required to learn the same content as everyone else, whereas he was able to independently follow his passion for string theory at Millennial.

On Reflection

This much is clear: a central premise of modern or innovative teaching and learning practice is that the teacher be decentred. Furthermore, teachers are required to shift the emphasis from acquiring knowledge to thinking about what knowledge can do (Bolstad and Gilbert 2012). I will reflect briefly now on this 'knowledge problem', but mostly will apply Vagle's notion of 'posting intentionality' (2015).

Personalisation and the 'Knowledge Problem'

Key components of 21st-century learning, or modern and innovative teaching and learning practice, are the notions of personalised learning and responsive curricula developed according to students' interests. Students should thus bring their own interests to bear on decisions about what will be learnt as a prerequisite. As I indicated earlier, however, it is argued by social realists of knowledge, notably McPhail (2016), McPhail and Rata (2015), Rata (2012), Young (2008, 2013), Young and Muller (2010) that the elevation of personal knowledge to the status of disciplinary knowledge not only undermines knowledge, but it harms the life chances of school leavers. Indeed, Young has made the point that it is those students who are marginalised, particularly by their economic status, who stand to lose most by the dilution of knowledge. Instead, those who firmly understand the relevance and use of enduring concepts of knowledge, and how knowledge is developed, maintained and renewed, are able to cement positive life chances in the future. Thus, long-standing socioeconomic and political inequalities are allowed to persist by an emphasis on social knowledge and pursuing personal interest.

While those who advocate for practices such as co-construction of knowledge will see in the social realist position a prehistoric attempt to hold onto decrepit classroom practices, Rata (2012), for example, maintains that social realist approaches to teaching and learning do not signify a return to Gradgrindian principles. This tension between the importance of students learning disciplinary concepts and the value of their engagement with a personalised curriculum (which is also a tension between organised teacher control against teacher facilitation) is not easily resolved. McPhail (2016), whose research participants work with integrated and personalised curriculum choices in a futures-oriented New Zealand secondary school, have, for instance, highlighted their concern regarding students potentially making choices that enable them to steer clear of difficult, nevertheless important, concepts. Settling this debate is not easily accomplished, however. Being a teacher in the 21st century may require finding the balance between providing opportunities for students to immerse themselves in a rigorous search for knowledge while at the same time supporting them to develop dispositions, skills and competencies, and doing so while drawing on their cultural and social life experience.

Intentionality

Principal aspects of the concept of intentionality include reference to a powerful sense of personal being and a bodily connection to the lifeworld as one is being with the world. That state has an ethical dimension, as suggested by Heidegger's *Besorgen* or concernful having-to-do-with (Gorner, 2000). Further, as Vagle suggests, intentionality is a conscious and sub-conscious moving toward, and interrelating of self and the lifeworld. And, the researcher is implicated by virtue of his or her placement in the lifeworld of the phenomenon of interest.

The discourse of the teacher participants reveals a unified belief that they are being different teachers, as evidenced by some of these focus group comments

> **Innovation Primary**: "having a growth mind-set and not being afraid to make mistakes" (teacher); "really awesome opportunity to try new things and really to look at teaching in quite a different way. Because everything that most of us would have known is completely different…A lot of us came in almost feeling like beginner teachers all over again" (senior leader); "You kind of challenge everything that you ever did before" (teacher).
>
> **Millennial College**: "a disposition to openness, flexibility and wanting to try new things and being able to see beyond their subject silos…was what we were looking for [among the foundation teachers]" (senior leader); "releasing some of the influence and actually being prepared to step down and work one on one with the [students] on an equal footing…I saw a lot more space to really explore values and understandings around those things that I felt was really limited in a traditional school" (teacher).
>
> **Angelus School**: "quite a liberating way of teaching for me personally" (teacher); "we had to change our thinking and also the [students] have had to change their thinking. Going from…one teacher…[to]..talk to, to…three now" (teacher); "since we've been working together and doing more research and seeing other schools…my thinking…has changed in that student agency looks more like the students initiating their own learning. It's not all about me taking the responsibility" (teacher).

In keeping with these altered (and altering) mindsets in respect of their work as teachers, a common element in the three schools reviewed here (and indeed, Holyoake College, not referred to in this chapter) is the evident orientation of teachers towards their students, and their patient care and concern in relation to the progress of their students. Reflecting the insights offered by Bishop (2011), Gay (2002), Freire (1998), Wlodkowski and Ginsberg (1995), these teachers are responsive to their students not simply as human beings, but as cultural beings. This may translate in various ways, such as greeting the children in their home language at morning roll call, having student work prominently displayed, or using Te Reo Māori[5] in various informal exchanges. In particular, the dispositional focus of curriculum activity, as a central feature of modern or innovative teaching practice, lends itself to teachers finding themselves in positive and affirming relationships with their students. Harsh words are not heard to be spoken, voices are not raised, and the learning climate across all three schools is productive. This does not mean

---

[5]The Māori language.

to say that teachers find themselves in fawning or obsequious relation with their students. On the contrary, firm expectations are evident—"being warm and demanding with the students" (senior leader, Innovation Primary, DB). When errant behaviour or conduct is remarked upon, it is done so by reference to the underlying dispositional values of the school.

All three schools are committed to restorative justice practices in their approach to behaviour management. This is unsurprising, given the positive, non-judgemental student-teacher relationships in clear evidence at each school. The Millennial staff are well trained in the use of restorative justice and its language permeates all matters arising out of behavioural issues. Additionally, students are trained to know what to expect of the restorative justice process. The principal of Innovation Primary specifically referred to the work of Russell Bishop, and was pleased to say, "we haven't really had to use it". Angelus School works strongly on ensuring teachers know each child individually, and connect meaningfully with the family when there are issues. Restorative justice is an explicit approach at Angelus School:

> Not labelling or damning the child at every instance, [rather to] work through right to the end because often with children like that they can become labelled and every incident that happens they get blamed for it, but we don't do that. We look at what was underneath, what happened before and work it through (Principal, IV).

I was able to observe a particular instance of restorative justice practice at Innovation School, couched as a 'committee meeting.' I recalled the event in my field notes on May 26, 2015 as akin to

> a family meeting. The committee of students...had got together to discuss a problem that's emerged in the last day or so...someone in the class threatening someone else...the committee...nutted out the problem and what to do about the problem. They'd come up with a Google Doc...The document was then projected up onto the big plasma screen. At the end of the period before time finished that group presented their document [of solutions to the rest of the class] on the plasma screen.

The teachers at these schools thus consciously weave a continuous thread between student conduct and the dispositional curriculum. At the same time, however, teachers are not exempt from calling their own conduct into question, judged too against the dispositions. This may be seen in terms of their active and vocal self-reflection, for instance a teaching team referring to its overestimation of the ability of students to follow a task when the teachers have in fact been unclear in their instructions. These are people who may therefore be seen to be constantly reaching out towards their students in concernful ways.

There were other instances that revealed inner thoughts, perhaps held in check in the sub-conscious, but triggered into speech in the context of private discussions. Here I think in particular of those participants at Millennial College, who "grieve" and "mourn" the loss of subject disciplines and private classrooms, now replaced with a skills-focussed integrated curriculum, and deprivatised, open spaces. Leaders used definitive and uncompromising language to indicate that the learning areas had to be pared back, and have the 'fat' trimmed off them, and that it was their responsibility to ensure that the curriculum was not 'disengaging for kids'. Passion was evident in the voices of those teachers who enthused about, and embraced, integrated curriculum.

Being a teacher in the 21st century, in the voice of my participants, and my observations of their practice, means then being a person of self-conscious dispositions, such as openness to practice differently, being willing to challenge oneself, and having a persistent focus on self-learning. For teachers, their being so clears the way to their recognition of the Being of students, and to repeat a phrase I frequently heard, "taking them from where they're at". This, ironically, presupposes no presuppositions. From this perspective, coming to know one's students as human beings is, as Freire (1998) would have it, an ethical duty, but one that a teacher opts to identify with. The voices of my participants reveal that there is significant pain, anguish and frustration to engage as a teacher in the 21st century, with much to lose —yet much to gain from the deepened relationships with work, colleagues and students.

In Conclusion

The participants in this research are bounded by their commitment to engage a policy impetus to develop modern, technologically rich, pedagogies (portrayed as both thinking about their work and actual classroom practice). The focus of this chapter has been on the manifestation of modern or innovative teaching and learning practice, conveyed primarily from my perspective as an embedded researcher/observer, but through the lens of both practitioners and students. My main concern is with the practitioners, and to establish what it means to be a teacher in the 21st century. Quite evidently, it is not to be a person who believes s/he has a fixed and certain body of knowledge to impart to a passive, compliant audience. On the contrary, as MacBeath (2012) pointed out, teachers now find themselves in a policy milieu that endorses the development of a range of dispositions, skills and key competencies, requiring teachers to seek ways of being innovative on a daily basis. They are also required to be responsive to a range of student needs and diverse backgrounds.

The participants in this study were attitudinally unified by their willingness to engage with futures discourses and, ironically, by their certain notions of an uncertain future. Implicit in their approaches to supporting their students for this uncertain future was their recognition of the emphasis given to the dispositional curriculum and the direct focus on skill development (over content coverage). Yet, the policy directives of the Ministry of Education are contradictory—on one hand, it encourages (indeed, through its building programme, demands) the adoption of innovative teaching and learning practices that will have dispositions, skills and key competencies at its core, while on the other hand, it advances just as firmly, its national assessment agenda through National Standards and the NCEA. Several participants across the three schools referred to in this chapter, including the principals, were united by their frustration with a reporting system (indeed, the systems within their own schools) that required them to report not on student development of dispositions, skills and key competencies, but on student achievement against scholastic standards.

Being a teacher in the 21st century thus means leading a double life of balancing the competing tensions of progressive pedagogy that should have as its outcome students who grow and develop to be citizens able to lead a meaningful and satisfying life in the current century, against the traditional demands for a scholastic education that requires teachers to teach to predetermined standards. Being a teacher in the 21st century also requires a significant level of critical acuity. For one, the question of dispositions and competencies pose significant critical difficulties, as I have previously indicated (Benade 2011), in particular in terms of manufacturing consent to an agenda combining social cohesion and the promotion of autonomous selfhood encased in a materialist and globally competitive economy. I further suggested (Benade 2012) that this agenda interferes with teachers' ethical effort to develop right relations with their students.

The participants each manifested evidence of engaging with modern teaching and learning practice, an overriding policy impetus both in New Zealand and more widely across the globe at this time of writing. Recapturing Vagle's notion of 'tentative manifestations', the participants did not necessarily manifest this engagement in the same ways or to the same extent, though I have tried to demonstrate that there are significant similarities among them. Despite being in three different schools with different visions and missions, effectively, they speak a common language with respect to what may be termed modern or innovative learning practice. In this chapter, I have portrayed this practice as developing unique approaches to curriculum, personalisation of learning, including respect for students' social and cultural backgrounds, restorative justice practices, and developing teaching and learning strategies that will support the development of student agency and engagement. In the following chapter, I will turn my attention to the spaces of learning.

References

Benade, L. (2011). Shaping the responsible, successful and contributing citizen of the future: 'Values' in the New Zealand Curriculum and its challenge to the development of ethical teacher professionality. *Policy Futures in Education, 9*(2), 151–162. doi:10.2304/pfie.2011.9.2.151

Benade, L. (2012). From technicians to teachers: Ethical teaching in the context of globalized education reform. New York, NY: Continuum.

Bishop, R. (2011). Freeing ourselves from neo-colonial domination in public school classrooms. In R. Bishop (Ed.), *Freeing ourselves* (pp. 31–73). Rotterdam, The Netherlands: Sense

Publishers. doi:10.1007/978-94-6091-415-7_2. Retrieved from http://link.springer.com.ezproxy.aut.ac.nz

Bolstad, R., Gilbert, J., McDowall, S., Bull, A., Boyd, S. and Hipkins, R. (2012). *Supporting Future-Oriented Learning and Teaching: A New Zealand perspective*. Report prepared for the Ministry of Education. Wellington: New Zealand Council for Educational Research and Ministry of Education. Retrieved August 8, 2015, from http://www.educationcounts.govt.nz/publications/schooling/109306.

Chapman, A., Randell-Moon, H., Campbell, M., & Drew, C. (2014). Students in space: Student practices in non-traditional classrooms. *Global Studies of Childhood, 4*(1), 39–48. doi:10.2304/gsch.2014.4.1.39

Freire, P. (1970/1996). *Pedagogy of the oppressed* (M. Ramos, Trans.). London: Penguin Books.

Freire, P. (1998). *Pedagogy of freedom: Ethics, democracy and civic courage*. Lanham, MD: Rowman and Littlefield.

Gay, G. (2002). Preparing for culturally responsive teaching. *Journal of Teacher Education, 53*(2), 106–116.

Gorner, P. (2000). *Twentieth-century German philosophy*. Oxford, United Kingdom: Oxford University Press.

Green, H., Facer, K., Rudd, T., Dillon, P., & Humphreys, P. (2005). *Personalisation and digital technologies*. Bristol, England: Futurelab. Retrieved February 6, 2016 from http://www.nfer.ac.uk/publications/FUTL59/FUTL59_home.cfm

Griffin, P. (2009, January). What makes a rich task? *Mathematics Teaching, 212*, 32–34. Retrieved from http://www.atm.org.uk/write/MediaUploads/Journals/MT212/Non-Member/ATM-MT212-32-34.pdf

Kay, K. (2010). 21st century skills: Why they matter, what they are, and how we get there. In J. Bellanca & R. Brandt (Eds.), *21st century skills: Rethinking how students learn* (pp. xiii–xxxi), Bloomington, IN: Solution Tree Press.

MacBeath, J. (2012). *Future of teaching profession*. Cambridge, England: University of Cambridge. Education International Research Institute. Retrieved from http://download.ei-ie.org/Docs/WebDepot/EI%20Study%20on%20the%20Future%20of%20Teaching%20Profession.pdf

Matters, G. (2006, October). Good data, bad news, good policy making…*QTU Professional Magazine*, 18–24. Retrieved from http://www.qtu.asn.au/files/8713/2268/2363/vol21_matters.pdf

McPhail, G. (2016). From aspirations to practice: Curriculum challenges for a new 'twenty-first-century' secondary school. *The Curriculum Journal (online first)*. doi:10.1080/09585176.2016.1159593

McPhail, G., & Rata, E. (2015). Comparing curriculum types: 'powerful knowledge' and '21st century learning'. *New Zealand Journal of Educational Studies (online first)*. doi:10.1007/s40841-015-0025-9

Ministry of Education. (2007). The New Zealand curriculum. Wellington, New Zealand: Learning Media Limited. Available from http://nzcurriculum.tki.org.nz/The-New-Zealand-Curriculum

Rata, E. (2012). *The politics of knowledge in education*. New York/London: Routledge Taylor and Francis Group.

Smardon, D., Charteris, J., & Nelson, E. (2015). Shifts to learning eco-systems: Principals' and teachers' perceptions of innovative learning environments. New Zealand Journal of Teachers' Work, *12*(2), 149–171. Retrieved from https://teachworkojs.aut.ac.nz/autojs/index.php/nzjtw/article/view/31/56

Vagle, M. D. (2015). Curriculum as post-intentional phenomenological text: Working along the edges and margins of phenomenology using post-structuralist ideas. *Journal of Curriculum Studies, 47*(5), 594–612. doi:10.1080/00220272.2015.1051118

Wlodkowski, R. J., & Ginsberg, M. B. (1995). A framework for culturally responsive teaching. *Educational Leadership, 53*(1), 17–21.

References

Young, M. F. D. (2008). *Bringing knowledge back in: From social constructivism to social realism in the sociology of education*. London, England/New York, NY: Routledge.

Young, M. F. D. (2013). Overcoming the crisis in curriculum theory: A knowledge-based approach. *Journal of Curriculum Studies, 45*(2), 101–118. doi:10.1080/00220272.2013.764505

Young, M. F. D., & Muller, J. (2010). Knowledge, truth and the sociology of education. In R. Moore & K. Maton (Eds.), *Social realism, knowledge and the sociology of education: Coalitions of the mind*. London, England: Continuum Books.

Chapter 5
The Impacts on Teachers' Work: Working in Flexible Learning Environments

> The generative source for a materialist interpretation of spatiality is the recognition that spatiality is socially produced and, like society itself, exists in both substantial forms (concrete spatialities) and as a set of relations between individuals and groups, an 'embodiment' and a medium of social life itself. (Soja 1989, p. 120).

The initial impetus for the research on which *Being a Teacher* is based was the policy direction taken by the New Zealand Ministry of Education to implement a programme of building new schools as flexible learning environments, and to retrofit existing schools by refurbishment, or adding new facilities. These challenging new spaces must be thought of as a technology like any other, and be given similar critical and theoretical treatment as any other technology would. This is so because these spaces have the potential to disrupt and modify existing practices, and encourage or even demand new ones. Uncritical responses may take the direction of enthusiastic zealotry or ignorant dismissal. Neither, I would argue, is satisfactory. The former fails to acknowledge possible and real flaws in the idea that learning spaces be altered to accommodate three times as many students and teachers working both collaboratively and independently on multiple, personalised, tasks. The latter is simply ignorant, and is often linked to a view that likens these contemporary spaces to the failed open plan classrooms of the 1960s, and/or to the view that "there is no research". It is, coincidentally, a view that does not acknowledge learning to be possible without the teacher at the front teaching. Against this background, it is therefore imperative to develop a theoretically robust research base. I flagged this in Chap. 3, with reference to some key ideas drawn from materiality theory and the work of Henri Lefebvre. The following critical discussion will review the context of the development of flexible learning environments in New Zealand, drawing on some key sources of research that have influenced the Ministry of Education. I will also reflect further on some of ideas relating to spatiality and Lefebvre in the context of the physical spaces of learning I refer to as flexible learning environments.

© Springer Nature Singapore Pte Ltd. 2017
L. Benade, *Being a Teacher in the 21st Century*,
DOI 10.1007/978-981-10-3782-5_5

Flexible Learning Environments and Space: Some Critical Perspectives on Policy

Some years ago, Green et al. (2005) suggested that the learning environment is more than just the built environment. If it is assumed that knowledge can no longer be considered either the preserve of teachers alone, or possible for any one person to retain, then experts outside the school must become key ingredients in the learning environment. It is for the school to act in ways that will facilitate these important connections (2005). Practical steps include schools enabling 'anywhere, anytime' access to digital assets that bring experts into the school, or to physically enable outside experts to connect with students in the school, perhaps by running workshops (2005). Therefore, not all learning takes place in the formal classroom (Dumont and Istance 2010). A learning environment is "crucially focused on the dynamics and interactions between four dimensions—the **learner** (who?), **teachers and other learning professionals** (with whom?), **content** (learning what?) and **facilities and technologies** (where? with what?)" (p. 29, emphasis in the original).

The New Zealand Ministry of Education remains loyal to the concept of learning taking place within a school's orbit, albeit not necessarily in a classroom. This is consistent with its own stated strategic intention: "School buildings will continue to be the primary and the preferred infrastructure from which education services are delivered." (2011, p. 2). As the key stakeholder in all New Zealand state schools (over 2000 in total), the Ministry of Education has a significant financial commitment to these schools, its Schools Property Infrastructure Service currently allocating some $500 mil annually to maintaining and upgrading school property (Ministry of Education 2016). Its vision of providing safe and inspiring learning environments is based on the beliefs that schools contribute to making vibrant communities, that investing in schools follows sound financial principles and, importantly, that school buildings *"empower students to learn and teachers to teach"* (2011, p. 4. Emphasis added).

One of the goals of the strategic plan is to ensure schools are fit for purpose, and here the Ministry of Education openly commits itself to "modern learning environments". Breaking with the tradition of a

> teacher-centred system that revolved around structured classroom lessons…[the Ministry of Education has accepted a]…Modern Learning Environment (MLE) standard that schools will adopt as they become due for their next round of property funding. Achieving this outcome is critical to modern education delivery and will ensure that *the performance of the physical environment is linked to educational outcomes.* (p. 13. Emphasis added)

Ambitiously, the Ministry of Education has set 2021 as the target year by which time all schools will have been expected to modernise all their teaching spaces. Some important points emerge from the evidence considered here:

- the concept of modern learning environments, or innovative learning environments, the term now used by the Ministry, or flexible learning environments, the

term used throughout this book, is not notional—this concept, in various forms, is the standard for school buildings in New Zealand moving forward.
- by virtue of this strategic commitment, the various pedagogical and relational implications flowing from these building designs have to feature as intrinsic to the daily life of teachers and students.
- in the minds of Ministry of Education planners, the built environment has a shaping and determining influence over pedagogy;
- pedagogy must be shifted from the model of single teachers directing learning in single cell classrooms;

A final point, not openly expressed in this strategic plan, but implied, is that the role of the Ministry of Education is not to dictate how schools, through parent-elected Boards of Trustees and the Principal, will use their educational spaces. Rather, the Ministry of Education sees itself "[s]upporting teaching and learning [by] [e]nsuring schools have the range and quality of teaching spaces needed to support education" (p. 15). Therefore, it could be argued that while the Ministry of Education is not dictating how teachers ought to teach, it is dictating that teaching and learning cease to take place in single cell classrooms of up to 30 students with one teacher at the front. What ideas may have supported this strategic plan?

The Ministry of Education is sometimes accused, in the context of 'teacher talk', or public discourse, of introducing reforms (such as the development of flexible learning spaces) without providing an evidence base, or what is sometimes simply referred to as 'research'. There are, however, some key documents that provide insight to earlier thinking by the Ministry of Education in regard to this particular innovation. In particular, these are the study carried out by AC Nielsen (2004), and a review of a learning studio pilot project carried out by the Ministry of Education (2012).

AC Nielsen Study: Best Practice in School Design

The AC Nielsen study, commissioned by the Ministry of Education in 2004, aimed to ascertain the views of a range of key stakeholders in regard to the role of school design in securing and improving learning outcomes. This knowledge would assist the Ministry of Education to support schools by providing appropriate infrastructure. Conducted in two phases, it had a mixed methodology, commencing with a qualitative round of interviews, followed by a semi-quantitative self-completion survey (and telephone survey of designers). Participants were drawn from teachers across the compulsory sector, students in Years 5–13 (ages 10–18), principals, Boards of Trustees and designers. The qualitative phase involved 20 participants based in Wellington; 433 from schools in Auckland, Bay of Plenty and one South Island school took the survey.

Key findings were:

- the importance of ensuring some consistency between school vision and the built environment;
- the important role that the built environment (specifically classrooms) can play in learning;
- the significant contribution made to learning by such factors as the size and flexibility of this space, its ventilation, its temperature and its acoustic performance; specifically

    - that the actual learning environment be spacious and equipped with flexible features, including furniture that is easily moved;
    - that deterrents to productive work were CO_2 build-up, stuffiness and intemperate learning spaces;
    - that natural lighting has a positive role to play;
    - that noise, especially in the classroom must be minimised, but so too from surrounding areas

- the importance of 'future proofing', to allow for easy integration of new technologies;
- the positive effect on motivation of a high-quality, well-kept environment, including

    - appropriate spaces for teachers to work;
    - a mix of outdoor and recreational areas;

- finally, that all the above need to take their place within a larger vision for the school building and surrounding grounds.

As the relationships among space and pedagogy (the how and why of teaching) are important themes in this book, there are some findings detailed this report that have added relevance. Of significance, only one-third of respondents believed space makes a "big difference" (2004, p. 56) to student learning outcomes, whereas well over 70% of respondents agreed that it was the teacher's own abilities that make the most difference (which accords, for example, with the work of Byers 2016). This was, however, when space was ranged against several other options. This variable was tested alone, and when asked to what extent classroom design affects or eases student learning, the vast majority of teachers, students and principals agreed it has an impact, with 30% of teachers and 11% of students rating this extent to be "major", and 57% of principals rating it to be "reasonable". (p. 57). Principals linked reduced teachers' stress to the enhanced flexibility of multiple classroom structures (as opposed, presumably, to single cells), whereas they linked stress to working in overcrowded and unhealthy environments. In respect of students, the principals linked enhanced pride in surroundings and the anticipated positive attitudes to learning with being in environments that have moderate ambient temperatures and are well lit. From the perspective of teachers, 60% of 139 teachers surveyed emphasised the importance of having adequate space for movement as a key factor in a well-designed space (p. 160). Thus lack of space, particularly for primary teachers, was rated as a constraint, while 42% thought that the 'best' classroom was one with ample space to move around (p. 163), and 52% thought the most 'inadequate' classroom was one that lacked space (p. 165). Environmental factors were important too, and there was a roughly even split between teachers wanting to control, (if they could), space, temperature and lighting.

The AC Nielsen researchers suggested that their findings would form the basis of a Ministry of Education strategy to develop guidelines that schools could use in planning classroom redevelopments and designs. Further, they suggested that the Ministry of Education ensure there be a link between such planning and consideration of the curriculum. Significantly, this advice came at the time the present New Zealand Curriculum (MOE 2007) was under construction. It is also significant in that it mirrored the views of Fisher (2005), mentioned in Chap. 3.

Ministry of Education: Learning Studio Pilot Review

The second document of interest that will have informed Ministry of Education thinking about flexible learning spaces is the learning studio pilot project carried out by the Ministry of Education (2012). Commenced in 2008, the Ministry of Education took its lead from Fisher's work, mentioned above, and also that of Nair et al. (2013).[1] The intention of the pilot was to invite schools that were entitled to classroom upgrades to participate in a project to build future-oriented schools that would point the way to appropriate design for 21st century school buildings. Five schools were selected from around New Zealand, and were free to design their sites in keeping with existing buildings, ensuring only that they remained within the specification they were provided. All designs had to meet the approval of a Ministry-appointed consultant. The Ministry had an expectation that schools would procure "appropriate ergonomic furniture...and furniture that allows for a variety of room layouts, i.e. not basic desks." (p. 5).

The schools were completed by 2010, and in 2012, the Ministry of Education undertook a post occupancy evaluation (POE), which included consideration of the teaching and learning outcomes resulting from the pilot project. The report is largely silent on the methodology that informed its production, and data gathering seems to have been limited to speaking with the "Principals, Studio teaching staff and some Project Managers, BOT representatives and Architects" (2012, p. 5). Surprisingly, it seems the views of the students were not canvassed, even though the pilot affected nearly 500 students across the five schools. Apart from isolated references in the report to students, in only one place is a summation of student perspectives to be found, though the teachers whose views were gathered may have

---

[1]While the 3rd edition of this text is cited here, its first edition was published in 2005, three years prior to the pilot. 'Learning studio' is a term found in Nair et al. (2013) and Fisher (2005).

provided these.[2] Further, of the nine points raised, four are 'project specific', that is, relating to a specific school.

The Ministry of Education was satisfied that participating schools had demonstrated a high level of approval in their responses to the POE. The review report consists of 32 PDF pages of text, including three appendices. These consist of three pages of design drawings, a page of demographic information and four pages providing a planning and technical brief for future projects, based on the positive and negative feedback received. There is a four page financial analysis and a page of bibliographic detail. Thus the actual 'feedback' aspect of the report runs from page 6 to page 22, therefore, some sixteen pages, though there are several photographs throughout. In the introduction, the report noted of the post occupancy evaluation that it

> ...evaluates the concept, the construction process and the completed project in use, to identify the positive factors (so that they can be repeated), the negatives, (so that they are not replicated) and aspects worthy of further consideration in future projects...The results showed overwhelming support for the concept, but, as with anything new, there were some disappointments, some frustrations and some design details that could have been improved. (p. 5)

The Ministry of Education is to be applauded for demonstrating its willingness to acknowledge the criticisms that its evaluation received, clearly to learn what to avoid in future projects. Precisely how honest it was in this regard is demonstrated by the fact that, of the sixteen pages of evaluative text, only the first four summarise the 'positives', while the following twelve pages detail a litany of concerns, frustrations and lost opportunities, expressed by the schools (pp. 10–17) and the consultants (architects and project managers) (pp. 18–22). Before reviewing these two (apparently uneven) positive and negative perspectives, I will draw attention to the financial analysis.

The financial analysis of the report (pp. 23–26) outlines details of the brief to the consulting accounting firm commissioned by the Ministry of Education—essentially "to undertake a high level review to consider appropriate means in which to advise MOE on whether five previously constructed Learning Suites provide a Value for Money solution to the Modern Learning Environment" (p. 23). The task of the consultant was thus to examine the building projects of five unique and discrete sites, to flatten out, or equalise, differences in building costs among them so as to allow a like for like comparison, and thus "determine whether a particular suite, for its $/m^2$, was providing an efficient learning/teaching space and therefore a value for money solution to the Modern Learning Environment" (p. 25). A significant finding was that the average cost of building the Learning Suites was $2750/m^2$. This figure well exceeded, in the 2011/2012 financial year, the Ministry of Education Gross Floor Area (GFA) budget for new builds of $2100/m^2$.

---

[2]The report indicates that direct quotes from participants are in italicised text. The text relating to students (on p. 9) is all italicised, and apart from its adult language usage, its register reflects a third person, reporting style. This indicates adults reporting what they have heard students say, or what they have witnessed of student conduct in the spaces.

This finding led the commissioned consulting firm, Davis Langdon, to question whether the Ministry had an adequate budget for new school buildings, and whether the Learning Suite concept offered value for money.

Turning now to the findings of the POE, the ones of most interest in the context of this book are those specifically in reference to teachers' work and students' perceptions and responses. Nevertheless, there were a number of 'non-pedagogic' views, concerning general satisfaction with suite layout, and matters concerning light, ventilation, temperature and acoustics. A frequent, anecdotal, question (usually intended as a point of criticism) is whether student learning is enhanced by flexible learning environments. Significantly, one of the participants in the POE reported as follows: "Learning benefits that accrue from the concept are very difficult to assess, but the range of spaces offer opportunities that support enhanced education outcomes" (p. 6). Nevertheless, many of the reported comments drew attention to the enhanced teaching experience. These included:

- benefitting from collaborative teamwork:
- being released from the isolation of single cell classrooms;
- deriving mutual benefit from shared expertise;
- having the mutual support of colleagues working in the same space. In addition, the teachers in the pilot study
- appreciating the possibility of working with greater student numbers in social and flexible surroundings that were motivating to all.

According to the views expressed in the report pertaining to students, their experience is positive in relation to such matters as student–teacher relationships, peer-peer relationships and their response to the physical aspects of the new studio environments. The students were found to have gained advantage by having multiple teachers to refer to, and multiple teachers could better cater to the diverse characteristics of students. The active, social nature of the environments positively influenced student relationships, with positive outcomes also noted in respect of student behaviour. This positive behaviour extended to their respectful enjoyment of the new facilities.

Earlier, I referred to a 'litany' of issues, complaints and critical reflections dominating the report. These referred to the project design phase, the construction phase (though this features so briefly, it will be ignored here), teachers' experience of using the spaces, and the experience of the architects and project managers, mainly of working with the Ministry of Education.

In regard to the project design phase, all stakeholders raised several interconnected and complex issues, but for simplicity, these issues can be reduced to questions of bureaucracy and questions of design. Despite the 'hands-off' form of school self-governance, introduced to New Zealand by the 1984 education reforms, the Ministry of Education, which controls the Vote Education[3] central government

---

[3]The spending allocated to the education sector in the annual Budget, usually tabled in the House of Parliament during May of each year by the sitting government.

budget allocation, effectively controls the schools. The Ministry of Education sets very tight requirements around the building design briefs, limiting the choices schools may have in regard to building design. In turn, it imposes these restrictions on designers, who attempt to work closely with the schools. In cases reported in the pilot study, these designers were, seemingly, ignorant of (newly emerging) educational requirements (and arguably, this may continue to be the case). Amongst the restrictions within which the designers were required to operate, was an independent peer review process, to ensure their designs met the requirements of the Ministry of Education (rather than the schools). Thus a Ministry of Education design brief that sometimes failed to allow for the obvious (such as coat and bag storage), a restrictive budget, and review process imposed on the designers all combined to leave schools and designers frustrated.

Teachers' lived experience in flexible learning environments is a central feature underpinning the research on which this book is based. Thus the views of teachers' use of space in the learning suite pilot are significant. Unfortunately, most of the comments bear on design limitations *per se* rather than on the pedagogical implications of these limitations. Thus, comments relate to such matters as design features that were not 'child-friendly', to poor design features, ranging from the absence of urinals in boys' toilets, to shelving units obscuring electrical sockets, and inadequate storage for student gear (not allowed for in the brief). Of most interest is where pedagogical implications can be inferred. The source of such inference includes the view that outdoor space was inadequate and not fit for purpose in cases, and the inadequate GFA allowance (generally 1:15 teaching to learning space). Arguably, these realities will have reduced the possibilities for flexible usage during teaching and learning activities. Of most interest however, despite ergonomic furniture being a Ministry of Education requirement, in some cases, schools persisted with a conventional 'one seat/desk per student' approach, which was found to be largely unworkable in the new spaces (compounded by the inadequate GFA allowance). In some cases, this seems to have been a consequence of budget overruns, whereas in other cases, it appears to have been teacher preference. In light of the findings referred to later in this chapter, it will be seen that persisting with conventional furniture significantly minimises the value of the flexibility offered by redesigned learning spaces.

Finally, the views of the design and project consultants were summarised in the report. While the designers were excited by the prospect of participating in a 'leap forward' that could "create enriched, dynamic and interesting ways of teaching and learning" (p. 18), they found themselves frustrated at many levels. Just as the schools felt frustrated by being caught in a bureaucratic web woven by the Ministry of Education, where they felt caught between the designers and the Ministry, so the designers felt they were caught between the unrealistic demands of the Ministry of Education and the unrealised aspirations of the schools. Specifically, they commented on the unsatisfactory relationship with the Ministry of Education, which included obscure communication and unilateral decision-making by the Ministry. The Ministry of Education had provided a difficult, overblown brief that was unachievable given budget constraints with no allowance for unanticipated costs.

This included the demand for a Green Star[4] rating, which, though desirable, led to expensive procurements in order to achieve compliance. "More emphasis should be given to creating an effective learning environment rather than achieving Green Star ratings" (p. 20). Designers also expressed their general dissatisfaction with the peer review process that was found in some instances to be excessively expensive and overly detailed.

There are important, provisional, conclusions that can be drawn from these two reports, which may have played a role in developing the Ministry of Education property strategic plan, referred to earlier. The reports reveal a concern with space conceptualised as the classroom, a container, in which teaching and learning may occur, but they also reveal silences regarding how the space might be used, and how space and people might interact. There appears to be considerable focus on the 'property' side of the equation, with very little emphasis on the 'pedagogy' side. Concerns with cost, budgets and the prominence of bureaucratic frameworks override all other considerations, particularly pedagogical and relational issues. Closer examination of some elements reveals, however, that teachers are concerned with spaciousness as an important factor in supporting positive learning outcomes (or lack of space in newly-designed buildings being a source of frustration). Nagging tensions seem to exist, however, between questions of the conceptualisation and construction of space, spatiality (space as a construction of the relationship between people and the material spaces they occupy and work in), the pedagogies developed in those spaces, and the lived experience of the spaces. In particular, predominating questions exist in regard to conceptualisation and construction, and non-pedagogic aspects of the lived experience (issues with toilets, bag space and storage of teachers' effects, for instance). I will not attempt to deal with these tensions now, preferring to incorporate them into the discussion that flows from consideration of the findings of the study of learning environments in three schools undertaken in 2015.

The Practical Studies: Working in Flexible (Innovative) Learning Environments

I will continue in this chapter to focus on the three schools exhibiting practice in flexible learning environments, namely Innovation Primary, Angelus School and Millennial College. While the elements of modern or innovative teaching and learning practice, the design of learning environments, the development of digital pedagogy, and teachers' reflective practice in relation to these elements are not necessarily discrete, for purposes of clear analysis it is important to separate them, considering each on its own merits. Each dimension yields its own range of data

---

[4]Green Star is a tool that rates and communicates the sustainability of New Zealand's commercial buildings. See https://www.nzgbc.org.nz/Category?Action=View&Category_id=217.

calling for specific responses. In what follows, I will attempt to contextualise the various environments, inviting the reader to step into the unique worlds of each of the three schools. Within each school, teachers work with students in a range of spaces, and as they do so, draw on various elements within this space. Conceptualising space as socially constructed (Lefebvre 1991; Soja 1989), means neither teachers nor students are regarded as passive, atomistic entities occupying containers; rather, they each develop and exhibit agency, so their actions and views are important in developing spatiality.

Innovation Primary

Innovation Primary presents as a continuous, linear building on one level. Internally, a spacious and wide walkway flows from end to end. Learning and workspaces are located off the walkway. There are few internal walls and the egg crate design of traditional schools is absent. Similarly, the administration areas are open plan, with no designated closed offices, so the principal and staff share common areas for work. Outside areas are visible through very large and generous glass walls and windows. A boardroom located near the entrance permits space for confidential meetings.

Angelus School

Angelus School is a two-storey school, and though designed using contemporary materials and techniques, the core design of its initial building (the first phase of building) is typical of egg crate or single cell traditional schools. The ground level verandah and covered upper walkway look on to a large quadrangular and playground area. The classrooms enjoy the benefits of natural light, with very large windows looking out to the quadrangle on one side, and the currently undeveloped land on the opposite side. The second building phase introduced, on both levels, two large flexible learning environments, so that Angelus School now has a blend of traditional single cell rooms accommodating one class and one teacher each, and three classes and three teachers in each of the flexible spaces.

Millennial College

Millennial College is on two levels, though presenting a low profile from the exterior. Like Innovation Primary, from the street it presents as a continuous, linear building, with playing fields adjoining. Internally, Millennial College is not unlike a contemporary 21st century airport concourse, providing a sense of large spaces that generously admit natural light. Here too, staff and administration areas are generally open plan, with few closed spaces, and as at Innovation Primary, the principal and staff share common areas for work. There is a boardroom space for confidential meetings. Built on two levels, most of the observations took place on the upper level, where large learning spaces open to either side of the wide and generous central walkway.

Design and Set-Up of the Working Space

All three schools are characterised by large learning spaces allowing the flexible arrangement of a variety of educational furniture arranged in several ways to suit various purposes (see Fig. 5.1). The learning spaces are designed to allow large groups of students to be brought together if required, with several 'breakout' spaces, some walled, in single cell design, others (notable features of Innovation Primary and Millennial College), less clearly defined and without walls. All three schools have designated space set aside as teachers' stations where they can plan and leave belongings—at Innovation Primary and Angelus School these spaces are within the learning areas, while at Millennial College, these spaces are located

Fig. 5.1 Multiple furniture and spatial options. Breakout centre *left*; wet area centre *back*; teachers' station to the *right* (obscured)

separately from the 'classroom' spaces, though adjacent to the walkways just described.

Innovation Primary and Millennial College had growing, but low rolls at the time this research was undertaken, in 2015. The largest number observed at Millennial College was around 40 (though one participant referred to a class of over 50); the least was 15. Innovation classes observed did not exceed around forty. Unsurprisingly then, the available space, especially at Millennial, is generous and uncrowded. By contrast, Angelus School has a full (yet growing) roll, and 90 students are located in each of its flexible spaces.

The flowing, non-defined (or less defined) space at Innovation, with its nooks and breakouts, creates opportunities for an increased range of activities. Millennial College and Angelus School have more clearly defined rectangular shaped central spaces, also with several breakout spaces adjoining the central area. Here too, students are able to move into, and utilise, these breakout spaces. All teachers observed encouraged their students to move freely in and about the spaces though in some cases, spaces have specially designated functions, such as offering a computer pod.

A range of furniture types in the primary schools offer teachers and students various possibilities, such as conferencing or running workshops at rectangular tables. 'Watering-holes' (Thornburg 2007) provide the opportunity to work on shared projects in circular groupings, while other places where work can occur includes fixed desktop computers, table groupings in a 'wet area', single, easily movable ergonomic stools, and high bar stool chairs at high tables provide 'lookouts'. Young children can easily move the furniture, and this was noted to be a frequent occurrence at Angelus School. There is not a seat for every student in the room, and many students may be seen siting on the floor or standing at tables. Millennial College, a secondary school, has more conventional furniture options, though still offering a range of options such as sofa-style and Ottoman seating. Innovation Primary offers the option of calling the entire group together in one circle, to create a 'campfire' (2007), consisting of small, portable Ottomans. Angelus School, while designating a full class grouping as a campfire, relies on students merely gathering close to the lead teacher (Fig. 5.2).

The walls (and indeed, the windows) become an additional source of information and support for the students. Here they may find reminders relating to their dispositional curriculum, various tools for keeping track of their individual and group progress, and pertinent, current information relating to aspects of the curriculum (such as numeracy 'basic facts' or exemplars). The walls show some evidence of the outcomes of large collaborative project work. The mass display of individual work typically associated with primary schools was, however, less overt in the observed spaces at Innovation Primary and Angelus School.

Fig. 5.2 Various breakout spaces, *front left*, *centre left*. Nearest breakout features a pod of desktop computers

Student Work and Attitudes

In order to understand and assess a selection of the student views, I will refer to some elements of the organisation of their working life in the flexible spaces. These points echo some of those already made in Chap. 4. The layout of the flexible learning environments across all three schools permits independent work, and differentiation is a prevailing pedagogic modality. For example, at Angelus School, in an observation of the Year 1 and Year 2 combined class, seven discernible and different groups were engaged in a variety of mathematics tasks while the remainder were generally working in small groups of three or so, working with mobile devices, all without teachers.

Ironically, the greater freedom of movement and ability to make choices over where to work and what to be working on in the flexible spaces is a factor in reducing student behavioural issues (Principal, Angelus School, IV). In single cell class spaces, with one teacher and twenty-five or thirty students, there are fewer spatial opportunities to redirect students who have become disengaged. Nevertheless, students working in flexible spaces are easily able to give the appearance of being productive: some students are "very good at going into corners", and potentially engaging in off-task activity (teacher, Millennial College DB).

Students expressed mostly positive feedback in favour of flexible learning spaces, and their views can be summarised in relation to student choice, personalised teaching and learning, flexibility and mobility, and relational possibilities. Readers will appreciate that some of these views touch on the issue of modern or innovative teaching and learning practice, nevertheless, some of the chief points justify repetition.

Almost invariably, when asked to justify why they favoured being placed in a large, flexible learning area with multiple students and teachers, students primarily cited freedom of choice. This includes choice over their learning programme or choices within a block of teaching or learning, providing them a sense of empowerment over their learning. Secondly, in relation to personalised teaching and learning, students realised their programme is not teacher-driven (see the examples of Ben and Francis in Chap. 4).

Several students favoured the shared learning spaces, as their flexibility and mobility offer possibilities for using a variety of spaces for different purposes, unlike the single cell classroom. Duncan, a Year 10 Millennial College student, enjoyed the freedom to spread around the big space. He also mentioned the more varied and intensive use of devices as a positive factor, a point made by other students too, suggesting that mobile devices are preferred over the fixed desktop computers more characteristic of single cell rooms. Nevertheless, in relation to questions about the experiences of his friends at competing, elite, schools compared with his own at Millennial, he told me that a friend from a notable secondary co-educational school does not lose the opportunity to tease him about coming to this school, which his friend labels 'kindergarten'.

Relational factors are also a consideration, and several students at Angelus School (where approximately 90 students work in one space) made positive mention of the sociability of the environment, noting that it enabled a wider network of relationships to develop. Also noticeable at Angelus, where a core team of three teachers are in each space, was the comment of several students who favoured having a range of teachers to work with or to seek out for support. There were, however, some contrary opinions expressed in regard to flexible learning spaces, all coming from some Year 5 and 6 students at Angelus School. While one preferred a single cell–single teacher arrangement because the teacher can ensure that students complete their work on time, the other comments focussed on the number of students and noise levels.

A group of about five boys (including Ben, mentioned before) working on maths in a small breakout room, told me they came to work in there to get away from the noise which they found distracting. Similarly, two girls (who previously were among those who commented favourably on the sociability element) told me a single cell classroom is preferable because there are fewer students and it is less noisy. Relatedly, they suggested that in a single cell, the teacher is easily able to identify noisy and troublesome students, whereas in the flexible space, it is difficult for teachers to establish who is making a noise.

One further, less enthusiastic view that does not easily fit into the categories above was that of Mick, a new student at Innovation Primary, who remarked that his previous school was "more of an outside school". When I asked for clarification, he said, of Innovation, "this school is one big building". He went on to explain he had more opportunities for outside play at his previous school. It is not clear whether this view reflected a new child's experience, or reflected the teaching and learning programme, or was indeed reflective of a design flaw. Suffice to say, from a researcher perspective, as the movement areas at Innovation Primary and Millennial College are fully internal, neither provided the sense of relationship with the outside I have come to associate with traditional schools over my years of experience in education. In contrast, as Angelus School retains some elements of a traditional school, such as the external verandah walkways, there is a more immediate sensory experience of the outside environment.

Classroom Management

As noted in Chap. 4, the three schools run large blocks of learning time, ranging between 90 min and 2 h. Classes at the three schools are characterised by minimal whole-class teacher instruction, with most activity focussed on student self-direction. And while much of their teaching activity occurs in small group conferences or workshops, teachers actively monitor the student work during the session. There was evidence of the widespread use of mobile devices and a range of educational software applications, the latter often playing a role in supplementing the teaching and learning process and objectives.

Several implications flow from placing a large group of students in a shared space with several teachers. One of these is a predictable rise in the level of noise and physical movement. Particularly in the two primaries, there are key points in the day when noise and movement reach a peak, such as immediately after break or lunch. Given the very open concourse nature of the architecture at Innovation Primary, the sense of movement by other students towards their learning area as other teachers are settling their own classes is apparent, and could be distracting. Once children have settled, however, usually within 5 min, the sound emanating from the various learning areas is muted. The learning spaces at Millennial College are fully open to the large concourses, thus any movement along the concourse is evident from the learning areas. With low numbers at the moment, however, the school has a quiet working atmosphere, and like Innovation, the acoustic effect is remarkably muted. The flexible learning areas at Angelus School are more clearly defined as individual 'classrooms', and are located at the end of the verandah walkway on the ground and first floors, respectively, thus external movement is not noticeable. Movement *within* the space is however noticeable, given that there are some ninety students present. As indicated in Chap. 4, the teachers at Angelus periodise each block (with the help of a small hand bell), thus movement intensifies every half hour or so, as children switch activities. Even with its smaller roll, students in the respective learning areas at Innovation Primary move about freely—within and between learning areas—once they have been released to begin their individual and group work.

Teachers' Work and Attitudes

Teachers in all three schools, as noted above, were observed to be actively moving among the students, evaluating by observation and engaging in supportive interactions with their students. At the two primaries, the teachers made selective use of public address devices. At Innovation Primary, the teachers' stations are equipped with a microphone, so teachers (and students) can broadcast general instructions, such as asking the children to return to class or to cease their various activities to come in to form a campfire. On rare occasion teachers use the PA system when the noise level rises noticeably. At Angelus School, the director teacher wears a mobile microphone, performing very similar actions to those just described. More frequent use was made of the PA system at Angelus School than at Innovation Primary to remind students to keep the noise level down, though this may be related to the larger roll at Angelus.

Working in non-traditional school environments requires teachers to develop deprivatised practices, notably collaborative planning, team teaching and joint reflection. While deeply unsettling to some teachers no doubt, deprivatisation creates opportunities for different members of the team to work to their strengths. During the period of observation, the teachers at Innovation Primary worked in teams of two (though with an increased roll in 2016, they have now begun to develop teams of three). Similarly, Millennial College teachers worked in pairs in 2015. While generally following a pattern similar to what was observed in the primaries, on occasion, two teachers can be working separately with half the students each, instructing, explaining, modelling and moving around the group as students attend to set tasks. This approach differs little from a conventional secondary classroom.

Innovation Primary focus group participants regarded teams, as "organic" and ever changing, like a "vine" growing around the needs of the children. Operations are smooth when teams are effective. Team construction was discussed in separate debriefing interviews at Innovation Primary with teachers and senior leaders, who provided insight to this process. The senior leaders put the teams together, based on such criteria as qualifications, previous experience, and likely 'fit' with a colleague, based on a clear understanding of the respective and relative strengths and weaknesses of individual teachers, and even their personality types. Team composition is vital to success, a view echoed in conversation with teachers at Millennial College and Angelus School.

One of the challenges of collaboration, especially for lead teachers, is to ensure the "team doesn't fall out" (teacher, Angelus School, DB). This lead teacher felt the weight of responsibility for ensuring the team was effective, given there are ninety students working in the shared environment. As she was both a member of a team and its leader, she felt the tension between the demands of leadership accountability and collaborative teamwork. This suggests that collaboration may imply some democratising characteristics, out of step with maintaining standards through forms of surveillance and an accountability regime.

Participants identified several benefits to teamwork. Just as students reported their preference for having a range of teachers to work with, so teachers in this study recognised the value to themselves of being able to allow a colleague to take control of difficult situations. (I had seen this in action at Millennial College, in the case of Dixon, a difficult Year 10 student, who did not respond well to one teacher, but cooperated when the other teacher discreetly stepped in and redirected Dixon). The close presence of team colleagues "releases...pressure on us as teachers because you do have those times when you clash with a student" (teacher, Angelus School, FG). A further benefit of teaching in teams in a shared space is that teachers use their different strengths to complement each other: "for me it's one stress less in a very stressful job that I have to worry about" (teacher, Angelus School, FG).

It is pertinent to ask whether the flexible learning environments bring about changes to teacher practices (and attitudes), or whether teachers must come to these environments with suitable attitudes and practices that will be further developed once in these environments. Comments already made in this section suggest the latter is the more likely scenario, however, it is relevant to trace some of the key responses of participants to the general question of which has the greater significance.

There is evidence in what several participants have noted, to suggest that their view is that space alone is not enough to shift practice. Larger, more complex strands include a dispositional curriculum and school values. There may, nevertheless, be a link between space and practice, and whether this was so, was teased out at various times. Teachers who desire control will find the radically altered teaching space confronting. Even well intentioned teachers may find themselves defaulting to practices not in keeping with personalised learning, "even though we're in an open plan environment" (teacher, Innovation School, FG), especially when fatigue sets in, as this teacher suggested. Put differently, innovative and progressive teachers do not necessarily require a unique space in which to perform —but they do require energy (and, as will be noted later, the support of the school).

Innovative teachers are not the product of innovative school design. As one teacher noted, in her previous school, which was a Nelson block school,[5] she seated her students

---

[5]The 'Nelson blocks' of the 1950s broke away from long rows of classrooms accessed by an external corridor. This design provided small self- contained blocks of six teaching rooms on one level, with a duplicate second level subsequently added to these designs. This design minimised student movement and eliminated corridor noise (McLintock 1966, "Modern Planning").

in the tightest little groups at tables…the stairwell [had]… a group. There would be a group sitting on the floor at the front because there actually wasn't physically the space to allow kids to talk and collaborate and whatever. (teacher, Millennial College, DB)

Nevertheless, even though space does not create innovative or progressive teaching, it presumably helps to support it. This is a complex relationship, in which furniture also plays a role. Teacher participants agreed that the set-up of traditional spaces encourages a default to traditional, didactic modes of teaching. Furniture can, however, play an important role in promoting choice for students—a fundamental characteristic of personalised learning—and it has the potential to encourage collaboration, "because you can move things, you can—there's some things that pod together much better" (teacher, Innovation Primary, DB).

On Reflection

The practical, lived experiences of the participants in this study must be located in the context of critical insights provided by scholarship that belies the cynical notion, "there is no research". In conducting this task, I will first rehearse some of the key ideas that relate to the particular theoretical approach underpinning the analyses in this book, namely space as a socially produced construct. The relevance of taking a theoretical (and philosophical) position on space is central to the way in which the scholarship I mention will be applied to the practical experience of the participants in the three schools. As in the previous chapter, I will later go on to apply the ideas of intentionality to the practical experiences the participants have of working in a flexible learning environment, and in conclusion, evaluate the relationship of these experiences to the case study design.

Spatiality

Brief references have been made to the term, 'spatiality' with little explanation. In providing some explanation now, I will draw on Lefebvre (1991), McGregor (2004), and Soja (1989). While the latter two are influenced by Lefebvre, these writers, and their collective notions of space, support, in turn, the work of other scholars mentioned in this book, such as Blackmore et al. (2011), Chapman et al. (2014), and Cleveland and Fisher (2014). These writers conceive spatiality as a construct that make a theorisation of space possible. Consistent with the notion of materiality mentioned in Chap. 3, space is not a passive or innocent concept. It has influence over human relationships, and for the purposes of this book, school organisation and learning are particularly implicated (Cleveland and Fisher 2014). McGregor (2004) regarded human interactions as capable of creating social space, thus 'space' depends for its existence on the social. These relations (between the spatial and the social) are continuous and dialectical, always underpinned by relations of power.

As McGregor pointed out (following Lefebvre), a common-sense notion of 'space' is to see it as a passive collection of physical or material objects and people, which is sometimes described as Euclidean space. In seeking a theory to span the gulf between the mental and the lived, Lefebvre rejected such notions of space. Instead, he argued for the concepts of *production* and the *act of producing*. He accepted that to "speak of 'producing space' sounds bizarre, so great is the sway still held by the idea that empty space is prior to whatever ends up filling it" (1991, p. 15). Nevertheless, he intended in his book to uphold the proposition that *social space is a social product*.

In her critique, McGregor (2004) argued that common-sense notions of space overlook the pervasive influence, power and agency inherent in space. These notions tend to regard space as transparent, homogeneous and apparently innocent, whereas spaces are not passive or uncontested, indeed, multiple conceptions of any particular space will arise from the network of many intersecting relations that co-exist in that space. The power or influence space is able to exert over those who occupy it and work in it was apparent even to Tessa, a self-reported highly gifted Year 10 Millennial College student. In response to my questioning whether a flexible learning environment might not suit some students like Dixon (her classmate who had been getting himself in trouble during the course of the observation), Tessa suggested the remedy was to ensure that *all* children, from early childhood, should experience flexible learning environments and self-regulated learning. And here too, recall the girls at Angelus School, who saw the advantage to teachers in smaller, single cell rooms, being the easy identification of noisy and troublesome students.

To dig a little deeper now, Lefebvre's key insights ought to be rehearsed. These include his position that capitalism, and what today would be termed, 'neoliberalism', deeply influences space. This influence is hegemonic and pervasive, touching multiple aspects of daily life. And here it should not be forgotten that the enactment of flexible learning arrangements by the Ministry of Education is regarded as supportive of its vision of "young people [who are] creative, energetic, and enterprising [and] who will seize the opportunities offered by new knowledge and technologies to secure a sustainable social, cultural, economic, and environmental future for our country" (2007, p. 8). Thus the provision of creatively designed spaces goes beyond mere facility upgrading. Lefebvre's notion was not rigidly deterministic, however. Whereas traditional Marxists would see only economic relations as determining social relations, both Soja (1989) and Lefebvre (1991) wanted to see geography or space as equally influential. The

> theoretical cornerstone for the materialist interpretation of spatiality [is] the realization that social life is materially constituted in its historical geography, that spatial structures and relations are the concrete manifestations of social structures and relations evolving over time, whatever the mode of production. (Soja 1989, p. 127)

Thus, Soja was led to the view that if spatiality is both the outcome *and* the method of social relations and social structures, then social life is both space-forming and space-contingent. Social life is thus producer and a product of spatiality. This is a critical insight as will be seen shortly, when considering further the relationship between space and pedagogy.

In his classic text, *The Production of Space* (1991), Lefebvre made use of several triadic formulations, which are helpful in constructing an analysis of flexible learning environments. In particular is his notion of *representations of space* (relating to the mental or conceptual constructions of space); *representational space* (being the perceived space, the symbols to convey those perceptions, and the lived experience of space); and *spatial practice* (the world of practice, the protocols shaping human interaction with space). In a further articulation of his triadic conception, Lefebvre referred to the *perceived, conceived* and *lived,* and these are simultaneously conscious and unconscious.[6]

This insight allows for a dynamic, or dialectical, understanding of the relationships between the bureaucrats of the Ministry of Education and the architectural firms they commission to design their schools; between these two groups and the building and contracting firms who actually bring concepts to a built reality; between all of the above and the communities on whose behalf these spaces are built; between all of the above and the school leaders who frequently have little or no influence in the process; and finally, between the 'end users' and all of the above, elements of which must seem very distant to these users of space. Ironically, however, it is the users of the space who are the most influenced and affected by the space, and who do more to influence and affect the space in their turn, through their explicit practices and implicit ways of being in the space. Nevertheless, the seemingly linear chain of influencers and actors described above each leave an indelible mark on the space; marks that become part of the fabric of (to use Vagle's term) the intentional relations within that space.

Design

What I propose to do now will be to briefly consider a light sampling of literature not covered in Chap. 3, in order to take insights from the work experiences of the participants, while at the same time, delivering some key messages about developing an informed understanding of flexible educational settings. I will consider this task in relation to design (which to some extent relates to Lefebvre's notion of conceived representations of space); the influence of environment on practice; and the (broken) links between learning spaces and student learning outcomes (these latter relating to the lived representational space).

---

[6]Refer to Chap. 3 for a fuller discussion of this triadic formulation.

Design Assumptions

As noted in Chap. 3, designers are motivated by the view that the 20th century building model has resulted in obsolescent industrial age classrooms (Nair 2014; Nair et al. 2013). Coupled to this view is the contention that the success of 21st-century learning demands dramatically reconceived building design (Blackmore et al. 2011; Cleveland and Fisher 2014). Amongst these ideas is the view that the attitudes, morale and practices of teachers and students (and therefore learning outcomes), will benefit by such new designs and buildings (Blackmore et al. 2011; Nair 2014; Nair et al. 2013). What is problematic in this view, however, is the linear relationship posited between these design assumptions and their purported benefits. Self-management, or self-regulated learning, a fundamental feature of personalised learning, was widely considered among the participants in the studies reported in this book to be an expected outcome of shifting students into large shared spaces with multiple teachers. Two teachers at different locations, however, captured the reality of life for 'supported learners', most in need of teacher direction and guidance:

> for some children it will take a long time [to adapt] and that's where our role is to support them to be able to plan so that eventually they can self-manage and then direct their own planning. (teacher, Innovation Primary, DB);

> That's a shift for some...they've had so many years of single cell or a very controlled environment to suddenly give them the freedom, that's actually quite hard for them. (teacher, Angelus School, FG)

Teachers moving into innovatively designed learning areas are required to make significant attitudinal shifts, and the words and actions of teachers across the three schools *did* display such shifts, typically captured by the notion of a growth mind-set over a fixed mind-set, releasing a teacher to be adventurous, and being willing to make mistakes without fear. The school leaders commented too from their perspective on the shifts teachers make (or are unable to make). For one of these leaders, teachers fall very easily into a mind shift paradigm, but some who may think they are amenable to shifting, find themselves struggling to make actual shifts. For these teachers "it's all about power and control. I control the classroom, I control learning, I control the planning, I control where you sit..." (Principal, Innovation Primary, IV).

The discourse of shifting the locus of power and control was repeated across the settings. Some teacher participants were finding it difficult to shake the pedagogical model of those who taught them, finding these approaches radically challenged in the new flexible environment. One of the "biggest shifts" is to change from being "the teacher at the front of a classroom... to [being] an advisor...working alongside students" (senior leader, Innovation Primary, FG). These examples suggest a relationship between the learning environment and certain teacher attitudes and practices, yet also indicate that this relationship is not unproblematic. A further point to note is that it is not the actual physical space making the sole difference, but rather the complex web of social relationships that can (or cannot) occur within a given spatial context. Thus it is not a simple matter (as I have attempted to achieve in this book) of separating the space from the pedagogy, from the wider digital technologies, and from teachers' reflective processes.

Design May (Not) Support Pedagogy

Ideally, new learning spaces will be characterised by flexibility, mobile, ergonomic furniture and ubiquitous digital technology, which will combine to support the development of modern teaching and learning practices (Blackmore et al. 2011), including collaborative, multidisciplinary teaching practices. It has long been suggested that effective school environmental design can contribute to the development of 'soft' skills (Moore and Lackney 1993). Changes to the physical environment of a school or classroom may potentially be the catalyst to improving education (Woolner et al. 2012).

There is a caveat, however. The point made earlier, rejecting a simple causal link between design and positive attitudinal or behavioural shifts, applies equally to pedagogy. Thus Woolner et al. (2012) found that pedagogical practices do not necessarily change in altered space. This is in part because of the entrenched practices that have developed over years in single cell environments. Furthermore, while spatial design changes may encourage teachers to commit themselves to altering their practice, significant change might not actually come about. This they attribute to

> two aspects of conservatism of practice...on the one hand, the unexamined culture of the educators' community of practice which resists change and, on the other, the tendency for change in teachers' ideas to have little influence on their practice. (p. 47)

Mention was made earlier of the response of various teacher participants to the challenge of shifting their teaching practices now that they find themselves in shared teaching environments. Among these challenges is the possibility of default to traditional practices due to stress and fatigue or when class sizes become unmanageable. Furthermore, the 'learner status' of those teachers new to innovative space and practice makes defaulting to traditional practices a distinct possibility (Principal, Millennial College, IV). The principal of Innovation School shares this notion of teachers as 'learners'. Teachers must come to realise "if we do what we've always done it's not going to work in these spaces". He proactively walks around among learning areas, being conscious of teaching practice. This enables him to raise questions with teachers in one-to-one conversations about their practice, particularly when this looks like traditional, teacher-directed practice.

Thus it is clear that the shift to flexible learning environments do not, by itself guarantee or necessitate a shift to modern teaching and learning practices, and here I specifically recall an observation note I made after one of my earliest observations:

> The class broke up into two groups; one taught by [teacher 1], one taught by [teacher 2]. My overall impression is mixed, I have to say…they…appeared to teach a fairly…standard kind of way, teaching a fairly standard topic…it looked to me like the two classes were quite separate.

Having said that, it may be expected that teachers will develop a mix of pedagogical approaches, although clearly they cannot work in traditional modes in uniquely furnished spaces designed to accommodate 90 or more students and up to five teachers. Managing that transition, and coping with the challenge of working in new ways, can be confronting to teachers, and some evidence of that may be seen when considering the notion of intentionality.

Intentionality

What are some of the tentative manifestations of being with new and radically reformulated spaces? How do the occupants of these spaces *live* their new reality? What are the conscious and sub-conscious ways in which they move towards this new reality? And what is it to be a researcher in such altered contexts, when keeping in mind that I, like so many others, am a teacher of a different generation?

While the students were not intended as participants, it is almost impossible not to (re)capture their views with intentionality in mind. They responded (the ones spoken with in casual conversation, in itself so radically unlike what is possible in a single cell space) with unbridled enthusiasm. They pointed to the relational possibilities, and the chance to move their bodies freely in space. The sociability of the space lent itself to peer support, and Afu, a new student at Angelus School, spoke of how surprised he was to find classmates being helpful. Perhaps Afu's experience bears out the views of Moore and Lackney (1993) that revitalised and flexible space can support the development of prosocial skills that indirectly support learning. And while Holyoake College is the subject of the next chapter, my experiences there as a researcher were so radically different, where I found myself locked into fixed seats in cramped single cell classrooms, barely able to communicate with more than just the one or two students nearest to me. My 50 min observations were characterised by my inability to move and flex; my observations of 90 and 120 min in the other three schools were typified by my own flexibility, and ability to get around to speak to any number of students I chose to engage with.

Teachers are highly active and energised when working in large, permeable spaces in which students are able to spread around at will (especially noticeable at Innovation Primary and Millennial College, with their lower rolls at the time). I observed teachers constantly moving among groups of students, covering significant distances. This was especially the case when a team member was absent, and was especially noticeable at Millennial College. In all three schools, team members cohere seamlessly between multiple roles of workshop facilitator, large group instructor, resident expert and supervisor.

This picture belies the tensions that lie beneath, such as the sense of loss and grief associated with the "phase of mourning about the loss of your classroom" once a teacher moves into shared teaching and learning space (senior leader, Millennial College, FG). Relatedly, in discussions with teachers, and based on observations across all three schools, it is evident that the teachers at these schools have ceased to use language such as 'my class', or 'my children'. The individualised language of 'my', 'mine' and 'I' is replaced with the collective language of 'our' and 'ours', 'we' and 'us'.

The work of teachers in flexible learning environments requires not only working together, but working in plain sight of each other, which is contrary to the traditional privatised practice of single cell rooms. High levels of trust are required, to offset the sense of team members being under the gaze of their colleagues in the team, of "being exposed", and constantly on show (teacher, Innovation Primary, FG). Arguably, deprivatisation represents a demanding change of teachers, and as Kyriacou (2001) suggested such demanding change is a source of stress for teachers at any stage of their careers.

Conversely, this same research indicated positive benefits to flow from collegiality and communication: "We challenge each other but it's not in that sort of I'm the observer or she's the observer kind of role" (teacher, Innovation Primary, FG). This is consistent with the comments made in the Angelus School focus group by a participant, who believed it important to be able to remark on the practice of her team colleagues, but to do so in a non-judgemental manner. Instead, she wanted such comments to be seen "as a sign of love and…wanting to help grow her and support her". The closeness of this working relationship had been noted in observations, where a brief word, or a non-verbal signal, such as a nod of the head, was enough to communicate a sense that one or the other had to actively reduce the noise level, for example. Relieving the pressure of working in deprivatised collaboration is achieved by engaging in some "light hearted banter" (teacher, Angelus School, FG).

These observations are simultaneously mundane and breathtaking. They speak of Be-ing through the emergent practices demanded by working in large, open and shared spaces. They speak of give and take, and care for one another. They speak simultaneously of loss and new gains. They speak, above all, of becoming a new Being—one who works so closely with teammates as to intuitively understand a simple look or nod; one who constantly interchanges roles; and one who gives up absolute control and anxiety. A radically revised identity of what it means to be a teacher is captured in the words and attitudes of those who are grappling with the emergent consequences of the changes associated with 21st century life.

In Conclusion

This chapter has a central concern with one of the tangible manifestations of the shift to reconceptualising education in this first quarter of the 21st century, namely the conceptualisation, design and construction of new spaces of learning. Known variously in New Zealand as Modern Learning Environments (or shorthand as 'MLE') innovative learning environments (also now earning the shorthand moniker, 'ILE') and flexible learning environments, these reconceptualised spaces bring together multiple groups of students who previously would have made up single classes, with multiple teachers, who previously would have taught their own classes as individuals. This chapter referred to research participants who are, in theory, 'cases' within schools, bounded by their commitment to engage with a state policy that intends, by 2021, to have flexible learning spaces within all schools in New Zealand (Ministry of Education 2016). This chapter has endeavoured to provide a flavour of the policy milieu informing the Ministry of Education, specifically by analysing and deconstructing key Ministry of Education documents. The engagement of participants with the fruits of this policy direction, as it is lived out in schools, helps to establish the intentional relationships the participants have towards each other and the flexible learning spaces.

This chapter has considered the spaces in which teachers work, and related this consideration to the perspective of the participants in the three schools. Their voice clarifies what it means, from a spatial perspective, to be a teacher in the second decade of the 21st century, and their insights are a signal to the growing number of teachers required to work in similar spaces. Being a teacher requires people who must *be* flexible in order to work in flexible spaces. They must give up control, ownership, privacy and anxiety. They must be willing to work in less ordered (yet highly organised) ways, for the spatial practice of flexible learning environments require certain 'consensuses' to be built around space (Lefebvre 1991). There are, for example, some unspoken agreements determining some spaces as quiet, and others that develop respect of private property.

The three schools referred to in this chapter have implemented many of the desired expectations of organisation within significantly revised and altered physical space, as indicated by Blackmore et al. (2011), Heppell (2016), and Nair (2014). These include combined classes, the reduction in, or elimination of, the use of a school bell (except at Angelus), the use of peer support, and multiple teachers working in one large space.

Space is not a passive entity that is shaped by humans; rather, their practices and the space are in a dialectical relationship, much as Lefebvre posited. To imagine people as active agents in a passive world presupposes the self as stable, whereas the self can be deeply influenced by materialities, such as the built environment. The built environment thus 'talks back' but does not dictate (for this reason, modern teaching and learning practice is equally possible in a single cell classroom or under a tree with slate boards). Recall, however, Reh and Temel (2014) who argued that the built space or environment does not plan, intend or reflect, yet acts on its users.

This leads to a crucial interpretation I will emphasise here: *space does not have agency nor does it cause pedagogy, yet it is an enabler. Pedagogy (i.e. practices and the thinking underlying the practices) evolves in response to space, and what it enables.* In much the same way, technology is neither passive, nor does it cause revised teaching approaches. It does, however, act as an enabler. This is the focus of the next chapter.

References

Blackmore, J., Bateman, D., Loughlin, J., O'Mara, J., & Aranda, G. (2011). *Research into the connection between built learning spaces and student outcomes* literature review, paper No. 22 June. State of Victoria (Department of Education and Early Childhood Development). Retrieved from http://www.education.vic.gov.au

Byers, T. K. (2016). *Evaluating the effects of different classroom spaces on teaching and learning.* Doctoral thesis, The University of Melbourne, Melbourne, Australia). Retrieved from http://hdl.handle.net/11343/115307

Chapman, A., Randell-Moon, H., Campbell, M., & Drew, C. (2014). Students in space: Student practices in non-traditional classrooms. *Global Studies of Childhood, 4*(1), 39–48. doi:10.2304/gsch.2014.4.1.39

Cleveland, B., & Fisher, K. (2014). The evaluation of physical learning environments: A critical review of the literature. *Learning Environments Research, 4*(17), 1–28. doi:10.1007/s10984-013-9149-3

Dumont, H., & Istance, D. (2010). Analysing and designing learning environments for the 21st century. In H. Dumont, D. Istance & F. Benavides (Eds.), *The nature of learning: Using research to inspire practice* (pp. 19–34). Paris, France: Organisation for Economic Cooperation and Development Publishing. doi:10.1787/9789264086487-3-en

Fisher, K. (2005). *Linking pedagogy and space* [slide presentation]. Retrieved from http://www.education.vic.gov.au/Documents/school/principals/infrastructure/pedagogyspace.pdf

Green, H., Facer, K., Rudd, T., Dillon, P. & Humphreys, P. (2005). *Personalisation and digital technologies.* Bristol, England: Futurelab. Retrieved February 6, 2016 from http://www.nfer.ac.uk/publications/FUTL59/FUTL59_home.cfm

Heppell, S. (2016). *Total learning.* Retrieved February 21, 2016 from http://rubble.heppell.net/three/

Kyriacou, C. (2001). Teacher stress: Directions for future research. *Educational Review, 53*(1), 27–35. doi:10.1080/00131910120033628

Lefebvre, H. (1991). *The production of space.* (D. Nicholson-Smith, trans.). Malden, MA: Blackwell.

McGregor, J. (2004). Spatiality and the place of the material in schools. *Pedagogy, Culture and Society, 12*(3), 347–372. doi:10.1080/14681360400200207

McLintock, A. H. (Ed.) (1966). *Modern Planning.* From An Encyclopaedia of New Zealand, republished in *Te Ara - the Encyclopedia of New Zealand*, updated 22 April 2009. Retrieved 12 August 2015 from http://www.TeAra.govt.nz/en/1966/architectureschool-buildings/page-4

Ministry of Education. (2007). The New Zealand curriculum. Wellington, New Zealand: Learning Media Limited. Available from http://nzcurriculum.tki.org.nz/The-New-Zealand-Curriculum

Ministry of Education. (2011). The New Zealand school property strategy 2011–2021. Retrieved from http://www.education.govt.nz/assets/Documents/Primary-Secondary/Property/SchoolPropertyStrategy201121.pdf

References

Ministry of Education. (2012). *Learning studio pilot review*. Retrieved from http://www.education.govt.nz/assets/Documents/Primary-Secondary/Property/School-property-design/Flexible-learning-spaces/LearningStudioPilotReview.pdf

Ministry of Education. (2016). *Property*. Retrieved June 5, 2016 from http://www.education.govt.nz/school/property/

Moore, G. T. & Lackney, J. A. (1993). School design: Crisis, educational performance and design applications. *Children's Environments, 10*(2), 99–112. www.jstor.org

Nair, P. (2014). *Blueprint for tomorrow: Redesigning schools for student-centered learning*. Cambridge, MA: Harvard Education Press.

Nair, P., Fielding, R., & Lackney, J. (2013). *The language of school design: Design patterns for 21st century schools* (3rd ed.). Minneapolis, MN: DesignShare.

Nielsen, A. C. (2004). *Best practice in school design* (No. 1407454/1407463). Report Prepared For the Ministry of Education. Wellington, New Zealand: Ministry of Education.

Reh, S., & Temel, R. (2014). Observing the doings of built spaces. Attempts of an ethnography of materiality. *Historical Social Research, 39*(2), 167–180. doi:10.12759/hsr.39.2014.2.167-180

Soja, E. W. (1989). *Postmodern geographies: The reassertion of space in critical social theory*. London, United Kingdom/New York, NY: Verso.

Thornburg, D. (2007). *Campfires in cyberspace: primordial metaphors for learning in the 21st century*. Retrieved from http://tcpd.org/Thornburg/Handouts/Campfires.pdf

Woolner, P., McCarter, S., Wall, K., & Higgins, S. (2012). Changed learning through changed space: When can a participatory approach to the learning environment challenge preconceptions and alter practice? *Improving Schools, 15*(1), 45–60. doi:10.1177/1365480211434796

Chapter 6
The Impacts on Teachers' Work: ICT/BYOD and Digital Pedagogy

> Overall, the evidence from PISA, as well as from more rigorously designed evaluations, suggests that solely increasing access to computers for students, at home or at school, is unlikely to result in significant improvements in education outcomes. Furthermore, both PISA data and the research evidence concur on the finding that the positive effects of computer use are specific—limited to certain outcomes, and to certain uses of computers (OECD 2015, p. 163).

Being a Teacher is focussed on how the notion of '21st-century learning' is playing out in a selection of New Zealand schools, and among a group of teachers and leaders in those schools. Coincidentally, the voices of students can sometimes be heard, though they have not been a focus. Nevertheless, their voices are important and thus should not be overlooked. In the face of stating this, many educators would hasten to point out that 'learners' ought to be at the centre, but it is precisely the marginalisation of the 'invisible teacher' I am challenging. It is the 'learnification' of the curriculum, as Gert Biesta terms it, that is but one manifestation of 21st-century learning, indeed, a component of modern teaching and learning practice. I have suggested that such practices are enabled by working in flexible learning spaces and by digital technology. These practices make increasing demands on teachers to be self-reflective and to reflect with others. Taken together, these various developments challenge school leaders in specific ways. In the preceding two chapters, I considered the case of modern or innovative teaching and learning practices, and by sharing the evidence gleaned from the work of teachers in three schools, have demonstrated how their work exemplifies these practices. The decision to shift schools towards flexible learning environments is located within a specific policy framework that seeks to promote modern teaching and learning practices. Thus, I considered the same three schools as exemplars of spatial environments that challenge conventional and traditional understandings of learning space. By analysis, the preceding chapters outlined how the implementation of these practices and working in flexible environments makes an impact on teachers' work. The widening implementation and use of digital technology creates a further point of reference in establishing the ways in which teachers' work is evolving as the world moves into the final quarter of the second decade of the 21st century.

To illustrate the influence digital technologies have on teachers' work, I will refer in this chapter mainly to the experiences of teachers in one particular school I have named Holyoake College, though where relevant, the experiences of teachers at Innovation Primary, Millennial College and Angelus School will also be considered. As in Chap. 4, this chapter will commence by providing a critical policy perspective that brings to the fore several key issues that may be overlooked in the excited rush to 'go digital'. The lived experiences of a range of practitioners working in a BYOD environment is at the core of this chapter. These experiences will be critically discussed in the context of questions around materiality and technology. As in the preceding chapters, this one will conclude by considering the manifestation of intentionality in the work lives of the participants, and their contribution to the case study.

Digital Technology Implementation in Education: Critical Perspectives

In 2016, as I write, digital technology is central to the lives of young people[1] (and has been increasingly so in tandem with the rapid advances in mobile technology). Various forms of digital technology and Internet developments (such as the expansion of Web 2.0 possibilities) are strongly oriented to personalised and customised use, hence, unsurprisingly, students desire greater control of their learning process.

Digital technology can enable teachers to support their students to engage in personalised learning in the classroom, by tapping into the skills and habits they have developed as users of technology. On its own, the use of digital technology in schools is not, however, a 'silver bullet', warned Green et al. (2005), as its use does not guarantee personalisation. Nevertheless, as the affordances of technology allow the unbundling and re-bundling of knowledge and information content in ways print and analogue do not, teachers, and educators more generally, who ignore devices and applications do themselves and their students a disservice.

Education struggles against inequality, however—the various digital divides referred to in Chap. 3. On one hand, variation in private access to digital technology, and on the other, variation in the educational value of private, home use. Nevertheless, OECD surveys (2011, 2015) revealed disadvantaged students making greater increases in access to a home computer than their advantaged peers. Similarly, the OECD found there to be rapid expansion in student access to the Internet at home. Still, lack of access to the Internet robs students of many freely available opportunities for formal and informal learning (OECD 2015). Furthermore, the OECD reports averages, which have a masking effect, as it is only by drilling into specific cases that greater global inequality becomes apparent.

---

[1]Indeed, to the lives of many people across age groups.

Furthermore, teachers and schools are not working on a level playing field, given inconsistent governmental support, globally, for ICT integration in education. At the school level too, there may be inconsistent approaches to integrating digital technology. As Groff (2013) argued, innovative schooling requires school-wide technology saturation, a point made earlier in New Zealand by Cowie et al. (2011). Yet the 2012 OECD PISA round discovered that desktops continue to pervade infrastructural provision in schools, despite the flexibility offered by mobile computing devices such as laptops or tablets.

Apart from institutional provision of, and support for, technology integration, staff support, as previously indicated, is a critical factor (Brečko et al. 2014; Shear et al. 2011). These arguments serve to support a position frequently repeated in this book, namely that teachers' work matters, and is central to the educational enterprise. The CERI research team of the OECD discerned 'first order' and 'second order' innovations in the course of its Innovative Learning Environments study (Groff 2013). At the first-order level, hardware, software and web applications are considered significant levers of change while at the second order of innovation, increasingly 'disruptive' technologies enable more creative and innovative practices and strategies. This means users can move beyond using technology merely as a tool. It would seem self-evident that both levels of innovation demand and require meaningful staff learning, particularly to ensure uptake and institution-wide application. Nevertheless, teacher resistance to change is a critical feature of the shift to modern, innovative practice underpinned by digital technology saturation. This shift is compounded by the evolution of teacher identity from direction to facilitation, encouraged by the integration of ICT in the classroom (Anderson 2010).

While linking ICT to inquiry-learning, the development of collaboration and problem solving, and the creation of personalised learning environments, Groff (2013) nevertheless dismissed a linear relationship between ICT integration and personalised learning, or the eradication of the teacher from the educational picture. These qualifications aside, while the use of digital technology by teachers is only the first step in developing e-Learning in the classroom, the prospects for developing innovative uses for that technology, and incorporating these into daily pedagogy, may remain dim. Shear et al. (2011) found that collaboration or 'real-world problem-solving' were the exception rather than the norm, even in the 24 'innovative case' schools across seven countries that they identified from an initial sample of 159 schools. For many of those teachers observed or surveyed in this research, 'innovative' use of ICT amounts to little more than using devices to present information for students to passively receive information or engage with in routine ways.

Herold (2015), writing for *Education Week*, cited a United States National Center for Education Statistics 2009 survey of 3159 teachers, which found that student in-school use of ICT was largely centred on text production, web-surfing and computing skills development. Rarely, according to the survey, did teachers facilitate students to use ICT for experimental, creative design and production, or content creation. I noted in Chap. 3 that the SAMR model (Puentedura 2013) enables an assessment of the cognitive challenge represented by digital tasks. These cited survey findings, and those of Shear et al. (2011) indicate that shifting students and teachers from digital consumption to (critical) digital production is challenging, and possibly out of the reach of many busy classroom teachers.

Thus, the OECD (2015) finding that "PISA results show no appreciable improvements in student achievement in reading, mathematics or science in the countries that had invested heavily in ICT for education" (p. 15) must be seen in the context of teachers' weak uptake of the content creation and manipulation possibilities presented by digital tools and software applications. It must also be seen in the context of computer use that fails to provide opportunities for personalised learning (Hattie and Yates 2013, cited in OECD 2015). Other conflicting evidence came from Shapley et al. (2009). Their quasi-experimental study of technology immersion in 21 Texan middle schools indicated that the teachers in these schools increasingly used technology to support their students' development of thinking skills by experiencing deeper and more complex inquiries. This same finding was less evident in the 21 control schools in the study that had not engaged in the state technology immersion programme. On the other hand, results on the reading and mathematics tests used in the study did not always show statistically significant advantages ensuing from technology immersion. Thus, the OECD comment captured by the epigraph at the start of this chapter will bring little comfort to those who promote digital technology integration.

The fault does not lie only with teachers and teaching approaches. The same OECD research found evidence that few students use ICT and the Internet out-of-school for much more than leisure (such as gaming) and social media communication. In the 2012 PISA round, 88% of students reported Internet browsing as their most common leisure activity when using computers (2015), closely followed by social networking, downloading music and gaming. "Only 31% of students use computers at least once a week to upload their own content, such as music, poetry, videos or computer programs" (p. 42).

Those who wonder whether ICT integration is having any meaningful influence on learning may be looking in the wrong place, or asking the wrong questions. The notion of 'connectivism' as an independent learning theory, proposed by Siemens (2005), highlights the ubiquity of digital tools and devices, accentuating informal and constant learning. This possibility, suggested by Siemens, means it is feasible to imagine that students will not be learning in ways that are traditionally understood (that is, according to a linear, routinised and analogue model). Young people and their teachers inhabit a complex world, now increasingly digitally mediated, that permits both the creation of new content, and manipulation of existing content, which may be achieved in physical or remote collaboration with others. As Bolstad and Gilbert (2012) argued, knowledge continues to be important, but rather in terms of what can be done with it than in terms of it being a bankable commodity.

An important strategic and pedagogic priority is therefore to find appropriate ways of developing complementary technology and classroom pedagogy. This may, potentially, now come in the form of a widening use of mobile devices and a range of educational software applications ('apps'), the latter often playing a role in supplementing the teaching and learning process and objectives. What follows is a more detailed exploration of the findings derived from observational evidence and data from specific interviews and focus groups, mainly at a secondary school I have named 'Holyoake College'.

The Practical Studies: The Challenge of Undertaking a BYOD Implementation

What follows will focus on the development of technology integration, primarily at Holyoake College, though reference will be made to Innovation Primary, Millennial College and Angelus School. The key difference among these schools is that the latter three were selected for their flexible learning environment design features. In addition, they engage fully with modern teaching and learning practices, including digital technology use. In contrast, Holyoake College was selected primarily for its emergent school-wide implementation of BYOD, a practice not in evidence at the other three. As BYOD is a school-wide policy at Holyoake, it may be assumed that the teachers would be required to engage in e-Learning and digital pedagogy as features of modern teaching and learning practice. Moreover, the teachers may be expected to exhibit reflective practices consistent with significant changes to their working practice, while their middle and senior leaders would be facing several implementation and practice challenges. Thus, while this study suffers from all the limitations of qualitative work (such as generalisability, validity and reliability issues), it remains possible to build an account characterised by veracity and verisimilitude, achieved in part through data triangulation. Thus, teachers working in a traditional school with single-cell classrooms will nevertheless be engaged in the process of evolving teacher identity formation through their shifting work roles, brought about, as at Holyoake College, by the implementation of BYOD.

Below, I will briefly contextualise Holyoake College, providing insight to the unique world of this school. The work and responses of the participant teachers to their engagement with BYOD will be presented, along with some insights derived from casual conversations with students. In the case of Holyoake, more substantive student comment was also elicited, in the form of a survey, in which approximately 10% of the Year 9 and Year 10 cohorts[2] participated, and one focus group from each year level. In addition, a small parent focus group was convened. I will continue the critical argument that neither the material world nor technology (as a specific instance of that world) exist in passive relation to people, nor are the actions people take overdetermined by either the material or technology.

---

[2]The first two years of secondary schooling in New Zealand (usually age 13–14).

Holyoake College

Holyoake College is a large metropolitan Year 9–Year 13 state coeducational school. As this book is largely motivated by changes to building architecture, it is of some interest to note that this college is built along traditional lines, characterised by single-cell classrooms, many of which are grouped in discrete two-level blocks consisting of four or six classrooms. Within classrooms, furniture is conventional, typified by uniform desks and chairs, usually arranged in rows. This arrangement is as much a function of the size of the rooms, the number of students per room and the furniture required for these students, as it is a function of traditional teacher approaches.

The BYOD Policy at Holyoake: Arguments for and Against

Ample reference has been made to the rapid advances in digital technology, particularly within the last decade. The penetration of the youth market by various digital technology providers of hardware and software, has dramatically increased the ubiquity of this technology. In turn, education systems are challenged to meaningfully respond, not only to capture the inherent value of using these technologies in educational settings, but also to maintain currency and relevance in the minds of young people. For its part, The New Zealand Curriculum (Ministry of Education 2007), now arguably well out of date, stated: "Schools should explore not only how ICT can supplement traditional ways of teaching but also how it can open up new and different ways of learning." (p. 36). Somewhat more updated, a recent visual discussion document (Ministry of Education 2015b) speculates on the education system in 2025, and outlines these ideas: "A pervasive digital environment is empowering learners as never before, allowing them to take charge of their own learning anywhere, anytime." (2015b, "Harnessing technology"); and: "Learners are always digitally connected—Locally, nationally and globally." (2015b, "Possible characteristics of a connected education system in 2025"). Thus there is an evident systemic commitment to the notion that schools become digitally connected and use the power of ultra fast broadband, for example, to network with learning opportunities beyond the walls of the classroom and the boundaries of the school.

In 2014, Holyoake College embarked on a policy of school-wide 1:1 or BYOD integration, beginning with Year 9 in 2014, to be followed progressively through the school over the following years, until the entire school is BYOD. The school committed itself to delivering a 'blended' model, combining e-Learning and digital pedagogy with more conventional pen and paper methods. Despite a period of planning, community consultation and staff preparation, the BYOD policy evokes both positive and negative responses among staff, students and parents. Apart from these attitudes, expressed in interviews, casual conversations, through the survey, and in focus groups, there are also claims made on behalf of the BYOD policy.

The implementation of the BYOD policy was undertaken in the belief that increased student engagement can be achieved through the use of technology. If so, the school's leaders hoped that student engagement would translate to achievement, then qualifications, and eventually to economic success for individual students: "there's an economic imperative for students to gain success in their qualification because that enables them to make that transition out and beyond the secondary environment" (Principal, Holyoake College, IV). Further, it was believed that increased student engagement would provide opportunities to those not achieving success by traditional means. Preparation for the workplace was a related motivator, buttressed by the view that students would require technology skills in the future. These views were, however, challenged in the parent focus group, which included parents in the ICT industry, who argued that these skills could be learnt on the job. Far more important, they argued, was the development of interpersonal skills, which, they believed, a focus on digital technology was eroding.

Students supported the BYOD policy for its contribution to their preparation for a digital world, one they know and understand. "Paperwork doesn't cut it anymore", and "…it's important for us to be tech savvy" were typical survey responses. Referring to student familiarity with the digital world, "our year 11 students were born at the turn of the century, they've never known a time when the Internet hasn't been ubiquitous…there's never been a time that they haven't been able to access YouTube" (Principal, Holyoake College, IV).

The BYOD policy has led to increased pedagogical opportunities to enhance digital literacy, and has opened the possibilities to develop critical thinking and problem solving. Most obviously, the BYOD policy connects with the New Zealand Curriculum key competency of 'using language, symbols and texts' (Ministry of Education 2007). Ready access to the World Wide Web has opened up new learning, and is enhancing the research skills of student users. Additionally, the accessibility and portability of devices requiring only a live Internet connection to permit access to learning resources, means that an 'anywhere, anytime' mindset has taken hold among students. No longer does routine illness, or absence due to school trips, mean that students have to miss out on work, or miss deadlines for submitting assigned work.

While the teachers themselves maintained a generally positive outlook to the policy, critical, or even negative claims and attitudes, were mainly expressed by the parents and several students. Oddly, given all that is claimed about the 'Net Generation', some students expressed the view that they learn more effectively using pen and paper, which they found to be less distracting than devices. Parents in the focus group associated the absence of pen and paper with the absence of teaching. Pen and paper organisation, it was argued, is easier for teenagers to manage than a multiplicity of websites, Google sites and applications. Furthermore, some parents argued they cannot support their child's learning at home when there is no textbook to refer to. One parent called the blended option 'chaos'.

A shift in teachers' roles to that of facilitator of learning, and attempts by several teachers to encourage self-directed student learning, seemed to parent focus group members (and some teachers) to undermine the tradition of direct, instructional teaching and the sense of a structured school environment, bounded by rules and regulations. This changing role of the teacher was also regarded as a threat to students' chances in the high-stakes assessment environment of senior secondary, which they would move into on reaching Year 11. Many students have an expectation that teachers will teach them, while some parents believed teachers' roles were being supplanted by online learning. Taken together, these threats were seen to degrade relationships between teachers and students (a view expressed by some teachers too).

Teachers in both focus group and in individual discussions expressed concerns that the BYOD policy has led to significantly increased workload pressure and associated stress for teachers. Students expressed health concerns regarding the development of poor postural habits (also commented on by parents), such as hunching over their laptops, and working on devices while sprawled across couches. Some students complained of developing eyestrain and headaches. Other health-related concerns pertained to parental (and some student) concerns that students are overstimulated by excessive screen time, and that they were losing their ability to relate to one another at a human level.

BYOD at Innovation Primary, Millennial College and Angelus School

A key point of difference here is that none of these schools (in 2015) had a policy requiring students to each have a device. Device purchase was a parental choice, and was not discouraged. Of the three, Angelus School was actively moving towards implementing BYOD, and has done so in 2016. Millennial College goes so far as to give parents advice on its website concerning preferable devices. The principal of Innovation School was actively resisting any move to BYOD, as this would prevent the school from seeking Ministry of Education support to purchase assistive devices for special needs students. Having said this, device use permeates the teaching and learning observed in these three schools. For students without devices in the two primary schools, there are mobile tablet devices and some desktop computers in each learning area to use. Millennial College students without devices (of whom there are few) are able to book out a laptop from the library.

Digital pedagogy: Holyoake College

In this book (as elsewhere), I have used the concept of 'pedagogy' to refer to both teachers' classroom practice, *and* the thinking that underpins this practice. I will thus highlight, under the broad heading of 'pedagogy', teacher assumptions of the

'Net Generation', the practice of e-Learning and the application of the SAMR model.

Teacher participants acknowledged that the students coming to school in 2015 are not the same as those who may have come to school 15, 10 or even 5 years ago. It seems a truism (repeated by these teachers) that technology is integral to the lives of teenage students, and this raises the question of how schools should respond. Student participants at Holyoake College confirmed these particular teacher views, as they expressed an inseparable (addictive, some suggested) link to their devices. Students aged 13 and 14 in 2015 will always have known the Internet, the World Wide Web, and more recently, the ubiquity of mobile devices. Some students (perhaps expressing parental views) noted that children are becoming too attached to technology from a young age.

Problematically, however, is the assumption made or implied by many teachers (including the participants), that computing skill and digital device expertise is a necessary characteristic of young people: "...some teachers...need to ask...their students how confident they are with using...devices because not everyone is." (Sn, Yr 10 FG). Students perceived that their teachers, sometimes lacking computing knowledge or skill, assume that students have sufficient know-how to help each other: "...sometimes the teacher isn't even that familiar with what area we're working in. So she gets someone else in the class to help that student sometimes" (L, Yr 10 FG).

For their part, the students who participated in the focus groups and who took the survey supported the OECD (2015) finding regarding the somewhat limited nature of student out-of-school device use. While some reported making use of creative tools, most simply engage with social media, videos and games. Communicating and playing online games with friends, and watching YouTube videos were mentioned by students. It is therefore unsurprising that students are not intuitively at ease with all dimensions of computer and application use.

The school's blended e-Learning approach allows technology skills to be developed alongside conventional paper-based reading and writing skills. Students in the focus groups (particularly the Yr 10s) reported ever-widening use by teachers of devices, and among the participant teachers observed, there was evidence of a combination of mixed or blended use of devices and pen and paper; non-device use; and primarily device use. Good practice looks like minimal teacher talk time, constant teacher movement around class, checking in on students, actively teaching small pockets while all are challenged with exercises requiring the use of devices, split screens, Google Classroom documents and the Internet.

There appeared, on observation, to be challenges in finding the balance between device use and the use of traditional teaching materials. Thus, despite an espoused commitment to *blended* e-Learning, observational evidence suggested that some teachers were still only developing their understanding of how to successfully integrate devices into their teaching, with inconsistent results. Furthermore, the BYOD policy at Holyoake College mandates device use, to prevent teachers defaulting to pen and paper, yet a blended approach implies a seamless integration of devices *with* pen and paper options, giving rise to confusion.

The inconsistent application of e-Learning across all teachers was reported by some students, and all the parents in the focus group. More concerning was the view that teachers were neglecting students by avoiding 'hands-on' teaching in favour of device-led teaching: "Like, in some classes she gives us these Google presentations to work on and we just do that for the whole lesson. That's it. That's all we do" (K, Yr 9 FG). Qualitative responses in the survey revealed similar comments

> The teachers expect us to know what to do and I don't like the way they're teaching. They don't interact with the students and build relationships, when we ask for help 99% of the time I'm ignored. And…the teachers completely neglect us and don't explain our work properly, it's all posted online and is confusing.

The sentiment that 'the basics' were being neglected was common to the teacher, student and parent participants. From the perspective of the student and parent participants, the teachers at the school assume the students will be able to fill in the gaps at home, using a combination of Internet and Google Classroom resources.

A perceived benefit of e-Learning is collaboration and sharing, and its potential to support the aims of enquiry learning. Several teachers reported that they recognised the potential of e-Learning to encourage students to be active learners. On the strength of the evidence to hand, however, there were missed opportunities to advance an e-Learning culture, including minimal evidence (at the time of the research) of the use of 'flipped' classroom techniques, or of teachers exploring the possibilities that grow from collaborative sharing or content creation.

Collaborative work in the observed context usually meant no more than working in pairs, though teachers' classroom layouts inhibited larger groupings. Teachers' competency may be another factor: "It really depends on who your teacher is. Because, like, you get the teachers who are technophobic and they don't use the Chromebooks at all so you can't really do collaboration with Chromebook if all your teachers are technophobic." (R, Yr 10 FG). The situation described here may have less to do with staff capability, and more to do with the difficulty some teachers have with recognising that ICT is more than simply a tool or teaching aid: "I think a lot of my colleagues see the technology as integral to their lives, but not necessarily as integral to their professional processes." (Head of e-Learning, Holyoake College, IV).

The Substitution, Augmentation, Modification and Redefinition (SAMR) model (first mentioned in Chap. 3) is well known to the Holyoake staff. The New Zealand Ministry of Education, through its portal, Te Kete Ipurangi (TKI),[3] vigorously promotes the SAMR model. SAMR

---

[3]Literally, an online basket (of knowledge), gathering and connecting a wide range of resources for use by teachers and schools.

is a framework through which teachers can assess and evaluate the technology used in the classroom. As teachers move along the continuum, computer technology becomes more important in the classroom but at the same time becomes more invisibly woven into the demands of good teaching and learning. (TKI, nd "Using the SAMR model")

SAMR therefore identifies the level of complexity at which ICT is being integrated with teaching and learning, and the demands e-Learning is making of students' engagement with ICT and associated software and applications. In this regard, at Holyoake College in 2015, a continuum of practice and application was evident. Notably, 87.5% of Year 9 and 10 students surveyed ($n = 88$) answered that using a teacher-made document was the activity that they were *most likely* to complete on their devices. In contrast, 72.7% indicated that creating new content was the activity they were *least likely* to complete with their devices. Observational evidence confirmed significant use of teacher-made documents (such as worksheets and presentations) uploaded to Google Classroom for student consumption and use. In some cases, very old-fashioned exercises were used, the only break with the past being that they were presented as online documents, rather than paper worksheets. Thus, teaching activities using ICT were likely to be closer to the 'substitution' end rather than at the higher end of the SAMR model.

The application of the SAMR model was significant to teachers, for several reasons. The model encourages reflection on the cognitive demands of any particular classroom task involving digital technology use, but it also becomes a measure of the quality of teachers' digital e-Learning strategies. Thus, SAMR becomes a tool of analysis not only for teachers, but also as a reference for appraisers and outsiders, such as evaluators from the Education Review Office. Teachers will recognise the risks involved in implementing high-stakes strategies; risks that are associated with possible failure, which may outweigh, in their minds, any potential benefits, as the following suggests:

> the whole redefinition [the highest SAMR level]...takes so long to get to that point where you're comfortable enough to be able to sit there and redefine how it is you... and you need the time to do that as well, the time to sit and think and play around and trial and re-do and all the rest of it. When you've got a class of 30 kids staring at you to go and trial something like that with them is really daunting because if it all falls apart what are you doing to do? You're going to have to have backup so it becomes, getting up to the redefinition level, becomes this big obstacle. (teacher, Holyoake College, FG)

Nevertheless, there were examples of teachers attempting to teach up the SAMR scale, including having students create their own documents, making Powerpoints, creating Prezi presentations and using other web applications that enable students to create and manipulate content. There was further evidence of some use of shared documents, with the use of the Google application, Padlet, specifically mentioned in the student focus groups. Some teacher participants may have aspired to the higher levels of SAMR, but the pressure to complete curriculum tasks, and to embed basics, inhibited the time and desire to attempt radical new redefinition tasks. And even when attempting to be innovative, student inertia is a problem:

I thought this [students creating a blog site] is going to generate some excitement, the kids are going to get into it and I'm going to start getting emails from the parents and phone calls and that sort of thing. Zero. (senior leader, Holyoake College, FG)

Digital pedagogy at Innovation Primary, Millennial College and Angelus School

Digital technology is well integrated into the practice of all three schools, thus all three sites yield some evidence of e-Learning and digital pedagogy. Like Holyoake, these three schools make use of the Google suite of educational applications. In the case of Innovation Primary and Angelus School, where student self-management of planning is critical, the basic structure of each week is located on Google Drive. Teachers at both schools communicate crucial planning and organisational information that is publically available to students and parents, to access each day, whether at school or home. Students at Angelus School are required to log their progress against their learning goals for the week on Google sheets, a spreadsheet application available on Google Drive. The teachers at Millennial College upload the learning intentions for the current day online for students to see prior to the class. The teachers at Angelus make significant use of shared Google Docs, for example to support their judgements of students' progression through various stages, which in turn enables them to more accurately group and regroup the students.

In reference to teachers using digital devices and applications to pitch teaching and learning up the SAMR scale, teachers in all three settings were observed to make decisive efforts to get beyond simple substitution. Observational evidence suggested that the 'worksheet', to the extent that it exists at all, acts as to guide student activity, rather than requiring students to engage in 'busy work' of the teacher's choosing. In some observed cases, however, it seemed that the activities required by teacher participants might have been too complex, or were not sufficiently well scaffolded. An example was an information retrieval exercise observed in a class at Innovation Primary, where minimal instruction was provided to guide the search, and the content, from what was observed, seemed at a level that was beyond the comprehension of the students I engaged with. This observational evidence is consistent with the comments reflecting the experience of some students at Holyoake College.

There were examples of collaborative work. The Year 4–6 teachers at Innovation Primary created and personalised a Google Doc for each group of students, who were observed completing a reflection using the document. The group document, focussed on their current project, was located on Google Drive. The students worked on this for some time (though in some observed cases, what some were doing looked like recounting, suggesting that the skill of reflection remains emergent for these children). The Google application, eblogger, is an important tool for reflective activity at Innovation and Angelus.

In the main, however, student use of digital technology is more modestly pitched at the 'augmentation' level of the SAMR model (Puentedura 2013). Examples include using video to support the completion of related exercises. A group of Millennial College students, for example, were required to view a video related to an important political protest event in New Zealand, and then to formulate an appropriate protest in response to one of several other political events, to highlight social justice issues. Going a step towards 'modification', students could select to generate a blog post written from several protest perspectives.

Potentially passive-consumptive use noted in observation include a phonics video watched by a class at Innovation Primary during their morning 'snack time', although the students happily interacted with the video as they ate. This gave their teachers some 'breathing space' time in which to set up for the next block of learning activities. At Angelus School, students regularly use their devices and fixed desktop computers to compete in 'Mathletics', an online mathematics learning platform, which covers the New Zealand mathematics curriculum from Year 1 to Year 13 (http://www.mathletics.co.nz), and a literacy program, 'Sunshine Online' (http://www.sunshineonline.com.au/about.php).

Critical questions may be raised concerning devices and software replacing the teacher in these environments, and what they teach students about teaching and learning, and the role of the teacher (questions that were raised at Holyoake College). In her interview, the principal of Angelus School, expressed satisfaction, however, noting that these kinds of programs served as "a maintenance or follow-up...[an]...activity that they can do...independently". The programs "run alongside the proper intensive teaching" that takes place in workshops. She also pointed out that the adoption of these electronic aids is school-wide, thus not confined to those classes that work in the flexible learning environments.

The Relationship Between Device Use and Student Learning: Holyoake College

In this theme, evidence is used to address the question of the relationship between device use, as mandated by the BYOD policy at Holyoake College, and student learning. I will make some general observations, and then focus on the distractions from learning.

Several Holyoake College teachers acknowledged that digital technology is engaging some students' attention, and encouraging ambitious work: "the kids will go with a passion for something that they're really interested in, like that Anzac stuff" (teacher, FG). This confirmed the view of others in the focus group, who noticed positive changes in attitudes to learning among the Year 9 and 10 students as compared to the (non-BYOD) senior students. The juniors will discuss and...share their work...and...critique each other's work or...[give]...feedback and...comments...I don't really see them as being afraid to get it wrong...[but the]... seniors, they still want everything to be handed to them. (Teacher, FG).

Thus, the non-BYOD seniors are less likely to take any kind of academic risks; whereas it was more likely that the younger students would be willing to take risks.

Students were divided regarding the relationship between device use and their learning, several expressing their concerns that their reading, spelling and writing capabilities are in decline as a consequence of their growing reliance on digital technology. Some students noted that copy and paste is a frequent student practice in the completion of homework and projects. There were observed instances, though not widespread, of students coming to class without a device, which was acknowledged by certain teachers as an on-going issue.

Some learning areas of the curriculum are more amenable to device use, and here, students indicated, their learning is maximised using devices. These areas include English, social studies, maths and food technology. Contrastingly, their device use was frustrated or limited in areas less amenable to device use. These included French (whose characters and accents, they suggested, are more easily handwritten) and maths. They noted no use at all in hard technology. The use of a device to help with working out calculations in maths was likely to allow cheating, according to one, which raises the question of non-productive use of digital technology.

Observational data revealed extensive use across several classes of off-task engagement with Facebook and gaming (sometimes up to 30% of a class). In student voice:

> They [other students] instantly feel like they've just got the golden key to play whatever game they like, whenever. *Because sometimes teachers just sit at the front of the class and don't even bother to get up and walk around and make sure everybody is on task.* Some people see that as like a gateway to play games and not even stay engaged at all. (E, Yr 9 FG. Emphasis added)

In classes where such (ab)use was not observed, the teacher was well organised, did not dominate the lesson, moved around constantly, and proactively kept students on task. In the main, however, the use of devices, according to the parents and several students (and acknowledged by some teachers) distract from learning, particularly manifested in game playing during class time. Links were made in the parent focus group between teacher digital capability and the school's powerlessness to keep students in check: "there seems to be quite a few games that are played in class, during class. And it's not monitored properly and you can't stop the games being downloaded either." (Parent, FG)

In the student survey ($n = 88$), 14 respondents (nearly 16%) were critical in their qualitative comments about students engaging in off-task, device-driven behaviour during class. Frequently cited examples were Facebook, music and games. A disgruntled student stated in the survey

> how the hell am I 'e-learning' when kids are playing music through their laptops? Why is my learning being stunted because of the Internet, or because other kids don't care about everyone else's learning? In fact I've gone downhill because of this 'e-learning' crap.

The Relationship Between Device Use and Student Learning: At Innovation Primary, Millennial College and Angelus School

This relationship did not form part of the overt enquiry at these schools, thus observations and questioning inquiries did not focus on this relationship. Some brief, generalised conclusions can be drawn, however, from the evidence recorded so far, in particular when compared with the evidence of the BYOD implementation at Holyoake College.

Across the three flexible learning environments, the use of digital media is seen to support and supplement learning; it is a well-integrated aspect of teaching and learning. Thus, device use is not indiscriminate, but where and when pertinent to particular learning tasks, devices are used by students in preference to using paper-based options. In these cases, teachers direct students to tasks that require the use either of various software applications, or web-based tools. The Internet is a well-integrated feature of teaching and learning in these schools. In the section on digital pedagogy, I provided a number of examples of student and teacher usage, and these do not require repetition here, apart from pointing out that the teachers in these three schools are developing pedagogical routines that call on high levels of student self-accountability, while many tasks I observed were pitched at more sophisticated levels than mere substitution of traditional activities. This includes active student involvement in producing videos and using applications such as Padlet to reflect meta-cognitively on their own learning journeys.

Of some interest, however, was the generally productive use of these digital affordances, and the lower level of off-task device use at these three schools, though there was somewhat more evidence at Millennial College of non-sanctioned usage. The relative freedom and flexibility associated with student-directed learning make it possible for some students to drift off, while appearing to look busy with their devices. While the large, flexible space provides these students opportunities to be able to be distracted in this way as "they're very good at going into corners" (teacher, Millennial College, DB), the responsibility, this teacher suggested, lies with teachers to ensure students remained focussed on their work. Indeed, my observations of this teacher and her colleague noted their active monitoring of student device use, as they moved among the students in the learning space.

Strategic and Management Considerations: Holyoake College

In this theme, the evidence is used to focus on considerations at a strategic and management level in relation to the BYOD policy, with specific emphasis on initial motivations, staffing matters and challenges moving forward.

Initial planning was motivated by the opportunities and challenges presented by the 'digital age'. Possibly too, the school was motivated by the 'moral panic', or at least the implied requirement for schools to act decisively to accommodate the experience of the 'Net Generation' (Bennett and Maton 2010; Helsper and Eynon 2010; Jones 2011). Furthermore, the new possibilities for digital assessment, which have the "power to completely change what happens in a school" (Principal, IV), were a motivating factor. The principal looked to the shift to individualised learning practices (in schools such as Millennial College), as a further impetus for change, suggesting new strategic thinking is required in all schools. One key focus of this strategic thinking is to recognise the collaborative possibilities of e-Learning.

The school signalled the significance of ICT in its daily life by nominating a senior leadership person to have general oversight of infrastructure, hardware and professional learning (in relation to e-Learning and device use). To reflect the overt shift to thinking about the reality of implementing e-Learning, the Holyoake College Board of Trustees decided in 2012 to appoint a Director of e-Learning, a position that comes with reduced teaching hours. In order to avoid a top-down change approach in favour of an inclusive approach, an e-Learning team consisting of staff volunteers was created to support the BYOD policy, and to work with the Director of e-Learning. The Director, in turn, worked to upskill the team, mentor other staff members, and support the delivery of e-Learning.

Recognising, as noted in research (for example, Brečko et al. 2014; Shear et al. 2011), the benefit of staff learning, the policy implementation was supported by visiting several schools that had already implemented BYOD. The senior leader responsible for the e-Learning strategy, captured a sense of urgency in this process during our interview: "...in 2013 we were furiously trying to put experiences of other schools in front of our staff". This included having representatives from known BYOD schools visit Holyoake College. Internally facilitated staff training provided an understanding of the technical aspects so teachers could confidently use devices in their teaching, though this may contradict the findings of Shear et al. (2011) that teachers preferred practical learning to learning the technical aspects of ICT. Nevertheless, for this senior leader, it was important that learning objectives drive the technical aspects, not the other way around. These reflections help to illustrate the rapid pace of change the onset of digital technology brings about in schools, which are often accustomed to moving forward at a rather more ponderous rate. No doubt, such rapid change places new pressures on schools, including staffing.

Staff recruitment has been focussed on seeking teachers with knowledge and experience of e-Learning. The principal ensures that questions around e-Learning and experience are always raised in interviews. Generally, when candidates are equivalent, those with e-Learning experience are preferred. Relief teachers are a different proposition, however, and the evidence of student groups suggested relief teachers have minimal understanding of the Google Apps for Education (GAFE) environment. They seemed to the students to be unprepared or unable to manage the work the teachers have left.

Given that infrastructure and technical support have been found to be significant (Cowie et al. 2011), it is noteworthy that an active strategic decision was taken to opt for Chromebooks. Nevertheless, the notion that "BYOD means bring the device we tell you, not bring your own device" suggests "a vision problem" (Head of e-Learning, IV). Although little more than a web browser, the Chromebook has a keyboard, which is critical in supporting students to create content and make best use of Web 2.0 tools. The senior leaders at the College favour these devices for being relatively virus-free, thus providing a workable and safe and reliable digital environment for students. These devices were, however, observed to have some limitations, with many students experiencing rapid battery deterioration. This suggests (borne out by observation) a challenge for teachers where not all students have equal access, an issue highlighted as a problem by Shear et al. (2011).

The Google environment has a pre-eminent place, though a student comment pointed out the tendency of teachers to work in a Microsoft Office environment, which not only requires a conversion of documents from Word to Google Docs, for instance, but potentially undermines the strategic value of the Google environment. Further evidence indicated a mismatch between the software teachers want to use, and what is available in the Google suite.

A further strategic consideration is finding ways to support teachers who are challenged by the significant re-planning and preparation of work required for effective e-Learning. This significant workload, symptomatic of work intensification (MacBeath 2012), has implications for their sense of personal well-being. Teachers have to grapple with the problem of how to integrate digital technology seamlessly into their work, and this too is an area requiring high-level support. A major challenge, for example, is helping teachers to move beyond a simple use of one-to-one to developing a higher level of student use of technology.

Some on-going, strategic challenges include the multiplication of devices across the large number of students, as an entire cohort is added to the network, ending with the entire school being connected. The emergent plans of the New Zealand Qualifications Authority for developing online NCEA assessments raises questions of assessment integrity and validity. Overcoming the problem of some students who come to school without their device is a challenge, but so is keeping students engaged—digital technology is not enough on its own.

Strategic and Management Considerations: Innovation Primary, Millennial College and Angelus School

These three schools share in common the important strategic and pedagogic priority to use appropriate technology, and to appropriately use technology to complement classroom pedagogy. For the Angelus leaders, it was important "to be up there with what is happening...to bring our digital technologies into the classrooms so that those children...[can] express [themselves] using...device[s] or...tool[s]" (senior leader, Head of e-Learning, Angelus School, IV). Accordingly, the staff at this school had "a whole year of intense ICT PD" in 2013, as an identified strategic priority was to provide developmental opportunities so the staff could use digital tools in ways that went beyond substitution. Here then is further evidence of the penetration into schools of the SAMR model (2013) and, as at Holyoake College, the sense of intensity and urgency occasioned by the rapid response required in relation to digital technology advances.

The principals of Innovation Primary and Angelus School have an expectation that teachers will use considerable discretion in their use of devices in their learning spaces. As "99% of our stuff is online for teachers to access", it is important to develop teachers' capacity "to be smart with the devices they use." (Principal, Innovation Primary, IV). He acknowledged that his teachers are on a continuum of personal development in regard to device use, ranging from some who "are incredibly talented and…some…[who] get scared by turning it on". Since the reported data above, the Angelus School staff have benefitted by further e-Learning professional development, particularly supporting their ability to use the SAMR cognitive model.

Innovation Primary explicitly opted for mobile plasma screens when the school was established, in preference to fixed interactive whiteboards (as were seen in evidence at Angelus School), "because that then states this is a teaching space, this is where I'm at." (Principal, Innovation Primary, IV). The availability of mobile plasma screens and mobile whiteboards allows the teacher the flexibility to shift the focus to a range of areas within the learning space. Despite their installation in her school, the principal of Angelus School took a similar line, questioning the on-going relevance of fixed interactive or electronic white boards, given the limitations inherent in the number of students who can be comfortably seated in front of such devices. She too, preferred the interactivity and flexibility of mobile devices.

In the 2013 phase of research, the senior leader responsible for ICT at Millennial College, echoing Green et al. (2005), suggested during our interview that the ubiquity of digital devices enabled the shift to self-directed learning, thanks to its 'anywhere, anytime' nature: "It enables you to facilitate a whole lot more choice in your classroom. Again, that increases student ownership". Differentiation and collaboration were further advantages afforded by digital technology. As noted previously, none of these schools had opted for a BYOD policy at the outset, but all have an invitational policy, encouraging parents to provide their children with appropriate devices.

On Reflection: Critical Perspectives on Technology and ICT in Education

As in preceding chapters, some critical, theoretic, reflections will provide a deeper level of engagement with the practical studies, and the lived experiences of participants, which will largely be captured by considering their intentional relationships to and with technology and their material world.

Materiality

In maintaining my ontological stance that human beings are capable of making a positive, transformative difference to the world through deliberate and ethical actions, there is merit in considering what may be an appropriate human orientation to the material world. As fundamental as the material world is to human existence (Miller 2005), only a rigidly anthropocentric understanding of that world will imagine that people are the only active agents in an otherwise passive world—a naïve perspective (Pickering 2013). Materiality is a significant concept, and is relevant to other reflections on teachers attempting to forge modern teaching and learning practices, precisely because what is to be a teacher in 2016 does not carry the same meaning as what it meant to be a teacher twenty or thirty years ago, and certainly not fifty or more years ago. An important reason why this is so, has to do with changes to the material world in which teachers work. One element of this world is ICT and its developing ubiquity. ICT and digital technology have transformed the way teachers conduct their work, arguably equivalent to the work transformations Marx was describing in the wake of mechanisation. To be clear, the way material artefacts mediate the relationship between teachers and their students, has arguably distanced or disconnected teachers from their traditional work so that this work would now be unrecognisable, certainly unfamiliar, to teachers who retired from teaching as recently as twenty or thirty years ago. Furthermore, as Dant (2005) argued, material technology is no substitute for human *im*materiality—"imagination, creativity, ideas, passion, love" (p. 34). A critical challenge is thus to understand how the benefits and advantages of technological developments can be aligned to the desire many teachers express, namely to play a transformative role in the lives of their students.

Technology

In addressing this challenge, it is helpful to engage with a more critically textured understanding of technology and it potential to play a meaningful role in the lives of teachers and their students. For this purpose, I will digress by referring in some detail first to what Heidegger said about technology, from his perspective of phenomenology, and then somewhat more briefly at the critical theory-informed view of technology suggested by Horkheimer and Marcuse.

Heidegger

Heidegger's analysis of technology is spelled out in *The Question Concerning Technology* (1977), first published in 1954. His analysis of technological development is underpinned by his emphasis on the ontological, revealing his concern that humans have steadily forgotten, neglected, or overlooked what it is *to be*. Because of this steady neglect, a tendency has come about to treat technology as a mere means by which further technology is developed, or a means to other ends. On this limited conception, technology is there simply to be mastered, so it can be manipulated in the service of its users. An equally limited view (arising from the same neglect) is that technology controls humans. There must be a way, Heidegger believed, of thinking about technology that will overcome the weakness and narrowness of this way of thinking.

To develop a critical understanding of technology, Heidegger argued it is important be open to recognising and understanding the 'essence' of technology. This essence is not to be understood as the general idea of technology or specific technological artefacts. Nor will simply promoting, putting up with, or avoiding technology help our understanding of its essence; and the least favourable response is to treat technology as neutral. This response merely blinds us to the essence of technology. The problem with characteristic understandings of technology is that they are, what he terms, instrumentalist and anthropocentric. This is so, he argued, because these understandings typically hold that technology is either the artefacts or the human activity that brings these artefacts to life (from conception through procurement of resources to the manufacture of the end product). Instrumentalism will not reveal the true essence of technology.

Among the problems with modern technology is that its form and content is in keeping with humans challenging or demanding of nature to provide a 'standing reserve'[4]. Heidegger compared the difference between the rural peasant and the mechanised, commercial farmer. Instead of allowing nature to take its course once the seed has been planted, the commercial farmer challenges the land in multiple ways, using modern insights of physics and chemistry to maximise the yield. Rivers become water power stations, lands become coalfields. Thus, the hidden assets of nature are revealed, transformed and stored for later use.

On this view of technology, this form of revealing (exploiting resources, for instance), requires people to themselves be challenged to be in place to participate. People are subordinate to the higher demands that are placed on nature, and are themselves a standing reserve. People are challenged to challenge nature. Heidegger cited physics, as an exact science, as a particular way in which the human mind is able to challenge nature in order to harness its potential.

A further consideration arising from this desire for an ordered world that can be called upon to reveal its potential is captured in the concept of 'enframing', which is the essence of technology. To articulate this concept, Heidegger took the concrete idea of a bookrack, turning it into the abstract idea of the mind as operating within a strict frame in relation to technology. This enframing of human thinking allows technology to become a pervasive influence in daily life, because our way of thinking about technology and the world is rigid. There is nothing that cannot be

---

[4]This insight is similar to the Marxist interpretation of capitalism which functions in part by creating surplus value beyond what is required for simple survival.

exploited for its technological potential; there is nothing that cannot be measured or controlled.

To be clear: Heidegger did not favour a view of machines as evil, or the devil incarnate. Nor did he take a fatalistic stance by suggesting people are powerless in the face of technological advance. What he was careful to point out, nevertheless, is that technology must not be thought of simply as an instrument (or a tool, I would suggest). To do so, is both to be mastered by technology and to fail to recognise its essence—enframing. This essence, on the one hand, leads to a frenzy of control by numbering and ordering, yet on the other, makes clear to humanity that it carries a significant responsibility for revealing the truth. Here, Heidegger seems to have in mind a transformative role for people, who assume some responsibility for their world.

Horkheimer and Marcuse

Critical theory contributes further critical insights to thinking about, and responding to, technology. One of the leading figures in the Frankfurt School was Max Horkheimer. In *Eclipse of Reason* (2004), he claimed that humans had developed a new instrumental reason that was driven by technological progress. Writing in the context of the Second World War and the rise of Fascism preceding it, Horkheimer argued that independent thought and action was replaced by a dependence on patterns, systems and authorities. Objective reasoning, that is, intrinsic, moral reasoning that seeks truth and meaning, and focuses on ends, had collapsed into irrationality through its emphasis on instrumental concerns. Instrumental reasoning was, he argued, wholly focussed on practical and purposes-driven outcomes, with no reasoning on the ends. Horkheimer wanted a return to seeking the grounds of good reason, for without objective reason, democracy is subject to individual (economic) interest, in which values become simply a question of seeking greater economic value. This notion of instrumentality has parallels with Heidegger's notion, insofar as Heidegger too was concerned with one-dimensional understandings of technology. A key difference, however, is that Heidegger did not have an explicitly political or ideological orientation in his thinking.

Marcuse (1998), also a member of the Frankfurt School, regarded technology as a social process, and regarded people and technology as interconnected

> Technology, as a mode of production, as the totality of instruments, devices and contrivances which characterize the machine age is thus at the same time a mode of organizing and perpetuating (or changing) social relationships, a manifestation of prevalent thought and behaviour patterns, an instrument for control and domination. (p. 41)...

Writing this in 1941, Marcuse, a German exile, reflected on the way the Nazi Reich maintained its control by both brute force and the "ingenious manipulation of the power inherent in technology" (1998, p. 41). Marcuse extended Horkheimer's notion of reasoning, suggesting the notion of 'technological rationality'. Given their capacity, power and efficiency, the machines of technology have steadily replaced the need for individual human function, and have therefore favoured mass production and large-scale enterprise. This has led, in turn, argued Marcuse, to a form of thought that prioritises and preferences the apparatus of technology, suppressing individuality. The human element is reduced to that of mere operation—and increasing consumption of the products of technology. Thus, those controlling technology are able to use its mechanistic characteristics to generate conformity through the processes of semi-skilled, patterned usage. This conformity spills over into various forms of social organisation, eventually reaching into the private "realm of relaxation and entertainment." (p. 48). This conformity deadens the critical impulse, technological rationality encouraging instead self-discipline and self-control, and standardised thought among the mass of individuals who have, in fact, lost their individuality.

Drawing on Weber, Marcuse noted that bureaucracies develop so as to coordinate the isolated, atomistic units of specialised technological functions in society. By maintaining order and direction, the bureaucracy comes to be seen as representing objective rationality, thus providing some meaning to the work of individuals. Rationalisation and efficiency are the watchwords of the day; performativity the measure of an individual's work; and individualism but a nostalgic and irrelevant philosophic ideal. The development of technology has replaced the need for the individual to be asserted; its functions mean individuals no longer have to quest for survival.

Marcuse, like Heidegger and Horkheimer, could do little in the face of technological advance but to ask people to be more critical and discerning; to be more subversive in their thinking. Yet, even as Marcuse said that he felt cheated by realising that his brand new car will one day be old and lose its value, and that "the car is not what it could be, that better cars could be made for less money", he was also aware that "the other guy has to live too…[that] turnover is necessary; we have it much better than before. The tension between appearance and reality melts away and both merge in one rather pleasant feeling" (Marcuse 1991, pp 230–231, quoted by Dant 2005, p. 48).

Thus technology, paradoxically, can both enslave and liberate, and its influence is inescapable. So it is for teachers faced with rapid advances in technologies of communication and technologies of space. At once, they may seek to avoid, flee or engage these technologies. Simultaneously they realise that these technologies spell both the end of their traditional approaches and their known spaces. Technological advance portends different approaches to reach radically changed outcomes for young people who are, besides, somewhat different than any their teachers have experienced in the past. Such (hypothetical) responses may be weighed up against Dant's summation of the critiques of technology. A product of technological advance is the erosion of humanity that seems to rob people of their imaginative and creative powers, and of their social capabilities (who of my generation would have imagined you could one day ask for a date by text message?) Automation serves to distance people ever further from their work—they become alienated from their labour. Associated with notions of control is the concern with technology being used to control lives by agencies or structures that have power over others.

Here we might think of the question of the imposition of technologies on people, such as the blanket decision by schools to be paperless and 'digital-only'.

Intentionality

This chapter has given a sense of the issues and developments that bring to life the possibility of a school choosing to engage with devices (in the way Innovation Primary, Millennial College and Angelus School have) and adopting a BYOD policy (such as Holyoake College has). It has provided a better-informed sense of the notions of materiality and rationalities of instrumentality and technology. Given that backdrop, what tentative conclusions can be drawn from the practical evidence of the participants (notably the teachers) regarding how they come to shape their Being in a context that has developed rapidly? And how are they be-ing in this context? Is it possible to discern some unacknowledged relationships and tensions? Of importance too is how the participants move towards each other, *in relation to* the technology. As the central focus of this chapter has been Holyoake College, most of the evidence here is drawn from those participants. My comments focus on the bearing the adoption of a BYOD policy has had on individual teachers.

It is at the nexus of adoption and resistance that individual relationships to the phenomenon of digital implementation and pedagogy are clearly evident. A key to the success of new initiatives is to get buy-in by involving teachers in the planning. Even the champions and early adopters will "be a lot more resistant if the technology fails" (Head of e-Learning, Holyoake College, IV). What is manifest here is the tenuous nature of people's optimism and willingness to experiment with new technology, perhaps because they have not fully resolved the precise nature of their human relationship with manufactured technology. As Heidegger (1977) cautioned, technological artefacts are not merely passive objects in a passive world, and human influence over those artefacts is, in turn, embedded in other layers of power and control. Exercising this influence requires recognition of the struggle to bring forth the potential embedded within the technology without either believing that human users are somehow manipulated by technology, or can themselves easily manipulate technology. Nor should they lose the essence of their human immateriality, as Dant (2005) argued. By re-reading the words of the participants reported earlier in this chapter, it may be seen that even as they are struggling to come to terms with new technology, they feel in the process, simultaneously in control and controlled.

The comment above concerning power and control being embedded in extended layers of power and control are manifest in the thoughts of one teacher in particular, who, on observation, appeared to have limited her device use to simple substitution. It seemed to her that institutional pressure to implement the policy had robbed her of the pleasure of traditional teaching: "you feel this overwhelming push to do everything online and to come up with exciting stuff…but actually coming up with different things and making it meaningful…I just feel that I've lost touch with my students." (Teacher, Holyoake College, FG). For this reason, she had planned not to use Chromebooks in the unit she was planning next: "I'm going to do other stuff, which was the stuff that we were shouted down for by the previous regime".

Her defiance has an underlying echo of the instrumentality of Horkheimer (ends-focussed) and the bureaucratic technological rationality referred to by Marcuse (1998), whereby independent human functioning is superseded by the superior efficiency of technology. An interesting contrast to this thinking is provided by the principal of Innovation School, for whom, it will be recalled, digital technology represents only one of a number of choices for teachers to select to complement their work. Another view saw digital technology going "hand-in-hand with our teaching" (teacher, Angelus School FG). These perspectives do not overstate the case for digital technology, yet seeking to give it an appropriate place in the lives of teachers.

Nevertheless, the introduction of digital technology, and implementation of effective e-Learning has imposed itself on the health and well-being of some participants, as these initiatives require significant replanning and preparation of work:

> I'm also signing up for lots of weekends sitting at home at the kitchen table writing whole units of work in collaboration with my department, writing resources for this new world. I'm a bit sick of it already and I'm not looking forward to next year but it's not going to go away. Someone has to do it and it's people from one end of the country to the other who are doing this. (senior leader, Holyoake College, FG)

This participant is relating here not only to the implementation process as it affects him directly in his leadership role, but also to his department colleagues, and indeed, to teachers who find themselves in a similar situation around the country. Two of his colleagues in the same focus group, demonstrated the pressure on teachers

> I've felt that I need to do everything on the Chromebook, that I need to show that...I'm up there with all the latest technology and I can do all this exciting stuff.and,...the pressure to be expert and to constantly have new things...is overwhelming...when you're not an expert at it because everything you do it just becomes too much, seriously.

Not only do these collective words reflect the pressure on teachers to succeed, and to 'fake it till you make it', but they reflect the warnings of Marcuse (1998) that technological rationality in bureaucracies determines performativity as a measure of one's success.

Ubiquitous technology imposes itself on teachers' lives in other ways. The teachers at Innovation Primary and Millennial College are encouraged to have Twitter accounts. Though not overtly encouraged at Angelus School, nevertheless some staff have activated such accounts, though, at this stage, appear to make minimal use of these. In contrast, some of their peers at the other two schools are very active users, and have attachments to several hundred, and even over a thousand, follower accounts. There are also examples of some of these people maintaining regular web blog accounts. The effect on their personal lives of this ubiquity was described thus

...we're all so heavily invested we don't switch off. I used to go home and I didn't think about work...But now...I go home and I'm still thinking about work and we're still checking emails and we're still texting each other. There's a higher...investment and level of responsibility and care taking involved for each other and the kids. (senior leader, Innovation Primary, FG)...

These words highlight the work intensification highlighted by MacBeath (2012). It may well be asked why teachers opt to respond to emails after hours, why they feel impelled to post frequent examples on Twitter or their blog pages of the shifts in their thinking, or the ways their teaching exemplifies innovative pedagogy. At one level, they are responding to the demand that teachers be reflective; at another, they are manifesting their changing identity. The demands of e-Learning can cause teachers to "feel like their whole professional identity [is] being taken away by having to work in a team" (Head of e-Learning, Holyoake College, IV), while the mix of traditional teacher knowledge and lack of digital knowledge in classrooms where there may be students who know more than they do, can be confronting. "So how do you exploit that knowledge of that student whilst still maintaining your rightful position as the captain of that ship?" (senior leader, Holyoake College, FG). It is not certain he has resolved this for himself, stating: "I'm confused about what my purpose is. I'm confused about what I'm doing in the classroom". That may simply have been one of his dark days.

In Conclusion

The participants featured in this chapter have, in the main, been those I met, observed and interviewed at Holyoake College, though where pertinent, I have introduced participants working at Innovation Primary, Millennial College and Angelus School. The intent of this chapter has been to explore a further dimension of the notion of '21st-century learning', namely the imperative to work with digital technology if for no other reason than to ignore to do so flies in the face of daily student life. The underlying question remains: what is it to be a teacher in the 21st century? This question was particularly focussed in this chapter on what happens when overt policies require teachers to implement e-Learning and deploy digital devices in the classroom.

Digital technology implementation, I have argued, must take into account such factors as frequent, but often low-level use by school students of digital technology (OECD 2011, 2015), and must occur with the understanding that it is not necessarily true that there is a 'Net Generation' of expert young users and an older generation for whom technology is alien (Bennett and Maton 2010; Helsper and Eynon 2010). Appropriate staff preparation is significant (Brečko et al. 2014; Shear et al. 2011), nevertheless, the likelihood exists that staff will resist (Anderson 2010).

There is no simple relationship between digital penetration and personalised learning (Green et al. 2005; Groff 2013), and more thought may need to be directed towards understanding different kinds of learning being made possible, such as in reference to connectivist understandings of digital learning (Siemens 2005) and complex, networked relationships (Bolstad and Gilbert 2012).

In this chapter, evidence suggests that teachers (in all four schools) reflect a continuum of capability, and the extent to which they use digital technology, and the way they use it, reflects this continuum. The vaunted surrendering of control, and the shift to facilitated and self-managed learning, leads to fears of teachers giving up their traditional role. Being a teacher in the 21st century *does not* mean ceasing to be vigilant, highly active and participatory alongside students. The examples of observed best practice were teachers who actively engaged with students and did not encourage passive learning. As the analysis of teachers' intentional relationships with the phenomenon of digital pedagogy suggests, teachers find themselves in a confusing space, moving uncertainly between their known trusted and traditional approaches and approaches that place more responsibility on their students and rely more on the power of digital technology to convey learning experiences. This continuum of practice leads, as suggested in this chapter, to inconsistent results.

Nevertheless, being a teacher in the 21st century requires teachers to see the possibilities and the potential of digital media and tools, and to have the courage to explore and experiment. This means, in part at least, being a person who seeks to overcome the limitations of time, capability and the pressure of mandated curriculum and qualifications demands to integrate activities and learning that will stretch students cognitively. Where the evidence suggests only some of the participants capitalising on these opportunities, there may be a link with spatiality. Exploring collaborative opportunities seems to come more readily to teachers in flexible spaces—even though they were not necessarily any more competent in their use and manipulation of devices, yet they were better able to integrate e-Learning with their general teaching and learning processes. Relatedly, the school-wide adoption of modern teaching and learning practice is critical to supporting innovative e-Learning, and teachers working in a largely traditional context are, arguably, less free to develop the attributes a teacher requires at this time in the 21st century.

Finally, through the struggles and successes of the teachers reported here, it is important to see that digital devices and affordances are not merely passive tools that stand independently of their users. Reflective teachers in the 21st century will recognise the potential and limitations of these, and seek to make digital technology an integral part of their practice, without the technology subsuming their practice or who they are as human beings. It is a consideration of the role of reflective practice in what it is to be a teacher in the 21st century that will be the subject of the next chapter.

References

Anderson, J. (2010). *ICT transforming education: A regional guide*. Bangkok, Thailand: UNESCO. http://unesdoc.unesco.org/images/0018/001892/189216e.pdf

Bennett, S., & Maton, K. (2010). Beyond the 'digital natives' debate: Towards a more nuanced understanding of students' technology experiences. *Journal of Computer Assisted learning, 26*, 321–331. doi:10.1111/j.1365-2729.2010.00360.x

Bolstad, R., Gilbert, J., McDowall, S., Bull, A., Boyd, S., & Hipkins, R. (2012). *Supporting future-oriented learning and teaching: A New Zealand perspective. Report prepared for the Ministry of Education*. Wellington: New Zealand Council for Educational Research and Ministry of Education. Retrieved August 8, 2015, from http://www.educationcounts.govt.nz/publications/schooling/109306

Brečko, B., Kampylis, P., & Punie, Y. (2014) *Mainstreaming ICT-enabled innovation in education and training in Europe: Policy actions for sustainability, scalability and impact at system level*. European Commission, Joint Research Centre. Luxembourg: Office of European Union. doi:10.2788/52088. Retrieved March 6, 2016 from http://ipts.jrc.ec.europa.eu/publications/pub.cfm?id=6361

Cowie, B., Jones, A., & Harlow, A. (2011). Laptops for teachers: Practices and possibilities. *Teacher Development, 15*(2), 241–255. doi:10.1080/13664530.2011.571513

Dant, T. (2005). *Materiality and society*. Berkshire, United Kingdom: Open University Press.

Green, H., Facer, K., Rudd, T., Dillon, P., & Humphreys, P. (2005). *Personalisation and digital technologies*. Bristol, England: Futurelab. Retrieved Feb 6, 2016 from http://www.nfer.ac.uk/publications/FUTL59/FUTL59_home.cfm

Groff, J. (2013). *Technology-rich innovative learning environments*. OECD CERI innovative learning environments project. Retrieved from http://www.oecd.org/edu/ceri/Technology-Rich%20Innovative%20Learning%20Environments%20by%20Jennifer%20Groff.pdf

Heidegger, M. (1977). Question concerning technology. In D. M. Kaplan (Ed.), (2004) *Readings in the philosophy of technology* (pp. 35–51). Lanham, MD: Rowman & Littlefield Publishers.

Helsper, E. J., & Eynon, R. (2010). Digital natives: Where is the evidence? *British Educational Research Journal, 36*(3), 503–520. doi:10.1080/01411920902989227

Herold, B. (2015, June 10). Why ed tech is not transforming how teachers teach. *Education Week*. Retrieved June 24, 2016 from http://www.edweek.org/ew/articles/2015/06/11/why-ed-tech-is-not-transforming-how.html

Horkheimer, M. (2004). *Eclipse of reason* (revised edition). London, United Kingdom/New York, NY: Continuum.

Jones, C. (2011). Students, the net generation, and digital natives: Accounting for educational change. In M. Thomas (Ed.), *Deconstructing digital natives: Young people, technology and the new literacies* (pp. 30–45). New York, NY: Routledge Taylor & Francis e-Library.

MacBeath, J. (2012). *Future of teaching profession*. Cambridge, England: University of Cambridge. Education International Research Institute. Retrieved from http://download.ei-ie.org/Docs/WebDepot/EI%20Study%20on%20the%20Future%20of%20Teaching%20Profession.pdf

Marcuse, H. (1998). Some social implications of modern technology. In D. Kellner, (Ed.), *Technology, war and fascism: Collected papers of Herbert Marcuse* (Vol. One, pp. 39-65). London, United Kingdom/New York, NY: Routledge. (Original published in 1941).

Miller, D. (2005). Materiality: An introduction. In D. Miller (Ed.), *Materiality* (pp. 1–50). Durham, NC: Duke University Press.

Ministry of Education. (2007). The New Zealand curriculum. Wellington, New Zealand: Learning Media Limited. Available from http://nzcurriculum.tki.org.nz/The-New-Zealand-Curriculum

Ministry of Education. (2015b). *New Zealand education in 2025: Lifelong learners in a connected world*. Discussion document. Retrieved from http://www.education.govt.nz/assets/Documents/Ministry/Initiatives/Lifelonglearners.pdf

Organisation for Economic Cooperation and Development (OECD). (2011). *PISA 2009 results: Students on line: Digital technologies and performance (Volume VI)* http://dx.doi.org/10.1787/9789264112995-en Retrieved March 4, 2016 from http://www.oecd-ilibrary.org/education/pisa-2009-results-students-on-line_9789264112995-en

Organisation for Economic Cooperation and Development (OECD). (2015). *Students, computers and learning: Making the connection*. Paris, France: PISA, OECD Publishing. doi:http://dx.doi.org/10.1787/9789264239555-en. Retrieved February 7, 2016 from http://www.oecd-ilibrary.org/education/students-computers-and-learning_9789264239555-en

Pickering, A. (2013). Living in the material world. In F-X. de Vaujany & N. Mitev (Eds.), *Materiality and space: Organizations, artefacts and practices* (pp. 25–40). Basingstoke, United Kingdom: Palgrave Macmillan.

Puentedura, R. P. (2013, June 13). *The SAMR Model explained by Ruben R. Puentedura* [Video file]. Retrieved from https://www.youtube.com/watch?v=_QOsz4AaZ2k

Shapley, K., Sheehan, D., Sturges, K., Caranikas-Walker, F., Huntsberger, B., & Maloney, C. (2009). *Evaluation of the Texas Technology Immersion Pilot: Final outcomes for a four-year study (2004–05 to 2007–08)*. Austin, TX: Texas Center for Educational Research. Retrieved from http://files.eric.ed.gov/fulltext/ED536296.pdf

Shear, L., Gallagher, L., & Patel, D. (2011). *Innovative teaching and learning research 2011 findings: Evolving educational ecosystems*. SRI International. Retrieved from http://www.itlresearch.com/images/stories/reports/ITL%20Research%202011%20Findings%20and%20Implications%20-%20Final.pdf

Siemens, G. (2005). Connectivism: A learning theory for the digital age. Retrieved from http://er.dut.ac.za/bitstream/handle/123456789/69/Siemens_2005_Connectivism_A_learning_theory_for_the_digital_age.pdf?sequence=1

Chapter 7
The Impacts on Teachers' Work: Practitioner Attitudes and Reflective Transitions

> A key function of the mass education systems of the 20th century was to turn out people with the knowledge, dispositions, and skills needed in 20th century economies and societies…Now, in the 21st century, our education system needs new goals. The educator's job must go beyond imparting already known knowledge…To survive and thrive…people need…to be able to produce new knowledge, on their own and with others. Doing this requires a well-developed intellect. It requires intellectual capacity, intellectual "processing power" and flexibility…If the 21st century educator's work is to design experiences to build these capacities in students, then they themselves need to have these capacities, in well-developed form. (Gilbert and Bull 2015, p. 3)

> …the practice of critical teaching…involves a dynamic and dialectical movement between 'doing' and 'reflecting on doing'…in the process of the ongoing education of teachers, the essential moment is that of critical reflection on one's practice. (Freire 1998, p. 43. Emphasis added)

> Effective teaching is much more than a compilation of skills and strategies. It is a deliberate philosophical and ethical code of conduct. (Larrivee 2000, p. 294. Emphasis added)

The 'learnification' of the curriculum (Biesta 2014) means the focus in many educational systems falls now on the 'learner' and the skills and dispositions required to learn successfully for a 21st century future. To the extent the learner is emphasised, the teacher is de-emphasised. Regardless, however, of the various policy intentions to de-emphasise the role of the teacher, I concur with the view of Gilbert and Bull (see the epigraph) that it is the teacher who requires these skills and dispositions if these are to be successfully imparted (assuming of course these skills and dispositions are what is required to live a good life in the 21st century). Making this kind of shift places teachers in a unique relationship with their work, with their colleagues, their students and their places of work. Arguably, if Freire and Larrivee are to be believed, then critical reflection on practice is not only among the foremost skills and dispositions to be cultivated by teachers in their lifelong development as teachers, but one that is their ethical duty to develop.

In Chap. 3, I made reference to the requirement that licensed, practicing New Zealand teachers have to demonstrate their ongoing commitment to continually improving their practice by engaging in evidence and research-based critical inquiry and problem-solving, that is both conducted in the company of peers and in private, and that requires an openness to feedback and a willingness by teachers to be critically self-reflective of their personal beliefs (Education Council, n.d.). This very well sums up what it may mean to be a 'critically reflective practitioner'.

This will be a shorter chapter than the previous considerations of modern teaching and learning practice, flexible learning environments and digital technology. It is, nonetheless, an important chapter insofar as engaging in new ways of teaching and learning in technology-rich, flexible environments calls on teachers to make significant shifts in their practice. In so doing, and in order to do so requires, I argue, significant mental shifts. These are substantial and substantive shifts requiring significant investments of reflective energy in order for sustainable shifts to occur. School leaders, specifically principals, have their own unique reflective challenges and are thus not immune from the demand to alter their mind-sets. Readers of this book will benefit from the experiences and reflective practices of those practitioners working with digital technology and in technology-rich, flexible environments. Thus, most of the focus of this chapter will be on the experiences, practices and mental attitudes of the participants who were observed and who participated in interviews and focus groups. First, however, I will briefly traverse some ground on reflective practice I have covered elsewhere.

Critically Reflective Practice, Trust and Teaching as Inquiry

As the research study on which this book is based has evolved, three separate and distinct articles have appeared in publication, each considering elements of the reflective practice focus of the research. I will briefly outline each here, as together they provide a useful summary of ideas on this subject.

Teachers' Critical Reflective Practice in the Context of Twenty-First Century Learning

This article (Benade 2015b) was based on the '21st-century Learning' study (see Chap. 2). Its basic assumption was that a link exists between reflective practice and the demand to engage in 21st-century learning (essentially modern, or innovative, teaching and learning practices). Understanding this link is significant both for the reason that teachers are required to make significant mind shifts to engage differently with teaching and learning, and in order to sustain these shifts requires the ability to be critically self-reflective. The context for considering this link was the development of digital pedagogy and working in the context of technology-rich and flexible learning environments. Both contexts were considered to be manifestations of 21st-century learning.

Beginning from the position that "... reflective practice must assume a level of directed, proactive cognitive activity by an individual, who is disposed to such activity" (p. 44), the following six principles of reflective practice were put forward:

- The individual ought to be able to sustain the practice of reflection on an ongoing basis in a self-directed manner;
- Groups of individuals ought to be able to reflect together, either in pairs or in bigger groups;
- Reflective activity focuses on peoples' practice, and has a temporal character—taking place before, during and after practice episodes;
- Reflection is cognitively challenging and unsettling;
- It has an ethical dimension;
- Correspondingly, reflection leads to action, typically with a social justice focus (or at least a desire to improve the lot of others).

In an attempt to draw out some key differences in thinking, I contrasted the views of the school leaders (and ex-school leaders) with those of the teachers. Thus, I treated each of these groups as cases. In the former case, there appeared to be a more generous and wide-ranging understanding of reflective practice, though the leader group linked reflective practice to appraisal. In the teacher case group, there existed a much narrower notion of reflective practice, with the emphasis on classroom work. Arguably, the constitution of both these positions may be influenced by the various work roles of the two groups. A somewhat subdued conclusion was that while some of the six principles of reflective practice were in evidence in the thoughts and words of the various participants, the leader case group seemed ultimately focussed on the contribution of reflection to accountability demands, while the teacher case group was motivated by student achievement data. This finding gave rise to the next article.

The Role of Trust in Reflective Practice

Perhaps suggesting a seventh principle of critically reflective practice, I argued in this article (Benade 2016) that trust underpinned in particular the principle of collaborative reflection. The impetus to explore the concept of trust in relation to reflective practice stemmed from leaders linking reflective activities (such as writing) to performance appraisal. The notion that teachers' critical self-reflection about their practice in public and in writing be utilised in appraisals seemed to contradict the very basis of reflective activity. At the very least, it is difficult to imagine that teachers will be critically forthcoming if they know these thoughts may appear in their performance appraisal documentation.

Several factors associated with trust make a relationship between critically reflective practice and performance appraisal problematic. A most obvious matter is that openness to personal failings or (possibly flawed) beliefs makes people vulnerable to betrayal. A less obvious dimension is the close link many writers make between trust and competence (see 2015c for the elaborations of these points). In the matter of workplace relations, individuals have to believe the other has the skills if they are to trust that person. Knowledge of (or belief in) the competence of the other makes trusting that person more likely, and with it, a willingness to be open to betrayal.

Teachers being open and transparent about their practice (and thus laying bare their soul, as it were) is an important step in the process of altering their mind-set, so as to fully embrace new technologies of digital media and space, and to approach teaching and learning in innovative ways. By sharing their success and failure with others, they both sustain shifts in their own practice, while supporting others also engaged in this process. This is a view held by several participants, and will be a theme I return to shortly, when discussing the practical study.

In the article, I referred to two distinct approaches to the relationship between reflective practice and appraisal. One view was that appraisal enables reflective practice—arguably, this is a weak account of the relationship. The other account, which could be characterised as a strong version, regarded the product of reflective practice to be an instrument of appraisal, such as being a form of evidence contributing to the verification of teacher practicing standards. A reason some participants (specifically leaders) had for linking appraisal to reflective practice strategies is to embed yet another mandated requirement of the New Zealand Ministry of Education, namely 'teaching as inquiry'. Precisely what this is, and why it requires critical evaluation, was at the centre of the third article.

Teaching as Inquiry: Well Intentioned, but Fundamentally Flawed

The subject of this article (Benade 2015c) was 'Teaching as Inquiry' (TAI), a cyclic model of teacher reflection found in The New Zealand Curriculum (MOE 2007, p. 35). TAI consists of three inquiring questions: What is important given where my students are at?; What strategies are most likely to help my students learn this?; What happened as a result of the teaching, and what are the implications for future teaching? (p. 35).

This article, like the other two, drew on the evidence from the 21st-century learning study. In it, I persisted with the argument that teachers' reflective practice is a collaborative and critical activity. Here I argued that this practice has an epistemological element, namely that teachers require some knowledge and skills to effectively engage in reflection. Further, this practice has an ontological element, that is, practitioners must be disposed to engage in reflective activity, particularly the willingness to put their own beliefs and theories under a critical microscope, so to speak. In explaining this ontological element, I drew on the six principles of reflective practice referred to in the first of these articles.

These principles were reviewed, in the words of the participants, and in light of TAI. Even though there are other models and approaches to teacher reflection available to New Zealand teachers, the Ministry of Education has effectively authorised this as the default option by including it in The New Zealand Curriculum (MOE 2007). This apparent lack of choice is problematic, which I tried to show by arguing in the article that the basis of this particular model is flawed.

Reasons for these flaws include the deletion of important dispositional characteristics that appeared in the original version of TAI from the version in The New Zealand Curriculum (Benade 2015c). The model in The New Zealand Curriculum is instrumental, requiring little practitioner engagement beyond moving through the three questions. Further, the model does not guarantee or even encourage collaborative engagement. At best, the model implies social justice and ethical concerns (without being stated); at worst (or, in reality), it is a mechanism for ensuring accountability in reference to the Ministry of Education focus on targeting low-performing students.

While TAI may be a beginning point for teachers unfamiliar with self-reflection, the evidence provided in the article (2015c) suggests it is not uniformly well understood or applied, and the participants to the research tended to see it in bifurcated terms, as a form of reflective practice, or as a parallel activity to reflective practice. These views, and those reported in the previous two articles were based, as I stated, on the 21st-century learning study, which took place between October 2013 and December 2014. What these articles did not (and could not) reflect on, were some of the views that emerged in the second phase, namely the 'Being a Teacher' study. It is to a consideration of some of those findings I will now turn.

The Practical Studies

Introduction

In the course of this study, an attempt was made to discern and understand teachers' positioning in relation to a range of issues. These came to light in the course of informal conversation between and during teaching and learning episodes, in more formal, but semi-structured discussions with individuals or teams of individuals, and in the course of focus groups. The wide scope of change demanded of participants at Innovation Primary, Millennial College and Angelus School, has provided a rich mine of data. The scope of change at Holyoake College has been significant, but being limited to the introduction of a BYOD policy, the focus of the impact has been on the implementation of an e-Learning model. Thus the weight of evidence provided here reflects the work with the three schools that have flexible learning spaces. Where relevant, the Holyoake experience will be specifically referred to.

A frequent objection to 'modern teaching and learning practice' is that it reflects what 'good' teachers have been doing for decades. Several points can be read into such objections. At a cynical level, this objection could be interpreted as denial. At another, the objection could be read as a more general objection to the zealous promotion of 'the next big thing', where the objection can be interpreted as 'old hands' dismissing zealots as too young or too ignorant to realise that some of these ideas have been in circulation for decades. Writing as I do from the perspective of an old hand rather than a young zealot, I have some sympathy for the objection. There are, however, many differences and these are fundamentally driven by significant attitudinal shifts, such as those displayed in the words and actions of the participants to this study. These shifts require openness to new learning, and the willingness to make mistakes. This shift in thinking requires teachers to place themselves in vulnerable positions. An important area to operationalise this mindset shift resides in teachers' reflective practice. There were many examples in evidence of participants self-consciously recognising the value to their practice of active reflection, and of quickly recognising significant shifts in themselves.

Open to New Learning

The development of flexible learning environments requires teachers to cede control in many ways, especially if the pedagogy of choice is to be self-directed and self-initiated learning: "I've realised I have to totally change my thinking…and… [recognise]…everyone's equal, we all have something to give, students, teachers… We all respect each other's thoughts, students included". (Teacher, Angelus School, FG.) This cession of control goes with ceding anxiety, and placing greater faith in students' ability to initiate learning and locate the resources they require.

Participants in the Innovation Primary focus group spoke of undergoing a complete overhaul in their thinking about their practice as teachers, to the point of questioning practices that came naturally, one participant wondering if any previous practices that seemed effective, "actually worked at all". Self-doubt is a characteristic of being open to new learning, and although unsettling to some, can be productive. The teachers in this focus group questioned the 'tick box', mechanistic approach to schooling and teaching practice they had been led to believe was accepted practice.

Being open to new learning requires the disposition to be growth-oriented, open and flexible, characteristics, which teachers in the Millennial College focus group expressed. This does not mean there is no pain associated with new learning for these teachers to work through, especially in light of losing their right to their own classroom space. On the other hand, these participants found giving up traditional power and influence was compensated by the reduction in administrivia in this particular school.

The points highlighted by the participants across these three focus groups go to the heart of some of the changes that are most perturbing for many teachers. It is a confronting notion that teachers, long accustomed to the practice of working alone in a closed room with 30 students, should now agree to practice with two or three colleagues in large shared space with perhaps 100 students. Deleuze and Guattari developed the idea of territorialisation, de-territorialisation and re-territorialisation in their book, *Anti-Oedipus*. The concepts are linked to their broader critique of Freud, and address the idea of personal and bodily investment in particular spaces in the capitalist economy, the withdrawal of investment from these spaces, and its reinvestment elsewhere (Holland 2013). The idea was in keeping with the general rejection by Deleuze and Guattari of discrete, enclosed and bifurcated (either/or) concepts in favour of their notion of the *rhizomatic*.[1] Territorialisation, de-territorialisation and re-territorialisation also entail a process of encoding, un-encoding and recoding (2013), thus it may be envisaged that learning to be a teacher in a single cell space with 30 students requires a teacher's mental frameworks to be coded in a particular way, consistent with notions of privacy, teacher agency and ownership over a particular territory. The turn to non-discrete, semi-boundless spaces in the flexible learning environment requires an openness to new learning, and a renegotiation of mental codes. Positively, this turn does set teachers free to reimagine their practice and, as suggested in the Angelus School focus group, give away feelings of anxiety associated with teachers taking most control over student learning and movement.

Reflection–In, –On and For–Action

Argyris and Schön (1974), and Schön (1983) delimited reflective activity into temporal phases. Teacher reflection-in-action (that is, 'on the spot' reflection) was frequently in evidence, especially at Innovation Primary. There teachers were heard talking self-reflexively to students about the teachers' own actions and thoughts, in which they endeavoured to model to their students the characteristics of adaptability and flexibility, and their ability to change activities or direction as required. This action of 'thinking aloud' is an important way of promoting the use of school learning dispositions at Innovation Primary:

> Our dispositions were all set up around whole brain thinking, so…for our learners to understand that, they need to have that modelled. So we're modelling our analytical thinking, our creative, holistic, visionary type side but also our emotional, interpersonal and then our organisational side. (teacher, Innovation School, DB)

Other very important forms of reflection are those that focus on action (that is, backward looking) and for action (that is, future looking). Resolving perplexity over action that is not evolving as planned "*is the steadying and guiding factor in the entire process of reflection*", suggested Dewey (1910, p. 11. Emphasis in the

---

[1]A rejection of hierarchical, ordered and finite concepts in preference to multiplicity and endless variety.

original). The process of team construction and developing a collaborative approach at Angelus School, for example, had not been easy, and in particular, achieving the correct approach to classroom pedagogy was an ongoing project. According to one of the team leaders, this process of development was, however, encouraged by the willingness and ability of the team members to acknowledge that they were 'not doing it right' at first, often defaulting to what they knew and felt comfortable with. This included breaking the cohort into three 'classes', which team members found themselves teaching in breakout spaces. Confronted by the 'puzzle' (Argyris and Schön 1974) of this default to traditional practice, the process of reflection enabled these team members to square up to problem-solving and informing (Larrivee 2000; Smyth 1992) their practice, thus shaping a different approach. This is, however, as Larrivee (2000) noted, a confronting process, but one that builds professional capacity (Reid 2004).

Backward-looking reflective activity can support forward-looking reflection. Amongst teachers at Innovation Primary School, the construction of teams in terms of 'critical-friend' relationships enable teachers to make supportive, yet critical, comments to each other in support of changing their practice moving forward. This experience of non-judgemental, supportive critical-friend relationships was echoed at Angelus School. That focus group added, however, the requirement of high levels of trust if team members are to benefit by the supportive comments of their team colleagues.

The principals of the three schools each strongly believe that there is a link between self-reflection, collaborative critical conversations, and effective teamwork. It was noted in Chap. 6 that teachers at Innovation Primary and Millennial College are encouraged to have active Twitter accounts, providing them an outlet for displaying elements of their personal practice to a wider audience. This kind of reflective activity may be used as evidence by the staff of working towards the Registered Teacher Criteria, which include being a reflective practitioner. This linkage of reflective activity to appraisal was first noted in the '21st-Century Learning' study, and referred to earlier in this chapter.

The processes of self-reflection and collaboration combine powerfully at Millennial College. Weekly opportunities are created for the teachers to share their evolving teaching strategies in the flexible spaces, so that a mutual bank of expertise is developed. Here discussion of issues includes how student voice may be utilised, finding links across learning areas, and ways of effectively collaborating in planning and delivery of the curriculum. This is a form of reflective practice, and a time of honest self-appraisal, a time and place where the teachers 'celebrate failure' (Principal, Millennial College, IV).

The Changes that e-Learning Demands

The overt adoption of a digital culture in a school has significant implications for teachers. Considering that as recently as 2011, Holyoake College was only just at the stage of "making that momentous decision to allow the students to use their cell phones at break times" (Principal, IV). From the perspective of her leadership team, freeing up rules around cell phones at school acknowledged the pace of change being created by digital technology, and demonstrated the realisation by 2015 that students then coming to school were not the same as those who may have come to school in 2000. Adopting new technologies and techniques is not, however, a natural approach for some teachers, and while some have "got a more natural inquisitiveness, reflectiveness...[and] really pushed their comfort zone" (teacher, FG), others were making little or no effort to shift.

Green et al. (2005) argued "creating personalised learning environments...[is not possible] without using the communication, archiving and multimedia affordances of digital resources" (p. 5), while Groff (2013) pointed out the intersection of new innovations, current staff skill level and teachers' preparedness for change may be a site of conflict. Still, this may be a battle worth fighting for some: "the benefits of e-Learning [are namely] real collaboration and sharing and the knocking down of the classroom walls, which builds professional capital." (Head of e-Learning, IV). For this participant, e-Learning is "a foundation for reflective practice and collaboration", and, arguably these practices will support changes to teaching, such as greater individualised attention, and less front of class teaching. Among the challenges she identified, is to get teachers to see digital technology as complementary to their teaching, while not becoming panicked by this shift.

A transition most keenly felt by Holyoake College teachers as they moved into a BYOD environment, was the way they prepare for classes. Going beyond a simple use of one-to-one to develop a higher level of student use of technology represented (and continues to represent) a significant challenge to the Holyoake teachers. This is paralleled by their realisation that some students enjoy technical superiority over their teachers. Students are able to (very quickly) develop new proficiencies and skills as a result of using technology in a BYOD/e-Learning context. In similar vein to their colleagues working in shared, flexible environments, these teachers have experienced a loss of power and control. The resulting feelings of inferiority can be alienating, and, potentially embarrassing for some.

On Reflection

Intentionality

A useful context from which to think about intentionality is provided by the theme of transition, which has special significance to any discussion of reflective activity. This is especially as I argue that critical reflection on practice, and, in particular, a willingness to engage in deeper reflection is specifically a way in which modern or innovative pedagogy breaks with the past. It cannot be assumed that all teachers come 'ready-made' for working in radically different ways; thus, they must undergo some kind of transitional experience if they hope to be successful. In making these shifts, they are becoming, effectively, 'different people'; they are reconstituting their professional selves. Thus, transitional experiences open a window to what it is they become, and how they perceive this new way of Being, and be-ing.

Of particular interest in the 'Being a Teacher' study was thus to see the nature of the shifts participants make or experience as they progress in their practice from traditional forms to forms of teaching that can be variously described as modern, progressive, innovative and personalised. These terms each have unique meanings, but in all cases, they refer to styles of teaching that represent a break with didactic, teacher-controlled, universalist approaches to classroom relationships and activities. 'Pedagogy' is taken to mean more than just classroom strategies in this study, however. It is also taken to refer to what teachers think about their work and role as teachers, what their views are concerning education, and what their underpinning values are. That is to say, 'pedagogy' has an axiological (values) component, as much as it has epistemological (such as pedagogical content knowledge) and ontological (such as teacher–student relationships) components.

Transitions in Flexible Learning Environments

While some teachers fall very easily into a mind shift paradigm, others may imagine they are amenable to shifting, yet they find themselves struggling to make actual shifts:

> So [for] some [new teachers]…all they've wanted to do the whole time is challenge their practice. Others have…*thought* they challenge their practice, and it's taken them a while to realise, "actually, no, I've never challenged my practice, now I'm challenging my practice, and this is bloody hard"…that ability to think…differently about learning has been a different journey for everybody. (Principal, Innovation Primary, IV)

A major shift (THE major shift?) is for those teachers transitioning from a school with rigid routines and fixed approaches to planning. Personalising learning requires teachers to move away from being able to determine uniform content that leads to uniform learning outcomes for all students in the class. A traditional, teacher-focussed approach enables a teacher to predict precisely the topics to be covered at any given time of the year; now, "we redesign and reshape to the needs of the kids, not us" (teacher, Innovation Primary, FG).

Teaching in a personalised environment requires teachers to learn to use time more productively. In conventional schooling, there is wasted 'wait' time, while all students come to a common understanding for example. This may allow a teacher to carve out periods of low-key or slow activity. In a personalised environment, however, by the start of day, students "have already planned their day half an hour before the day starts. So they're gone" (teacher, Innovation Primary, DB). Certainly, many participants indicated that personalised teaching is physically and mentally demanding, and that exhaustion holds the ever-present danger of slipping back into 'default' modes of teaching.

The decision at Angelus School to move from being a school with ten single cell classrooms to one that included flexible learning environments was not taken lightly. The principal, recognised "it wasn't just about the buildings, it was more about what was going to happen within". She therefore recognised the fundamental pedagogical shifts required of the teachers at Angelus School, and realised that this was to be a "step into the unknown".

Precisely what this transition might mean to teachers was captured by the reports of one who spoke of her struggles with shifting from a traditional siloed, disciplinary curriculum, to an integrated curriculum, in which content knowledge transfer is supplanted by skills and dispositional development:

> I think my first term I was a bit confused about the whole thing. The second term I tried to teach too much. I tried to do too much. And by the third term I'd gone, *'Okay. I need to teach twenty percent of what I'd normally teach and I need to do it more like this'*. I think by the third term I'd found my feet. In the first and second term I did feel a little bit incompetent and I did feel like I wasn't doing the kids, you know, justice. Yeah. But I've got it now. (teacher, Millennial College, DB. Emphasis added).

The analysis of the discourse of transition in the thoughts and comments of the participants referred to here provide, as I suggested earlier, a window to the changing worlds of these teachers; changes that may be deeply unsettling to teachers who are accustomed to control; to those who may model their teaching on their school memories; or to those shifting from a siloed model to an integrated one. The notion that teaching innovatively in flexible spaces is little different to, or no different from, the teaching of 'good' teachers over the past few decades, belies the lived experience of practitioners who are challenged on a daily basis to do their work differently, and in the process, to *be* different people. The changes and challenges are no less magnified for the practitioners at Holyoake College.

Transitions in a BYOD Environment

To demonstrate intentionality in this context, I have selected an extract from my focus group discussion with the participants. In that discussion, I asked them to recall their initial response to the onset of the policy, and to articulate these recollections as labels. Labels provided included, *terror, anxiety* and *concern*, but also included *excitement, enthusiasm* and *determination*. Their words, spoken in a focus group, are revealing:

> Initially terrified of the unknown, particularly with the workload. So ran home and spent all that holiday working on…our own sites.
>
> I was really, really concerned because…I was terrified because I did not have the skills that I needed to implement effectively and I wasn't sure that we were going down the right track.
>
> I was quite upbeat about it at the start. Of course there were down parts in between and a few tantrums, but that's okay.
>
> …something you've been teaching forever and all of a sudden it's kind of going to be a new thing, a new direction.

I felt very resolute about it. I felt quite nervous knowing that it was a huge change for our staff and...as a school leader...I had these quiet little moments of terror...visions of half a class without a device and...those thoughts consumed me at the last quarter of 2013.

What manifests here is the tension between the promise of creativity and fresh beginnings, coupled with the visceral, embodied reaction to the unknown—'ran home'; be-ing 'terrified'; experiencing 'tantrums'; taking 'a new direction'; and 'consumed' by terrifying visions of the device programme being an utter failure.

When asked to label their experience eighteen months into the BYOD implementation, participant teachers used such labels as *fantastic, amazing* and *wonderful*, but conversely, some felt *frustrated, confused* and *disappointed*. Again, their words are revealing:

I think it's really a lot of work, but it's so fantastic. It's just amazing. I think the differentiation that you can produce with individual students and the tasks you can come up with; your imagination just flies with this.

The implementation and the process of learning that I have gone through has changed the way that I see teaching and learning, so actually the implementation of BYOD has had huge impact on the way that I see teaching.

It's more comfortable now. It's kind of like you know what you're doing and you go in there and you can do it and you can do just about anything, it's amazing. I found that it gives you a lot more one-on-one time with individual students.

I'm still excited [but] I've had to develop strategies of tracking their [students'] progress and not just assuming that they're doing the work because they're sitting quietly.

I dreamt about doing virtual field trips like...taking my kids 'to Antarctica' [or] taking them 'into a volcano'... [but s]ome days it's pretty ordinary, not because I want it to be but because it is.

These responses combine the enthusiasm of the ideal with the starkness of real, daily life in a classroom. On the optimistic side of the scale are people who see themselves as learning and acquiring new skills and dispositions, while on the other, are those who express some disenchantment, or the realisation that introducing Internet-connected devices is not going to revolutionise education—certainly not overnight. Again, the body and mind seem to work in tandem here, as the participants 'see', feel 'comfortable', dream, have flights of imagination, yet experience the mundane ordinariness of days that require dull (but significant) tracking.

In Conclusion

This chapter has considered reflective practice as a manifestation of 21st-century learning—or, it could be regarded by some as a by-product or a necessary ingredient. Reflective practice is not an uncomplicated characteristic, as the opening pages of this chapter demonstrated, when I considered some of its key features, problematised its relationship to appraisal, specifically by drawing attention to the role of trust, and then by taking a critical stance towards the officially-sanctioned form of reflection in The New Zealand Curriculum, namely, 'Teaching as Inquiry'. When taken as a case, the teacher participants in the '21st-Century Learning' study had a mixed understanding of this model; the leaders, as a case saw a relationship between reflective practice and appraisal. For some, the former informed the latter; for others, the latter enforced the former. Clearly, the leader participants spoke, to at least some extent, with their accountability hat firmly on. As for the teacher participants, their focus was also narrowed by accountability, in their case, to student assessment performance, seeing reflective activity as a narrow exercise in establishing how to correct deficiencies in student performance. The earlier study reached the glum conclusion that reflective practice—at least in the case of teacher participants—was not manifesting as well as I might have hoped, while among the leader participants, there was at least, in theory, a deeper notion of reflective activity, albeit being somewhat domesticated by accountability demands.

The important question is to establish how these participants, as individual cases or as a group (of teachers, for instance) move towards, or establish an intentional connection to the phenomenon of reflective practice, considered as an important characteristic of teachers working with modern or innovative pedagogies. This I attempted to establish by considering the theme or concept of transition, as this seems to me to capture one of the most (if not *the most*) fundamental aspects tied up with the phenomenon of modern teaching and learning practice—namely making significant mental shifts in order to come to terms with this altered way of Being a teacher. I have argued forcefully that being a teacher in the current times of the 21st century is to be a person in a state of constant unsettlement. In order to cope with that radical lack of certainty and control that teachers once laid claim to, requires teachers to be open to learning, and to be willing to reflect constantly, looking back, looking at the here and now, and looking forward; and to do so in deprivatised settings and in collaboration with others. Here we could recall Dewey's definition of reflective activity: "*Active, persistent, and careful consideration of any belief or supposed form of knowledge in the light of the grounds that support it, and the further conclusions to which it tends*" (1910, p. 6. Emphasis in the original).

In tandem with Freire (1998) and Larrivee (2000), I would also argue that teaching is an ethical matter, not a technical one, thus the reflective focus of teachers could do well to shift from instrumental accountability demands to a wider social justice and ethical focus—largely absent in the discourses of the participants, and at best only implied. Teachers' reflective activity is only a part of the change equation. The other is what takes place at an organisational level, which is my final area of focus.

References

Argyris, C., & Schön, D. A. (1974). *Theory in practice: Increasing professional effectiveness.* San Francisco, CA: Jossey-Bass.

Benade, L. (2015b). Teachers' critical reflective practice in the context of twenty-first century learning. *Open Review of Educational Research 2*(1), 42–54. doi:10.1080/23265507.2014.998159

Benade, L. (2015c). Teaching as inquiry: Well intentioned, but fundamentally flawed. *New Zealand Journal of Educational Studies, 50*(1), 107–120. doi:10.1007/s40841-015-0005-0

Benade, L. (2016. Online early). The role of trust in reflective practice. *Educational Philosophy and Theory.* doi:10.1080/00131857.2016.1142415

Biesta, G. (2014). Pragmatising the curriculum: Bringing knowledge back into the curriculum conversation, but via pragmatism. *The Curriculum Journal, 25*(1), 29–49. doi:10.1080/09585176.2013.874954

Dewey, J. (1910). *How we think* (pp. 1–13). Lexington, MA: D.C Heath. doi:http://dx.doi.org.ezproxy.aut.ac.nz/10.1037/10903-001. Retrieved from http://ovidsp.tx.ovid.com.ezproxy.aut.ac.nz

Education Council New Zealand. (n.d.). *Practising teacher criteria.* Retrieved March 25, 2016 from https://educationcouncil.org.nz/content/practising-teacher-criteria-0

Freire, P. (1998). *Pedagogy of freedom: Ethics, democracy and civic courage.* Lanham, MD: Rowman and Littlefield.

Gilbert, J., Bull, A., Stevens, S. & Giroux, M. (2015). *On the edge: Shifting teachers' paradigms for the future.* Teaching and Learning Research Initiative Research Completed Report. Retrieved from http://www.tlri.org.nz/tlri-research/research-completed/school-sector/edge-shifting-teachers'-paradigms-future

Green, H., Facer, K., Rudd, T., Dillon, P. & Humphreys, P. (2005). *Personalisation and digital technologies.* Bristol, England: Futurelab. Retrieved February 6, 2016 from http://www.nfer.ac.uk/publications/FUTL59/FUTL59_home.cfm

Groff, J. (2013). *Technology-rich innovative learning environments.* OECD CERI Innovative Learning Environments project. Retrieved from http://www.oecd.org/edu/ceri/Technology-Rich%20Innovative%20Learning%20Environments%20by%20Jennifer%20Groff.pdf

Holland, E. W. (2013). *Deleuze and Guattari's 'A Thousand Plateaus': A reader's guide.* London, England/New York, NY: Bloomsbury.

Larrivee, B. (2000). Transforming teacher practice: Becoming the critically reflective teacher. *Reflective Practice, 1,* 293–307. doi:10.1080/14623940020025561

Ministry of Education. (2007). The New Zealand curriculum. Wellington, New Zealand: Learning Media Limited. Available from http://nzcurriculum.tki.org.nz/The-New-Zealand-Curriculum

Reid, A. (2004). Towards a culture of inquiry in DECS. Government of South Australia, Department of Education and Children's Services. Retrieved March 25, 2016 from https://www.researchgate.net/publication/242749924_Towards_a_Culture_of_Inquiry_in_DECS

Schön, D. (1983). *The reflective practitioner: How professionals think in action.* New York, NY: Basic Books.

Smyth, J. (1992). Teachers' work and the politics of reflection. *American Educational Research Journal, 29*(2), 267–300. Retrieved from http://www.jstor.org/stable/1163369

Chapter 8
Responding to 21st Century Learning Policy Demands

> The general effects of policies become evident when specific aspects of change and specific sets of responses (within practice) are related together…I would suggest that in the UK at least (probably also the US, Canada, Australia and New Zealand) the cumulative and general effects of several years of multiple thrusts of educational reform on teachers' work have been profound. (Ball 1993, p. 15)

Policy: The New Zealand Context

These words by Stephen Ball may have been written 23 years ago, but I do not know of a single person of my acquaintance in the teaching profession who would disagree that Ball's analysis is as apt today as it was then. An underlying premise of this book is that 'being' a teacher in the 21st century is being a person who is responsive to, and is responding to, a policy scenario of global origins, taken up at national and regional level, and finally implemented into schools, where teachers (and school leaders) are at the sharp end. In so many ways, this is not new—certainly, in New Zealand (and in many similar countries around the world), the reform drive has been a fact of professional life since the mid-1980s. What changes is the emphasis of the reform, often driven by the political interests of those in government at specific points in time. Esteemed, long-time New Zealand educational policy critic and scholar, John Codd, suggested that policy outlines a course of action that selects goals, defines values and allocates resources (1988), while for Bell and Stevenson (2006), policy states what is to be done, who will benefit and why, and who will pay. From these definitions, it is clear why there is a link between governance and policy, and thus no surprise why their efforts to make good on election promises often results in policies designed to 'fix' the problems highlighted in election campaigns.

That being said, policy design, planning, implementation and evaluation is not a simple or linear process (for example Bell and Stevenson 2006). "There is ad hocery, negotiation and serendipity within the state, within the policy formulation process" (Ball 1993, p. 11). Similarly, there is not a simple and linear relationship between the government of the day and policy; that is to say, there is some consistency and stability across governments, and in this regard, New Zealand has been a good example. The processes and content of educational reform put into train by the Fourth Labour Government in 1984, considered by Codd (2005) to mark the advent of neoliberal education reform, have been maintained by successive governments, to a greater or lesser degree.[1]

These neoliberal reforms in the New Zealand context focussed initially on disengaging the state from a 'hands-on' role by creating mutually independent structures, such as the Ministry of Education and Education Review Office, and developing a strong school self-governance system. Multiple services previously provided by the central state now operate independently, often in a competitive, tender-based structure. Significant reform has influenced curriculum and assessment, while teachers' work has been systematically regulated by appraisal and teacher licensing techniques and structures. Attention has progressively shifted to developing policy that addresses perceived deficiencies in 'literacy' and 'numeracy', and increasingly, New Zealand is following the global emphasis on STEM (science, technology, engineering and mathematics). Specific attention is focussed on ensuring the educational success of Māori and Pasifika. Government policy in relation to education is aimed at all levels of the education system (from early childhood to tertiary), though many of the policies indicated here affect the 'compulsory sector' of primary (elementary) and secondary schooling, which is under the agency of the Ministry of Education.

The 'Briefing to Incoming Minister' issued by the Ministry of Education to successive governments provides a sense of its priorities for education. Its most recent briefing opens with these words: "It is important for New Zealand's future that we have a strong, learner-centred education system". (2014a, p. 4). The Briefing is replete with the terminology of 'the learner' and 'learning', and a key policy focus is to 'meet the needs of the learner', thus "we need to do more to improve achievement" (p. 18). Notable strategies to achieve this aim are to "improve educational leadership, and the quality and relevance of teaching and learning" (p. 18). Considered to be "the most important contribution the education system can make to improve learning" these elements, it is suggested, are supported by "emerging technology...which will transform how the system works". (p. 18). Additional supports now being trialled include the development of initial teacher education in a postgraduate format (a Master of Teaching and Learning degree compressed into one year that creates very strong links between providers and schools), and a 'Community of Learning' system that clusters schools around an achievement focus and that shares expertise across the schools in a cluster. The Briefing makes, interestingly, no reference to school buildings, though there is the *New Zealand School Property Strategy 2011–2021* (MOE 2011), referred to in

---

[1]The Fifth Labour Government of 1999–2008 implemented a slightly more 'humane', Third Way version (see Benade 2012) of educational reform, ushering New Zealand into the 'knowledge economy' and attempting to position New Zealand as a 'knowledge society'.

Chap. 5: "The Ministry of Education, as the owner of state schools, requires a portfolio of well-maintained schools supporting a modern education system that produces skilled people who can contribute towards a productive economy". (p. 3).

The Ministry of Education, which sees itself as "the stewards of the education system" (2014a, p. 50), has reached a high level of policy sophistication that comes from almost three decades of both proposing and producing education policies.[2] Its policy-making processes are subject to multiple influences, which go beyond the Ministry of Education simply being an agency of state power. Policy-making does not occur in a vacuum, but can be contextualised globally (Bell and Stevenson 2006; Robertson 2005). Furthermore, policy processes are not neat, thus, for instance, the relationship between global and local in the policy process does not reflect a simple, linear and downward relationship from global to local. Local (national-level) policies will reflect local variation on the global theme, while simultaneously lessons from the local level can be taken up into global thinking about education policy. This contention helps to inform the current chapter, which will suggest a critical perspective on the broader global policy agenda influencing the local level, and will then attempt to theorise some of the ways that the local can influence the global. These ideas will be illustrated by way of an examination of evidence from the studies at Innovation Primary, Millennial College and Angelus School, with particular reference to the strategic dimension of implementing practices associated with the broad policy emphasis on 21st century learning. This dimension in the life of Holyoake College was dealt with in Chap. 9, thus no reference will be made to Holyoake in this chapter.

Critical Considerations

The Policy Framework: A Critical Perspective

The upsurge in interest in, and increasing demand for, modern or innovative teaching and learning practices has to be understood in the context of a far broader policy framework and discourse in public and academic arenas. The demand for a shift to teaching and learning (with the decided emphasis now on *learning*) that meets the needs of school-leavers in the 21st century is both an implicit and explicit critique of the view of schooling as a period of initiation into past traditions (Loveless and Williamson 2013; Robertson 2005). Rather, there must be a forward-focussed view that sees knowledge not as fixed in tradition, but rather as a spring board for creating the new and previously unimagined possibilities for an indeterminate future (for example see Bolstad and Gilbert 2012; Gilbert and Bull

---

[2]Which is not to discount the many decades of experience of the earlier Department of Education, which operated from 1877 to 1989.

2015). A key to unlocking this door lies in the development of so-called 21st century skills.

Chapter Three referred to several versions and accounts of these skills, now frequently appearing in official policy documents, such as national curriculum statements. Documented lists of skills often include the ability to think critically and creatively, to be adaptable and flexible, and to be literate, numerate and skilled in the use of ICT. In addition, citizens of a 21st century world have to be competent team players to whom collaboration is second nature. Despite frequently emphasising autonomous action, there is the constant reminder of the importance of locating citizenship within the broader context of communities and societies, requiring the development of dispositions such as tolerance and commitment to others. Schools are required to ensure students emerge into the workforce with this battery of skills and dispositions. One of these dispositions, highlighting the focus on the future (rather than on past tradition), is lifelong learning.

The discourse of lifelong learning may be seen not only in relation to ongoing skill development, but in the context of providing broader social cohesion too: "thorough-going lifelong learning should not only be viewed as a means to a dynamic economy, but also for effective community and social engagement, participatory democracy and for living fulfilling and meaningful lives" (Dumont and Istance 2010, p. 23). Creating this social and economic success does not depend solely on government support for lifelong learning however. The trend to lifelong learning has shifted the emphasis of responsibility from society to the autonomous individual, who bears significant responsibility for ensuring that learning never ceases in adult life. The ideal "workers of the future are those…who willingly pay for their own continuous learning" (Coffield 1999, p. 488).

Knowledge becomes capital in the hands of such individuals who are now more or less desirable by virtue of their knowledge, adaptability, flexibility and portable skills. Human capital theory, popularised in the 1960s, suggested a link between personal investment in education and earning power. I previously noted that Brown et al. (2011) called into question the link between 'learning and earning'. The flaws in human capital theory (endorsed by the lifelong learning discourse that was well underway by the start of the 21st century) were clearly summarised in 1999 by Frank Coffield. The reasons he documented included the ability of human capital theory to steer the attention of politicians and public from underlying socio-economic contradictions that allow low wages to persist; its neglect of the value of other kinds of capital (such as social capital); its glossing over the persistence of gendered wage disparities, even among well-educated workers; and its contribution to credential inflation. Depressingly, the work of Brown et al. (2011) suggests that these reasons continued to be relevant a decade on. Also relevant over a decade later are the warnings Coffield sounded regarding the concepts of 'employability' and 'flexibility', where the former disguises the reality of an uncertain job market in which there may be periods of unemployment or underemployment for individuals, in which time they ought to be 'retraining', while the latter disguises the ability of employers to redeploy or underpay workers.

By the late 1990s, when Coffield was writing, policy-makers were locating lifelong learning discourse in the context of the 'knowledge economy' and the kind of 'knowledge society' such an economy required (Robertson 2005). The knowledge economy demanded workers capable of engaging in high-value, knowledge-based activities; this in the context of decreasing reliance on industrial manufacture. In a hard-nosed global 'knowledge economy', various nations seek to gain competitive advantage, hence the intensified discourse around lifelong learning and pressure on societies to support their citizens to acquire and develop the skills and knowledge appropriate for participation in the knowledge economy. Unsurprisingly then, as Dumont and Istance (2010) suggested, the rise of the notion of 'the learner' can be linked to the development of knowledge societies geared to the demands of the knowledge economy, in which digital and electronic ubiquity was increasingly apparent.

In the context of the knowledge economy discourse, global players have set policy direction for individual nations. An example is the OECD, with its key competency research (2003), and its PISA assessment programme. The OECD has, coincidentally, been a leading voice in highlighting what it sees as the shortcomings of 'industrial age' education. Its policy direction has emphasised the human capital value of lifelong learning and the cumulative effect of ongoing engagement with education:

> In modern knowledge-based economies, where the demand for high-level skills will continue to grow substantially, the task in many countries is to transform traditional models of schooling, which have been effective at distinguishing those who are more academically talented from those who are less so, into customised learning systems that identify and develop the talents of all students. This will require the creation of "knowledge-rich", evidence-based education systems, in which school leaders and teachers act as a professional community with the authority to act, the necessary information to do so wisely, and the access to effective support systems to assist them in implementing change. (2009, p. 3)

Thus, not only must the emphasis be on the learning side of the equation, but on the teaching side too, and in this regard, schools and school systems are directly implicated, as indeed they are in the *TALIS* report just quoted. The closing words of the quotation are apt in providing a segue to the next phase of this chapter, where I consider an alternative way to view change, namely as driven outwards from the local (micro) level, extending to the national (meso) level, and ultimately to the global (macro) level.

How Might Change be Effected? Theory and Practice

In Chapter Four, where I discussed the notion of 21st century learning specifically in reference to modern or innovative teaching and learning practices, I used the terms, *macro, meso* and *micro*. Chapter Three noted the influential global governance role-played by the Centre for Educational Research and Innovation (CERI) of the OECD with its 'Innovative Learning Environments (ILE)' research (2013).

The CERI research team worked from a micro to macro perspective (rather than the reverse) to define learning (Dumont et al. 2010). They did this by examining specific examples of innovative learning environments, which enabled the CERI research team to develop a set of ILE learning principles (OECD 2013). The OECD can now use this CERI research base to inform global (macro) system-level measures for implementation across member states.

Thus, in spite of the earlier suggestion of global policy-making influencing local, national policy, it is necessary to develop a sufficiently nuanced understanding to recognise how the local level can influence higher levels of policy and practice. Drawing on the disparate fields of economics, health science and sociology, I wish to evoke a notion of macro–meso–micro as distinct levels of promulgation, implementation and practice. This discussion will contribute insight to the transition from traditional notions of schooling to future-focussed ones.

Economists, Dopfer et al. (2004), regarded knowledge as a system of rules. Understanding is derived from generic rules that emerge from idiosyncratic rules developed over time in specific contexts, namely at the micro-level. These idiosyncratic rules alone, while providing variety, do not lead to understanding. Common or widely understood knowledge requires the development of groups of generic rules that are connected and exist in complementary relationship with other groups. Dopfer et al. (2004) regarded this level of connectedness to exist at a meso-level. Further abstraction and aggregation of groups of meso-level systems elevates understanding and knowledge to the macro level.

It is not that clear that the field of education provides anything like the deterministic regularity and certainty Dopfer et al. (2004) tried to apply to economic analysis. What is helpful though, is to think of a nesting of local, immediate, contextual actions and understandings developing in the context of a broader collection of more systematic and coherent actions and understandings, nested in turn in the context of wider national or even global actions and understandings. A further benefit is to be able to avoid falling into a simple bifurcation of macro and micro. Thus, in terms of policy, it is helpful to avoid a notion of a simple, linear promulgation of policy at a global, macro level (the OECD), its implementation at the meso level (the Ministry of Education), and its practice at a micro level (in the classrooms of individual teachers).

The use of the tripartite macro–meso–micro as a tool of analysis has been shown to be helpful elsewhere, such as in a study of resilience by Bergström and Dekker (2014) who likewise recognised the limitations of a simple bifurcatory macro–micro analysis. They advocated recognition by the health sciences of examining resilience at the individual (micro), organisational (meso) and societal (macro) levels. The meso level is seen to bridge the micro and macro.

In yet another context, that of sociology, Turner and Boyns (2002), argued for a 'macrochauvinistic' position, wherein they saw the macro level having greater influence over the meso and micro: "we will understand much more about the meso and micro by analyzing their embeddedness in macroinstitutional systems than we will by studying micro- and meso-events in order to gain an understanding of the macro level of reality" (p. 361). Importantly, Turner and Boyns did not regard the influence of the macro deterministically, but recognised a dialectical relationship (which they referred to as 'reciprocity'). Nor can the macro level simply be reduced to events and actions at the meso and micro level. A multiplicity of repeated events is required at the micro level to begin exerting influence on the meso level. Fewer repeated events are required at the meso level to influence the system as a whole, although meso-level events must be duplicated across many sets of meso structures in order to have a macro influence.

Macro-level demands emanate from global sources, such as the OECD, and national sources, such as state and Ministry of Education, requiring schools to do more to prepare their students for the 21st century. Individual teachers work at the micro level of their classroom contexts to make sense of, and implement, these aspirational and policy demands. Following the evolutionary microeconomic analysis of Dopfer et al. (2004), it may be suggested that individual teachers engage in problem solving within their professional contexts, evolving and constructing increasingly complex 'rules' (for present purposes, these may be understood as procedures, techniques and strategies). This evolution arises partly from mental and cognitive engagement with new and complex problems. What is missing in the account of Dopfer et al. (2004) is a notion of critically reflective practice, arguably a necessary requirement for this engagement. It is important that critical analyses of the transition from traditional ways of teaching and learning to modern, look beyond simple classroom techniques and strategies, to the more complex hidden mental assumptions teachers bring to their practice (see, for example Benade 2015b, c; and Chapter Seven above), and their ability and willingness to engage those assumptions regarding their professional work in critically reflective ways. Arguably, it is changes to these mental processes that are required if there is to be any change in practice.

For some (such as Bolstad and Gilbert 2012), such shifts are more than evolutionary; they represent a 'paradigm shift'. Coincidentally, in their explanation of 'evolutionary meso-economics', Dopfer et al. (2004), provided an account not out of place with Kuhn's notion of 'paradigm shift' articulated in his classic 1962 work, *The Structure of Scientific Revolutions*. They refer to the meso-level being in a state of disequilibrium, having to resolve the contradictions that arise from this disequilibrium, and managing the tensions between the micro and macro levels. At the meso level (and for purposes of the present analysis, this refers to schools across a region, jurisdiction or nation), change may be prompted by the introduction of new technology, which "creates a niche" (p. 270), filled by the adoption of new practices (in the terms used by Dopfer et al. 2004, a 'generic rule').

A 'meso trajectory' "can be viewed as a three-phase process of origination (emergence), diffusion (adoption and adaptation) and retention (maintenance) of a novel rule" (2004, p. 271). It may thus be theorised that the emergent stage is one in which individual teachers bring about novelty in practice (but, as argued here, preceded by significant shifts in thinking about practice, and in the context of a like-minded school). During the diffusion stage, the new beliefs and practices begin to gain purchase across several schools and among many practitioners.[3] The stage of retention is one of consolidation, new building and enhancement of the new ideas, beliefs and practices associated with teaching and learning, across the entire education system within the country. Taking up the 'macrochauvinistic' position of Turner and Boyns (2002), however, it can be theorised that the initial impetus for change requires the authority and power of the macro level (such as government or Ministry of Education), in the form of policies, directives, and the resourcing of technologies (such as ICT and flexible buildings and furniture). Within the theoretical construction proposed here, therefore, a dialectical relationship is a critical feature of policy formulation, promulgation and implementation, or what Turner and Boyns termed, 'reciprocity'.

Note here the confluence of several ideas in the foregoing:

- the OECD, a significant global originator of ideas, prompts and questions, has recognised the value of making sense of innovative education strategies at the local, micro level, in order to translate these into global, macro policy suggestions;
- the New Zealand Ministry of Education, a meso-level national policy-maker, has initiated the construction and development of technologies to enable personalised learning and skills for the 21st century economy, but does not dictate how this ought to occur; and
- individual teachers and schools (local, micro) develop the influence of their collective practice so that it is taken up more widely at a national (meso) level. This more so now that the 'community of learning' model, a development of the 'Investing in Educational Success' policy of the Ministry of Education (2016b), is gathering momentum.

The following evidential references to the strategic dimension of implementing practices associated with the broad policy emphasis on 21st century learning at Innovation Primary, Millennial College and Angelus School, will shed light on the impacts of this implementation at school level, while also demonstrating the potential of these implementation strategies to be taken up more widely. The chapter will conclude, again, with an analysis of these findings in relation to the concept of intentionality.

---

[3]Innovation Primary hosted approximately 2340 individual visitors from other schools since opening in 2013 till mid August, 2015, while Angelus School hosted visits from 27 schools between February and July 2015.

The Practical Studies

Introduction

Regardless of their source, education policies and initiatives call for specific practices to be brought forth in schools where they are implemented and put into practice. It is this implementation process that is most keenly felt by practitioners. School leaders, notably principals, play a pivotal role by introducing their schools to these policies and initiatives, negotiating the terms of their implementation (or, in negative scenarios, simply imposing these terms), monitoring the ongoing process of implementation, and finally, being accountable for this implementation process. The implementation process has implications across a range of aspects of the daily life of the school and those working in it, including its students and supporting community. All those associated with a school contribute to its culture, though the strategic development of that culture often falls to those in leadership, and, in the New Zealand context, those in governance, namely Boards of Trustees. It is thus important to understand the role-played by the overarching vision in each of the schools in supporting innovative practices. Consideration is also given to the construction of teams working in flexible spaces, teacher recruitment (including Beginning Teachers and relief teachers), support for staff, and the nature of the community relationships in evidence at the three schools.

Vision of, and Support for, Progressive Practices

Strategic and school-wide support for, and encouragement of non-traditional practices is important in developing a strong, single and school-wide understanding of what progressive approaches to teaching and learning look like. An ideal encapsulated by the concept of flexible learning environments is the belief that they provide an opportunity to liberate pedagogy (which is taken here to mean both teachers' practice and their thinking about their practice and education more generally) from the shackles of a traditional past. The schools in this study, by virtue of their commitment to developing pedagogy suited to flexible learning environments, have sought to develop a different vision of what might occur in schools now and in the future. Thus it may be suggested that the schools are supporting their teachers and communities to transition from a traditional vision of education to one that is more progressive, innovative, flexible and relevant to present times. There are several outward examples of this transition as the schools enact their vision of this education.

A common commitment of each school is to focus on developing relational pedagogies that seek to engage students positively with the learning process. One indicator is seen in the adult–student relationships encouraged within the schools. Innovation Primary and Millennial College embody these relations by permitting students access to areas that in traditional settings may be regarded as 'out of bounds'. Highly permeable spaces at Innovation Primary include the teachers' stations, located within learning areas. Despite having functions such as teachers interviewing individual students or preparing for class, students are able to move freely in and out of this area, and use the computers located there during class time. Innovation Primary is committed to the conscious eradication of hierarchies, thus students are welcome into the teachers' tea lounge area, and first names are the norm. At Millennial College, while the teachers' work areas are located away from the learning spaces, here too, students may enter the staffroom to speak with staff. Angelus School retains some traditional elements, embodied by clearer physical boundaries within and between spaces, such as the staffroom, nevertheless, students in the flexible environments are able to utilise the small staff breakout areas.

Various teacher participants across the three schools generally stated that their development of progressive and creative approaches to pedagogy relied on, and benefitted by, the institutional support of their schools, unlike some other schools they knew, where progressive pedagogies are kept behind closed doors, sheltered from the critical and disapproving gaze of colleagues and school leadership. It is liberating for the teacher participants to know "that you can just give things a go" (teacher, Innovation Primary, FG), a sentiment shared by the other focus group participants. Millennial College too, overtly sanctions innovation. Two teachers speaking in the Angelus School focus group mentioned their utter surprise at finding a colleague from a different school, who seemed to know nothing of student agency, "because that's all our school is about". It is equally important to note too that the teacher participants across all three schools shared a personal commitment to the values of their respective schools. The following comment may have been made on behalf of all: "Fundamentally you have to believe in the values of the school...It might look different for some of us but I know that we all do. And we all put children at the heart of what we do".

The principals of the three schools provided deeper insight to the ways in which their schools are able to project, promote and support visions that will enable (and require) staff to work towards a more liberating style of pedagogy—liberating for staff and students. The Millennial College principal referred to the school's firm commitment to relational pedagogy as suggested by Russell Bishop (for example 2011). This approach encourages teachers not only to centre the process of teaching and learning on the students, but also to validate their life experience as meaningful and significant to their education.

Particular discourses are created at all three schools, raising alternative notions about the experience of school. Language plays an important role in this process of discourse creation. At Millennial College, for example at the time of my interview with the principal, a 'pathways coordinator' was soon to be appointed. In traditional or conventional secondary schools, this would simply be a 'careers teacher'. This coordinator would work with the 'learning coaches' (approximates to a 'form teacher' in conventional secondary schools, though combines some of the pastoral role of a Dean). The pathways coordinator will support students to develop their personalised "pathway to a range of possible futures" (Principal, IV).

While Angelus School retains some traditional elements, such as referring to teachers as 'teachers', there is a firm commitment in school policy and practice to "modern learning practice" (Principal, IV). This is operationalised in several ways, such as focussing language on 'learners' and 'learning', 'student agency', and 'ownership of learning'. Practice goes beyond language signs, as there is a school-wide expectation that teachers will seek to model this language in talk and action.

Also common to all three schools is the dedicated focus to developing skills, dispositions and (in the case of Angelus School) virtues. Innovation School (like Millennial College) uses the language of coaching, and calls its teachers 'learning advisors'. Its principal discourages staff from overplanning, and expects the staff to think about the dispositions they will 'attach' to a 'big idea' in curriculum planning, to ensure that their students are "growing themselves as a learner and as a human being" (Principal, IV).

Recruitment and Team Construction

Angelus School

Staff recruitment is problematic in different ways for the three schools. The issue of recruitment presents somewhat differently for Angelus School than it does for either Innovation Primary or Millennial College. The chief difference resides first in the Catholic special character of Angelus School, requiring that it recruit a certain percentage of teachers to fill 'tagged' positions, exclusively held by practicing Catholic teachers. This requirement places constraints on the principal, and her Board of Trustees, who have to find not only teachers qualified and disposed to working collaboratively in flexible spaces, but who, in some cases, must also be able and willing to fill a 'tag', and in all cases, to be willing to uphold the special Catholic character. The second difference lies in the mixed nature of Angelus School, having begun its life in 2010 as a traditional single-cell school. Thus, the foundation teachers,[4] while recruited with an eye on their ability to support the school to reach its visionary aspirations (which included elements of future focus) did not join the staff thinking they might be teaching in collaborative teams working in large, shared flexible environments.

Against this background, in her interview, the principal made her recruitment commitments clear: "Special character comes first. I want to know what's in here" (pointing to her heart). When interviewing an applicant, she considers how the applicant will fit into the team in the flexible learning environments. "It's like a marriage", she believed, as the team members must be capable of open and honest communication and a commitment to "work things out". This metaphorical

---

[4]The first teachers employed at a new school.

reference to marriage was echoed by a teacher in the focus group at Angelus School, for whom team construction meant "entering a committed monogamous relationship with your team and commit[ing] to being there together through everything". Unsurprisingly, then, the principal is not attracted to applicants who make definitive 'I-oriented' statements in interviews. "We're a learning school" therefore, applicants have to have an open mind to learning, and should not imagine they have "conquered teaching" (Principal, IV).

Team building at Angelus School depends significantly on the display of attributes of flexibility and willingness to cede control. These are "bottom lines" that are essential to success. Teachers must be able to give up saying, "these are my children, this is my cupboard, my space…and even…this is my planning" (Principal, IV). To be successful in teams requires that team members see and acknowledge the strengths of others, and recognise their personal limitations.

On the other hand, both Innovation Primary and Millennial College were founded as schools with flexible learning spaces and a commitment to a full-blown futures orientation, underpinned by progressive pedagogy. This has had a bearing on the qualifications, experience, and, in particular, the dispositions, of teachers seeking to be recruited to those schools.

Millennial College

The prospect of working differently, in regard to collaboration, space and curriculum, act as magnets:

> for those teachers it's not necessarily about the subject…there's something about having more flexibility or being more open to things that's really appealing, that you're not confined by a whole lot of content, that you can actually take your concepts of what you value and how you work with young people to another level. (teacher, FG)

Not only does working in different ways appeal to applicants: "nearly every application…[received]…people are voicing the frustration of this system they're in" (senior leader, FG). This participant listed the dispositions a successful applicant to Millennial ought to display: "openness, flexibility and wanting to try new things and being able to see beyond their subject silos." This latter disposition is especially important at Millennial, because of its integrated curriculum approach. Ironically, the principal is clear that his teachers must be subject specialists, with a deep understanding of their specialism. This knowledge will enable teachers to quickly grasp what curriculum content to match to the individual interests and needs of students.

Up until late 2016, the school had not struggled to attract applicants, with demand for jobs outstripping available positions. More challenging at the outset was that most applicants lacked the experience, knowledge or understanding of working in a school such as Millennial. Since opening, however, potential applicants are able to visit, and form a view of teaching and learning in the flexible spaces. While many applicants are unsuccessful, several applicants make successive attempts at winning positions, "and a number of [recent] appointments...have been people who have put their hat in the ring second time round." (Principal, IV). Ideally, these applicants will have a working idea of what personalised learning may mean in a secondary environment, and will be committed to self-reflective inquiry. The willingness and ability to work collaboratively with others is critical, and applicants must be able to provide some evidence of their experience in collaboration. Significantly, applicants must be disposed to seeking and making links outside and beyond the school in order to make learning "relevant and authentic" for students.

Collaborative work is at the heart of the pedagogical practices in schools with flexible learning environments, thus correct team composition is critical. Despite his openness to inexperienced teachers, the Millennial College principal ensures that no team consists of two inexperienced teachers. The teams work in delivering the integrated modules to students, thus they bring together two learning areas. While he can control this team composition, he is unable to control for teachers coming from contexts where they never have worked in teams, and have possibly no experience of offering integrated curriculum units. A mutually supportive coaching model is applied to developing this experience within the teams, as each team member brings different curriculum knowledge and strengths. Nevertheless, one of the 'pairing principles' he and his leadership team apply is to encourage teachers to work with a person they can learn from, rather than someone with whom they are comfortable.

Innovation Primary

The principal has noticed a steady decline in the number of applicants for positions at his school as time has elapsed since foundation. He assumed this meant the school had exhausted the pool of likely applicants living in the vicinity of the school. His views concerning the kind of applicants he looks for echoed the sentiments of his opposite number at Angelus School. He looks for applicants who have a growth mindset and a disposition to being a learner, rather than someone "who thinks they've mastered teaching". Interestingly too, he wanted a commitment to the ideal of teaching as "an active service". Thus he encourages his teachers to take some interest in the extramural activities of their students.

This principal, like his colleagues in the other two schools, has to think carefully about team construction, partly because teachers are foreign to the idea of collaboration. A person's life experience as a student at school then university is generally not one of collaboration, but rather hierarchical relationships. The act of sharing physical working space with colleagues, and actively planning and working together as a cohesive team on a single project is not common in traditional single-cell schools, where teachers often develop individualistic ways of working. Thus, once teachers begin their careers, they quickly fall into the pattern of privatised practice. The teams at Innovation are on a continuum of development, some working "incredibly effectively and [some] that are still learning how to work together."

(Principal, IV). Creating team agreements, that outline agreed values and strategies for collaborative work, is a strategy currently under trial. A senior leader assigned to work with teachers to develop their pedagogical practice was supporting this strategy. The particular values given priority relate to learning, not behaviour: "What do we truly value about learning? If we truly value this, this means this is how we have to act to make that happen". (Principal, IV).

Beginning Teachers (BT)

The challenge of recruiting teachers includes a consideration of whether beginning teachers (BT) make successful or desirable recruits to work in the schools in this study. The evidence across the three schools is not clear-cut. Working in an environment with a radical commitment to personalised learning will make significant demands on teachers, who already find themselves in a time-consuming profession. The demands of modern teaching and learning practice, incorporating digital technology, and working in a team in shared environments all require teachers to carefully manage their time. While not all BTs are young, the likelihood of a growing Gen Y or Millennial[5] workforce is a consideration, and the principal of Innovation Primary noted evolving attitudes to work. He was seeing shifting attitudes regarding work hours among younger teachers differing from those who accepted the 70-h working week he experienced as a teacher, suggesting this may be a reason to prefer more mature, experienced teachers. For many now, "a big day is 8 until 4 and that's it". He stated his reluctance to appoint BTs, as they "have to be pretty bloody exceptional...[with]...an intimate knowledge of the national curriculum and...have a range of tools available at [their] fingertips". (Principal, Innovation Primary, IV).

These comments raise some interesting concerns and tensions. Social media is replete with notions of a new 'generation gap', this time between 'baby boomers'[6] and subsequent generations, particularly 'Gen Y' and more lately 'Millennials' who are claimed to have very different work attitudes to their older counterparts. Specifically, such notions as 'work-life balance' have become central to the way work is conceived, and is somewhat echoed by legislative attempts in various countries to enable employers and employees to build greater flexibility into working hours, for example. More negative notions abound in common discourse such as 'Gen Y' and 'Millennials' having 'entitled' attitudes to work that rankle with their older, experienced colleagues. Meanwhile, 'baby boomers' are accused of having caused various socio-economic problems, such as inflated house prices[7]. This is not to suggest that any of these attitudes necessarily prevail at any of the three schools in this study, and from a school teaching perspective, it is difficult to

---

[5]Gen Y or Millennials are generally understood to be born between 1980 and 2000.
[6]Those born post-1945 till around 1965.
[7]Some examples: Dyson (2014) and Stein (2013).

imagine teaching as anything like a 40 h a week job. Nevertheless, just as school children born in the last 15 years are presenting very differently than did preceding generations of school-goers, so teachers born in the last forty years come to their work with different attitudes and expectations than did their older counterparts who will have experienced the post-1945 world, the Cold War, manufacturing economies and emergent technologies.

While there is more openness to appointing BTs at Angelus School, the principal will do so as long as there are experienced teachers in the team who can act as mentors. One of the differences between these two schools that may account for this difference in attitude is their stage of development and size of staff. In 2015, at the time of the research, Innovation was running teams of two, whereas Angelus, from the time of opening its flexible learning environments, operated these with teams of three, and in the case of its Year 5/Year 6 shared environment, has four teachers working in a team. It is reasonable to suggest that the bigger teams allow the integration of a BT, whereas in a team of two, the experienced partner is likely to carry a significant burden. During the first two years of operation, Millennial had four BTs. In the final term of 2015, the principal sought to appoint ten new staff, and was "open to any of those being PRT" (Provisionally Registered Teachers).

Related to the question of BTs is the question of Initial Teacher Education (ITE), a point on which the principals of Innovation Primary and Angelus School both held strong views. To some extent, they conveyed the sense that ITE providers (the university schools and faculties of education) are failing in their task by not preparing new recruits for working in a futures dimension, and specifically for working in flexible environments. "At university you could be modelling what that's like in a shared environment and that would be part of preparing because [what is important is] actually being in the space and working closely with colleagues". (Principal, Angelus School, IV). The principal of Innovation Primary echoed this sentiment, as he regarded collaborative work to be foreign to most teaching graduates, thus helping to explain his reluctance to employing BTs.

These views regarding ITE require attention by providers (such as universities). Given the commitment of the New Zealand Ministry of Education to the provision of flexible learning environments in every school within the next half decade, and given the uptake in new generation building in other jurisdictions, such as Australia and various European nations, it is not unrealistic to expect that ITE providers will have to do more to prepare student teachers for eventual work in settings requiring collaborative team work, the development of dispositional and integrated curricula, and the development of strategies to deepen students' experience of personalised learning. A fundamental barrier, however, is the significant experiential gap that exists between lecturer experience and school classroom reality. For many teacher educators, their experience of schooling and school teaching is the very model that is challenged by modern and innovative teaching and learning approaches. Thus, not only are teachers having to learn new skills and strategies, but so too teacher educators, suggesting an area of both future professional learning, but also research.

Supporting Staff

A common challenge facing school leaders is experienced by the three principals in this study, namely to manage novelty and the challenge of the new, while supporting teachers to alter their mindset. All the while, prevailing attitudes and directions in teaching continue to encourage traditional mainstream approaches. Professional learning, induction and teacher experience are critical ingredients.

Teachers who have moved out from schools with very fixed routines and planning systems to work in flexible learning environments are required to radically re-examine their beliefs—"our big challenge is around creating opportunities for people to change their mental models of what school should be." (Principal, Innovation Primary, IV). This principal plays a role in providing active support to the teachers on his staff in managing this process: "So my job is to get to know them as learners and if I know them as learners I know when to impact on them and when to leave them alone or when to provide challenge". One way he supports their learning is by walking around, consciously looking at teaching practice. He then raises questions with teachers in one-to-one conversations, particularly when their practice appears to be traditional and teacher-directed. In the course of these conversations, he also welcomes staff feedback on his own performance, and is pleased when they begin to challenge him.

For this principal, professional learning (or 'PD' as its is often called) must be 'reimagined' and its starting point should always be to return teachers to the "wonderful triangle" of vision, learning values and desired pedagogy. Innovation Primary provides intensive staff induction training to prepare teachers to work in its environments, and teachers can provide reflective feedback on those aspects of induction that worked or did not work. An induction page on the staff portal contains readings as well as ongoing reflective comments by current staff concerning the quality and nature of their own experiences at the school. Importantly, this ongoing flow of information helps to shape the language of new teachers, meaning new teachers "can be slowly shifting their mental model of schooling as they come. It's baptism by fire." (Principal, IV).

It could be suggested that this process legitimates a particular discourse, also suggesting staff willingness to 'buy in' to this emergent and developing discourse of teaching and learning. Unsurprisingly then, the principal has an expectation that the teachers at Innovation Primary with experience, and who have successfully transitioned into being 'teachers of the future' have to also become the future leaders of the school, mentoring and leading others. Their role is not only that of being a mentor and guide, but also to be 'critical friends'. An Assistant Principal is assigned to work with various staff members as a mentor who supports their pedagogical practice.

Schools in New Zealand have to provide support for themselves and their teachers by using their operational grants[8] because the Ministry of Education is not

---

[8]The annual funding allocation schools receive from the Ministry of Education.

providing support. Managing roll growth means that the principal of Millennial College has more teachers to induct and support. This induction process took on a new level of significance as the college prepared for 2016, as no less than ten new teachers were to be appointed for the new year. The significant role played by experienced staff in evaluating the school's induction processes was noted as a feature, as their feedback is helpful in evolving the induction programme.

Like his counterpart at Innovation Primary, the principal of Millennial College too looks to the teachers as his 'class', and invites their feedback on his own performance, using strategies such as confidential staff surveys. These results have enabled him to be more reflective over aspects of his practice that he was taking for granted as effective for all. There is a level of irony in this notion of a principal thinking of staff members as a 'class' or as 'learners', in part because it seems to foster some of the traditional values and norms of the 'school of the past'. Clearly, these leaders take seriously their commitment to lifelong learning and the importance of supporting teachers to make this difficult transition from traditional pedagogical modes to innovative approaches, but there must be some self-management required to monitor the boundary between telling teachers what they should be practicing and sharing that learning journey with them.

At Angelus School, there is an ongoing requirement to support teachers, but that support is now geared towards developing modern or innovative teaching and learning practices. The principal and her leadership team are overtly committed to ensuring the school-wide uptake of these practices, to better meet personal learning needs. This process is perhaps more keenly felt as this school has a blended model of single cell and flexible learning spaces. Currently, in the course of their six years at this primary school, students move into, then out of, and then back into the flexible learning environments. It is thus a priority that they have coherent and consistent learning experiences across the range of classes. Thus opportunities are created for all teachers to develop their skill at collaborative teamwork, and by cross-grouping across cohorts, teachers (and students) begin to develop a sense of flexible and porous boundaries, rather than rigid ones. Of significant formative benefit to those teachers working in single-cell rooms is having colleagues working in flexible spaces, as they are able to (and are encouraged to) spend time in those spaces watching their colleagues at work.

Teachers must be willing to experiment, take risks, and be open to failure: "it's only when you go into that space and you actually have to work within it can you know what it feels like." (Principal, Angelus School, IV) This principal believes it is her role to be able to listen to teachers in order to support them. In supporting them, she takes the view that there is no single set way to approach being a teacher in a flexible learning environment. This is a cautionary message she repeats to visitors who are keen to replicate in their schools what they see at Angelus School. In this regard, she may taking a somewhat different tack to her two counterparts at Innovation Primary and Millennial College, who are perhaps more certain in their views concerning the practice they anticipate seeing as they walk about their schools. Both positions have their merits—on one hand, teachers (like students) appreciate some certainty about a school's pedagogical expectations, while on the other, teachers and leaders together negotiating and shaping a unique pedagogical approach is entirely consistent with the personalised and constructivist approaches flexible learning environments make possible. On balance, each of these principals would be committed to both ends of the spectrum I have just outlined, but each would prioritise different shades on that spectrum at different times.

Looking Outward—The Community

The Quality of Relationship

'Open door' best describes the nature of the relationship each of the schools have with their communities. For Innovation Primary, this relationship is "not as strong as we'd like it with all families, but it's a work in progress" (Principal, IV), representing a continuum from those parents who take a hands-off approach to those who are strongly involved. The staff focus group at Innovation Primary confirmed the open-door policy, and teachers encourage parents to enter the learning area, notably at pick-up time in the afternoons.

At Angelus School, "if parents want to ask any questions they know that they are very welcome" (Principal, IV). She described the school–community relationship as 'strong', though this is to be understood as the school was in its fifth year in 2015. The principal of Millennial College stated that "powerful partnerships" is a guiding concept, which helps to structure relationships with families. The school's 'open-door' policy is "the best thing we've done", (school leader, FG) because any parent is free to come into discuss their concerns.

Nature and Forms of Contact

Three-way conferencing at termly parent–teacher meetings is common across all three schools. These opportunities enable students to share their self-tracking documentation with their families, and to discuss their learning journeys and academic progress. Apart from teachers and students experiencing significant transitional experiences in education, it may be expected that parents require 're-education', because 'school' as they knew it is a far-cry from what is rapidly evolving now. Students are able support their own parents in this process of transition, and the practice of 'three-way conferencing' helps in this regard. Millennial has an open evening, when the students walk their families around the school to discuss their own learning journey. Regular newsletters are also common, and those from Innovation Primary include topical readings for parents, that are "challenging them to reimagine what's possible". (Principal, Innovation Primary, IV) Regular parent workshops are also common to the three schools. These give the leadership and staff at the schools the opportunity of sharing their vision of teaching and learning with the parents. At Angelus School, the introduction of BYOD and the nature of teaching and learning in the flexible spaces have been shared and discussed at parent workshops. The benefit of these is that "we learn from parents as much as they learn from us." (Principal, IV).

Cultural Connection

Questions relating to the cultural connections in the school, while they may not seem obviously relevant, are in fact central in at least two important respects—the first being to the question of culturally responsive pedagogy, the other to restorative justice practices (for a discussion of both, see Chap. 3). These are evident in all three schools. The principles of culturally responsive pedagogy have been particularly well developed through Bishop's *Te Kōtahitanga*[9] (2011) work. Its premise is that Māori students require approaches that are not typically Western, but rather more in keeping with the strongly relational, cooperative and community dimensions of Māori culture.

Cultural connections at Innovation Primary, like its general community-building processes, are considered by its principal to be a 'work in progress'. Although the school has tried to cater for unique Māori and Pacific Island[10] groups, these families prefer to be integrated with the mainstream community body[11]. The school roll, in late 2015, included about 28% Māori.[12] The principles of *Te Kōtahitanga* (Bishop 2011) underpin the approach taken by Innovation Primary in working with its Māori and Pacific Island communities. Important focal points include providing academic opportunities for both Māori and Pacific Island students to achieve; for Māori to learn their language; and for the school to live out the principles of the Treaty of Waitangi.[13] Millennial College is similarly committed to the principles of the *Te Kōtahitanga* programme developed by Russell Bishop (2011), and the belief that Māori can achieve as Māori. The College has a dedicated staff member who supports other teachers to develop culturally responsive pedagogies.

Angelus School is multi-ethnic (more than 20 ethnicities), consisting (at the time, in 2015) of 3% Māori. The special Catholic character of the school is its unifying vision: "we don't single out specific cultures generally in our day-to-day running....[but]...we are a very inclusive school." (Principal, IV). This special

---

[9]Meaning, 'unity'.

[10]This is an inelegant description applied to various, diverse and unique national groups originating from the many island nations of the South Pacific. Most notable in New Zealand are people from Samoa, Tonga and Fiji, but others include Niue and the Cook Islands.

[11]Legally, New Zealand is a bi-cultural nation, consisting of Māori in a special relationship with the British Crown government representatives in New Zealand. Nevertheless, New Zealand prides itself on being culturally and ethnically diverse. Individual national and cultural groups are encouraged to maintain and develop their rich diversity of language and culture. For many, however, full integration into the dominant, European, society is thought to be essential.

[12]Which exceeds the national figure of around 15%.

[13]The founding document establishing the relationship between Māori and the British Crown.

character is supported by the Māori community, as evidenced by the consultative feedback the school has received from its Māori community. Nevertheless, the school provides many cultural opportunities, such as offering a *kapahaka* group,[14] now enhanced by having a Māori-speaking staff member. This teacher also supports her colleagues as they offer Te Reo Māori[15] language classes. At Angelus School too, there is an emphasis on living out the bicultural spirit of the Treaty of Waitangi.

Community Attitudes and Expectations

The families may be in a more significant state of transition than the children due to the temporal distance between themselves now and when they were at school. They are required "to rethink the idea of what education is" (teacher, Innovation Primary, FG). Parental attitudes are strongly shaped by their own experience of learning, and there appears to be a disconnection between their experience and the emergent experience of their children. Teachers in the Innovation Primary focus group theorised that because parents' experience of "learning…was harder…miserable…painful…tedious and boring", they wrongly assume their children are "not learning anything", because learning now appears to be "fun and exciting."

This experience was repeated at Angelus School, where it was noted that parents suspected that device use in school equated to "just mucking around [whereas] they're actually writing on their blog" (teacher, FG). Similarly, some parents seemingly do not understand the use of play dough and blocks in construction, an area of work in the maths curriculum. Thus, a significant challenge is to help parents see that teaching has shifted from "the Stone Age…where it was the teacher…at the front and you sit there and copy what the teacher is saying" (teacher, FG).

Homework, or rather its absence, also affects parental attitudes, as their expectation is a homework regime. For some parents, there may be a linear relationship between the amount of homework provided and the likely academic progress of their child, yet this attitude is sometimes challenged by the reality of students achieving academically, despite minimal homework.

The principal of Angelus School noted that some parents may exhibit anxiety over their children being moved into the 'shared spaces' at Angelus, where a mixed model of single cells and flexible spaces are in operation: "It's not an easy thing for parents because it's so different from the way we all went to school". Here, the open-door policy of the school helps to allay parental fears. Still, negative media commentary on flexible learning environments may also shape parental attitudes, because "a nervous parental community" are fearful of their children being used as 'guinea pigs' (senior leader, Millennial College, FG). Critical (and from the perspective of the principal of Millennial College, uninformed) comment was reported

---

[14]A cultural Māori dance group popular in many New Zealand schools.
[15]The Māori language.

in certain media in 2015 (Johnston 2015; Morris 2015; Walters 2015). In the last of these, it was suggested by a principal of a traditional high school that to remain "at or near the top of the ladder" (Walters 2015), meant not risking the chance of a failed 'experiment' (flexible learning environments). In 'top' schools instead, the emphasis would remain on traditional teaching, including 40-min periods and teacher control.

Negative media reporting on schools with flexible learning environments place these schools under the gaze of the critical public eye. In an interview with the principal of Millennial College soon after the Walters article (2015) was published, he reacted firmly, questioning the wisdom of reporters seeking comment from school leaders with no experience of working with flexible environments and innovative pedagogies. He suspected too that there are discriminatory undertones in the critiques of some who believe that progressive teaching and learning practices in flexible learning spaces are designed for middle class students, and that Māori and Pacific Island students will not respond well in such radical structures.

Parents at Angelus have demanding expectations of the school in relation to formalised maths, reading and writing activities. This expectation is related to parents being "quite obsessed on assessment data" (teacher, FG). Community expectations that their children's progress at school should be reflected in increased reading age levels, maths stages and spelling ages are in tension and contradiction with the focus of the teachers on the development of dispositions. The Angelus teachers want parents to recognise "how much [the children are] taking responsibility, look at the skills they're developing". Although Innovation Primary is in a neighbourhood 40 km distant, its principal experiences similar pressures, finding himself having to challenge these expectations. As many of the Innovation parents are "high flyers… [who]…actually employ people", it is possible for the principal to help them realise their schooling did not prepare them for the workplace. Sometimes, however, the space between parental expectations and what the school provides is too stark and wide: "they'll wander down and see the big open spaces and [ask], 'where's my child's desk? They don't have a desk. Oh we don't want to go here'. They walk out".

On Reflection

Intentionality

This chapter has tried to capture some of the broader policy texture that rubs up against daily life in schools with flexible learning environments and that are dwelling with different ways of teaching and learning. I have endeavoured to provide a critical sense of the New Zealand education policy context, which has evolved steadily since the mid-1980s to a level of sophistication not realised at the outset. The intent of the 1984 reforms was regarded by critics (for example Codd

2005; Snook 2003; Thrupp 1998) to be a reflection of the neoliberal, monetarist political policies being adopted by many Western states in the wake of Reaganism and Thatcherism. As I suggested earlier, despite the shift to more sophisticated 'Third Way' politics in New Zealand during the Helen Clark[16] era, critics (such as Roberts 2005) contend that the broad neoliberal intent of the initial reforms remains, however, featuring a 'hands-off' state, represented by the Ministry of Education, devolved authority structures that remain accountable to the centre through such agencies as the Education Review Office, and various structures and arrangements that encourage competition and contestability within the education system. This policy thrust draws heavily on, and is influenced by, global players, notably the Organisation for Economic Cooperation and Development.

This global influence resides particularly in the manifestations of a global economy, specifically the notion of a 'knowledge economy', which has arisen in the context of the declining importance of manufacturing and Fordist conceptions of the economy. In its stead, has arisen, in tandem with the annihilation of space and time by the rapid evolution of digital technology, the demand for 'smart' workers and solutions that provide services and add value. The policy response has been to centre the 'learner' in a discourse of lifelong learning and the promotion of human capital ideology. In this policy scenario, 'learning is earning', and the stuff of schooling is no longer disciplinary knowledge, but skills for the 21st century. The place to develop these, and the manner in which they are to be developed, is not the traditional, didactic classroom dominated by the sole teacher, but technologically rich, modern and flexible learning spaces, capable of accommodating multiple students, facilitated by teams of 'coaches' or 'learning advisors'.

This chapter tried to deliver the argument that policy does not slide easily from promulgation through development, to implementation on the ground. Nor does the change invoked by policy necessarily emanate from the centre or from a global, macro, source. The changes can be effected at a local or micro level, and work their way up to the centre through a series of intermediate developments at a meso level. In the New Zealand context, the newly developed 'Communities of Learning' (COL), a product of 'Investing in Educational Success' (Ministry of Education 2016b) may, for example provide one such meso-level platform.[17] The contributions of individual teachers to social media, such as Twitter and blogging, provide another platform, by which the politics of change may be communicated.

For any of this to happen, however, requires that there be a unified, localised or micro level, strategic effort. Apart from the micro, local level being the harbinger and advocate of change, it is also at this level that policy implementation is most keenly felt. While preceding chapters have focussed on impacts on teachers, this chapter has focussed more consistently on school leaders', notably principals',

---

[16]The 37th Prime Minister of New Zealand, 1999–2008.

[17]The COL is a cluster of educational providers from early childhood to post secondary, usually in a common geographical area, working together primarily to raise student achievement in part by sharing practice.

actions and views. To illustrate the theme of intentionality, to capture the notion of participants moving towards the phenomena of interest in meaningful ways that attest to their attempts to make sense of policy intent, I have selected to consider some challenges for leaders of pedagogy in schools. I will do this again by probing into their voices, in this case, the three principals. I will consider three different aspects, as readers will learn valuable lessons from each. The three aspects that cross over both flexible learning spaces and innovative pedagogy are deprivatisation, school-wide pedagogical change, and collaboration.

During our interview, the principal of Innovation Primary discussed his perspectives on the notion of deprivatised practice. He linked it to *visible* practice, that is to say, practice that was capable of being shared around for the benefit of all the teachers. Practices of course are more than just physical actions in the classroom or learning space—they include ways of disseminating important assessment information:

> ...the idea of visible learning is really important and some of the stuff on the walls, you'll see—that's last year's results around national standards and things. That's on the wall in every learning space. So parents can see it, staff can see it, kids can see it. *We're not hiding that stuff*. (Emphasis added)

From the perspective of privatised, traditional approaches to schooling, to openly publish results, such as National Standards, which reveal the students who are above, at or below standards in literacy and numeracy, could be considered to place some teachers in a compromising position. By hiding results, potentially deficient practice (assuming there is a link between classroom practice and student achievement) remains hidden. Making results transparently public, places teaching practice in full view of everyone. This may, arguably, place undue pressures on teachers. From the policy perspective of the New Zealand Ministry of Education, however, "we need to do more to improve achievement" (2014a, p. 18). Thus to publish student results on the walls at Innovation Primary can be justified by its principal, as a step towards ensuring the "quality and relevance of teaching and learning" (p. 18).

There was a further, compelling, perspective he had on deprivatisation, which may be focussed on achieving the same end:

> Now, if you're in single cell classrooms what happens behind the closed door? For most principals, they have no idea. So the practice can be privatised. Here in this environment—and modern learning environments are great for it—you can't hide. So it's easy for me to see. It's visible all the time.

While this comment may appear overly punitive or Foucauldian in its intent, he qualified it by saying, "I will provide high challenge plus high support." Here he sees his task as supporting his teachers to raise their own standards and to be accountable to him for the practices he witnesses, when these do not meet his expectations.

As Angelus School would mix flexible learning spaces and single cell classrooms, the principal stated in late 2013, just prior to the opening of the flexible learning spaces, that she and her "leadership team is quite determined...[not]...to run two separate schools." The solution was to ensure a uniform approach: "We want the pedagogy to change right across the school." In the planning stages, this meant taking a whole-school approach to teaching and learning, and specific preparation, before the flexible spaces were ready to be handed over, included the division of the staff into a "junior team, middle team, senior team. And then those teams would cross-group for maths, or cross-group for reading."(Principal, IV, 2013). What this led to was the diffusion of students across teachers within a team, which would help to embed the notion of shared responsibility for students, and the minimisation of the language of possession or ownership over students. Making this mental shift, for any school, places new demands on teachers, who can easily lose the close relationship they have with 30 students in a single cell room.

Nevertheless, speaking in the middle of 2015, the principal remained resolved to her position of developing a school-wide pedagogy: "…it wasn't just about the buildings, it was more about what was going to happen within." She acknowledged the concern she and her fellow senior leaders shared when considering the real prospect of "both pedagogies and how do you hook those two together…?" As noted earlier, however, she is also resolved to the position that schools must work out the best solutions for themselves:

> …you don't know what you don't know when…[you first walk]…into those environments. So as a leader I'd never taught in a modern learning environment before, so there's no way I could say to the people this is how you do it and this is the way it should happen. *But I did have certain bottom lines* and one of them would be that it would be *our room, our space, our children* so the children would be shared and there wouldn't be your class, my class, her class sort of thing. (Principal, IV. Emphasis added)

A further guiding principle—in the midst of uncertainty—was to break decisively with tradition, and not "bring single room practices into a modern learning space", which required a radical reformulation of practice, though there was a period of trial and error. Quite simply, "there is no right and wrong way of doing things. It's basically you get in, try things and if it doesn't work fail quickly and try something else." A key to such working-though is collaboration.

Coincidentally, her opposite number at Millennial College made a similar comment about his lack of experience: "What I'm realising is that I'm requiring to show some leadership around a way of teaching that I'[ve] not actually experience [d] myself as a teacher."(Principal, IV). Realising that he is "not the font of all knowledge or much knowledge at all about…how you actually do this stuff", he has instituted a number of weekly meetings with his staff, when they have the opportunity of "sharing and developing expertise around how you teach in this place." There is much to learn—not only is an integrated curriculum being offered, but the curriculum is packaged into modules, the timetable reflects large blocks of time, rather than multiple shorter 'periods', so that teachers will see their students less often than occurs in a typical school setting, *and* the teachers are working in teams, with large groups of students in shared learning areas. A critical ingredient is collaboration: "How do you use student voice? How do you plan collaboratively, teach collaboratively? What are the ways that you can teach collaboratively?"

(Principal, IV). Team construction is a further critical ingredient, and so-called 'pairing principles' have been developed by the senior leaders. One of these principles is to steer teachers away from pairing "with somebody…they were comfortable working with…[pairing instead]…[with those who are]…good at this collaborative teaching." (Principal, IV).

In Conclusion

The success of bringing about fundamental change to the pedagogical practices of teachers—and this much seems a requirement of using new flexible spaces to their full potential—may be determined by some crucial factors. Among these is enabling implementation that is democratic rather than hierarchical (Woolner et al. 2012). The warnings of Blackmore et al. (2011), Cleveland and Fisher (2014), and Moore and Lackney (1993) must be heeded, that adequate account of pedagogy is taken, else teachers will merely default to traditional practice.

The three principals reviewed here make a unique and specific case, embodied by their lived experience of implementing policies in their respective schools. These policies are aimed at the successful uptake of flexible learning spaces, and the development of appropriate pedagogies suited both to such environments and to better preparing young people for a 21st century knowledge economy. It is possible to draw some interim conclusions based on the analysis above of their intentional relationship to these phenomena.

It is possible to say that innovative teaching and learning practice in a flexible learning space is designed to occur in full public view, and this is likely to cause some discomfort to teachers schooled in traditional practices. Deprivatisation, it may be concluded, does, however, create opportunities for difficult and constructive reflective discussion about practice, perhaps far more so than traditional practices admit, and this may actually reduce stress (Kyriacou 2001). The notion, however, that 'it's all about the space', or that flexible spaces are a necessary requirement of innovative practices, is challenged by the principal of Angelus School.

A further interim conclusion that can then be drawn from the lived experiences of the principals of Angelus School and Millennial college, is that there is no set formula for determining practice in a flexible learning environment, though there are guiding principles, and these seem to revolve around a firm commitment to a whole school approach that favours the basic elements of modern or innovative teaching and learning practice; a commitment to turning existing practice on its head; and a sharp willingness and determination to constantly communicate and work collaboratively. Common to all three, following the view of Alvy and Robbins (2010), is their keen desire to break with tradition. Further, is the passion they express for working through failure, and recognising that they do not know all there is to know—indeed, there is a level at which these practitioners are radically underprepared for the task of implementing policy, but they are certain of their uncertainties, and lead their way through the challenges.

References

Alvy, H., & Robbins, P. (2010). *Learning from Lincoln: Leadership practices for school success* [EBL version]. Retrieved from http://www.aut.eblib.com.au.ezproxy.aut.ac.nz

Ball, S. J. (1993). What is policy? Texts, trajectories and toolboxes. *Discourse, 13*(2), 10–17.

Bell, L., & Stevenson, H. (2006). *Education policy: Process, themes and impact*. London, United Kingdom: Routledge Taylor and Francis.

Benade, L. (2012). *From technicians to teachers: Ethical teaching in the context of globalized education reform*. New York, NY: Continuum.

Benade, L. (2015a). Teachers' critical reflective practice in the context of twenty-first century learning. *Open Review of Educational Research, 2*(1), 42–54. doi:10.1080/23265507.2014.998159

Benade, L. (2015b). Teaching as inquiry: Well intentioned, but fundamentally flawed. *New Zealand Journal of Educational Studies, 50*(1), 107–120. doi:10.1007/s40841-015-0005-0.

Bergström, J., & Dekker, S. W. A. (2014). Bridging the macro and the micro by considering the meso: Reflections on the fractal nature of resilience. *Ecology and Society, 19*(4), 22. http://dx.doi.org/10.5751/ES-06956-190422. Retrieved from http://www.ecologyandsociety.org/vol19/iss4/art22/

Bishop, R. (2011). Freeing ourselves from neo-colonial domination in public school classrooms. In R. Bishop (Ed.), *Freeing ourselves* (pp. 31–73). Rotterdam, The Netherlands: Sense Publishers. doi:10.1007/978-94-6091-415-7_2. Retrieved from http://link.springer.com.ezproxy.aut.ac.nz

Blackmore, J., Bateman, D., Loughlin, J., O'Mara, J., & Aranda, G. (2011). *Research into the connection between built learning spaces and student outcomes* Literature review, paper No. 22 June. State of Victoria (Department of Education and Early Childhood Development). Retrieved from http://www.education.vic.gov.au

Bolstad, R., Gilbert, J., McDowall, S., Bull, A., Boyd, S., & Hipkins, R. (2012). *Supporting future-oriented learning and teaching: A New Zealand perspective. Report prepared for the Ministry of Education*. Wellington: New Zealand Council for Educational Research and Ministry of Education. Retrieved August 8, 2015, from http://www.educationcounts.govt.nz/publications/schooling/109306

Brown, P., Lauder, H., & Ashton, D. (2011). *The global auction: The broken promises of education, jobs and incomes*. New York, NY: Oxford University Press.

Cleveland, B., & Fisher, K. (2014). The evaluation of physical learning environments: A critical review of the literature. *Learning Environments Research, 4*(17), 1–28. doi:10.1007/s10984-013-9149-3

Codd, J. (1988). The construction and deconstruction of educational policy documents. *Journal of Education Policy, 3*(3), 235–247.

Codd, J. (2005). Teachers as 'managed professionals' in the global education industry: The New Zealand Experience. *Educational Review, 57*(2), 193–206. doi:10.1080/0013191042000308369

Coffield, F. (1999). Breaking the consensus: Lifelong learning as social control. *British Educational Research Journal, 25*(4), 479–499. doi:10.1080/0141192990250405

Dopfer, K., Foster, J., & Potts, J. (2004). Micro–meso–macro. *Journal of Evolutionary Economics, 14*(3), 263–279. doi:10.1007/s00191-004-0193-0.

Dumont, H., & Istance, D. (2010). Analysing and designing learning environments for the 21st century. In H. Dumont, D. Istance & F. Benavides (Eds.), *The nature of learning: Using research to inspire practice* (pp. 19–34). Paris, France: Organisation for Economic Cooperation and Development Publishing. doi:10.1787/9789264086487-3-en

Dumont, H., Istance, D., & Benavides, F. (Eds.). (2010) *The nature of learning: Using research to inspire practice* Paris, France: OECD Publishing. doi:10.1787/9789264086487-3-en

Dyson, R. (2014, May 2). Baby boomers were handed 'free housing', says top insurance boss. *The Telegraph*. Retrieved November 16, 2016 from http://www.telegraph.co.uk/finance/property/house-prices/10804031/Baby-boomers-were-handed-free-housing-says-top-insurance-boss.html

References

Gilbert, J., Bull, A., Stevens, S., & Giroux, M. (2015). *On the edge: Shifting teachers' paradigms for the future*. Teaching and Learning Research Initiative Research Completed Report. Retrieved from http://www.tlri.org.nz/tlri-research/research-completed/school-sector/edge-shifting-teachers'-paradigms-future

Johnston, K. (2015, May 11). Grammar eschews beanbag lessons in $6 m classroom upgrade. *New Zealand Herald*. Retrieved from http://www.nzherald.co.nz/nz/news/article.cfm?c_id=1&objectid=11446451

Kyriacou, C. (2001). Teacher stress: Directions for future research. *Educational Review, 53*(1), 27–35. doi:10.1080/00131910120033628

Loveless, A., & Williamson, B. (2013). *Learning identities in a digital age: Rethinking creativity, education and technology*. New York, NY: Routledge.

Ministry of Education. (2011). *The New Zealand school property strategy 2011–2021*. Retrieved from http://www.education.govt.nz/assets/Documents/Primary-Secondary/Property/SchoolPropertyStrategy201121.pdf

Ministry of Education. (2014a). *Aspiration and achievement: Education system*. Briefing to incoming Minister. Retrieved from http://www.education.govt.nz/assets/Documents/Ministry/Publications/Briefings-to-IncomingMinisters/AspirationAndAchievementEducationSystem.pdf

Ministry of Education. (2016b). *Investing in educational success*. Retrieved July 12, 2017 from http://www.education.govt.nz/ministry-of-education/specific-initiatives/investing-in-educational-success/

Moore, G. T., & Lackney, J. A. (1993). School design: Crisis, educational performance and design applications. *Children's Environments, 10*(2), 99–112. www.jstor.org

Morris, J. (2015, May 15). Grammar wise to steer clear of the 'one size fits all' classrooms. *New Zealand Herald*. Retrieved from http://www.nzherald.co.nz/nz/news/article.cfm?c_id=1&objectid=11448816

Organisation for Economic Cooperation and Development (OECD). (2003). *Definition and selection of competencies: Theoretical and conceptual foundations (DeSeCo): Summary of the Final Report*. Retrieved August 17, 2015 from http://www.oecd.org/education/skills-beyond-school/definitionandselectionofcompetenciesdeseco.htm

Organisation for Economic Cooperation and Development (OECD). (2013). *Innovative learning environments*. Paris, France: Educational Research and Innovation, OECD Publishing. doi:10.1787/9789264203488-en. Retrieved 7 Feb 2016 from http://www.oecd-ilibrary.org/education/innovative-learning-environments_9789264203488-en

Roberts, P. (2005). Tertiary education, knowledge and neoliberalism. In J. Codd & K. Sullivan (Eds.), *Education policy directions in Aotearoa New Zealand* (pp. 39–51). Southbank, Vic, Australia: Thomson Dunmore Press.

Robertson, S. (2005). Re-imagining and rescripting the future of education: Global knowledge economy discourses and the challenge to education systems. *Comparative Education, 41*(2), 151–170. doi:10.1080/03050060500150922

Snook, I. (2003). *The ethical teacher*. Palmerston North, New Zealand: Dunmore Press.

Stein, J. (2013, May 20). Why millennials will save us all. *Time*. Retrieved November 16, 2016 from http://time.com/247/millennials-the-me-me-me-generation/

Thrupp, M. (1998). Exploring the politics of blame: School inspection and its contestation in New Zealand and England. *Comparative Education, 34*(2), 195–210.

Turner, J. H., & Boyns, D. E. (2002). The return of grand theory. In J. H. Turner (Ed.), *Handbook of sociological theory* (pp. 353–378). New York, NY: Kluwer Academic/Plenum Publishers.

Walters, L. (2015, October 18). Top schools give multi-million dollar classrooms a fail grade. *Sunday Star Times*. Retrieved from http://www.stuff.co.nz/national/education/73042309/Top-schools-give-multi-million-dollar-classrooms-a-fail-grade

Woolner, P., McCarter, S., Wall, K., & Higgins, S. (2012). Changed learning through changed space: When can a participatory approach to the learning environment challenge preconceptions and alter practice? *Improving Schools, 15*(1), 45–60. doi:10.1177/1365480211434796

Chapter 9
Lessons to Be Learned?

> I have never been good at good-byes. I tend to either ramble on and on, repeating myself and incessantly over-processing information—or I end really abruptly, leaving people wondering what just happened. (Vagle 2014, p. 148)

The value of these words lie not in their profundity, but in their ability to capture the challenges of ending off—be it an article, book chapter, or indeed, a project such as this one. What I will do is to suggest some provocative 'take-home' messages, without labouring through a mere repetition of what has already been stated within the various chapters. These concluding suggestions and comments are addressed to various constituencies amongst those who would read this book.

Lessons for Practitioners in Schools

This book had the aim of exploring, interpreting and thereby developing, greater understanding of modern, innovative or non-traditional teaching and learning practices. It intended to understand the transitions teachers and school leaders make as they grapple with the challenge of twenty-first century learning, the development of flexible learning spaces and the rapidly changing nature of knowledge and learning in a digital age.

In the lifeworld of the practitioners featured in this book, change is occurring at several levels: the spaces in which they work; the tools with which they work; the ways in which they work; and the ways in which they think about their work. The two latter elements are significantly influenced by the former two, namely the spaces and the tools.

Change introduced from the bottom-up rather than imposed top down is considered to be highly significant in both the literature reviewed in this book and the reported findings of the fieldwork. Where teachers are motivated by their personal desire for change or to work with progressive pedagogies, they seem more likely to work through the challenges and setbacks, whereas imposed change (such as in the BYOD example), may enjoy less success. Carefully managed change (as seen at

Angelus School) is called for when retrofitting or adding new flexible learning spaces to an existing single-cell model, yet even then, significant challenges present themselves, such as teachers falling back into default settings.

The role of reflective practice and honest collaboration is significant in supporting teachers through those challenges. What may be less helpful, I have implied, is to link reflective practice to performance appraisal. The performativity of the latter militates against developing the level of critical judgment needed for significant change to occur. This implies a desire to change, however, and arguably for teachers to change their orientation to their practice requires the desire and willingness to break with tradition. This desire may be borne of dissatisfaction with the past, as it was for several participants mentioned in this book.

Important questions remain, however, in both the contexts of schools with flexible learning spaces and the introduction of BYOD: What of the 'passive learners' or those who 'zone out'? How is the value of dispositional learning captured? Is there a relationship between improving school facilities and improving academic results? What does collaboration look like, why is it important, how is it practiced, and how is it learned? The answers to these questions, as earlier chapters have evidenced, are not straightforward. While there may be arguments that school design or the use of digital devices can make a compelling contribution to student engagement and therefore scholastic success, a counter view may seek the answer to improved student performance in teacher performance and attitude. The implication must be that 'a good teacher can teach anywhere'.

Lessons for Teacher Educators

There is a strongly held view in the ICT literature reviewed here and feedback from participants, in both the BYOD and flexible learning contexts, that professional learning is critically important. Before reaching the point of partaking of in-service professional learning, teachers require appropriate pre-service initial teacher education (ITE). Two of the principals participating in the studies discussed in this book suggested that teacher applicants lack the skill and understanding to enter schools that engage with non-traditional pedagogy in non-traditional spaces. Indeed, the growing number of schools adopting school-wide digital strategies such as BYOD, and particularly the development of flexible learning environments, will place increasing demands on teachers' competence and skill.

Teachers' practice is influenced by several factors, including their experience of growing up, attending school, and, particularly, what they learn at university. As the principal of Innovation Primary has suggested these experiences are overwhelmingly characterised by being talked to or at, and working individually. Changing the shape of these learning experiences at university may be challenging, however. Not only are university lecturers often many years removed from actual school classroom experience, but also traditional university buildings favour lecture theatres and single-cell seminar rooms. In the New Zealand context, the old teachers' training colleges were incorporated into universities as schools and faculties of education. Many of these buildings are deeply inflexible in their design and furnishing.

Do ITE providers attempt to create opportunities for their student teachers so they are able to develop an understanding of working in non-traditional spaces? And if so, what does this entail, and what are the challenges? In keeping with the argument suggested in this book, space and technology are neither passive, nor do they dictate; yet they do enable. So simply building large, non-traditional spaces, or installing modern furniture and mobile screens in existing traditional space, will not bring about pedagogical change. Introducing personalised pedagogy, collaborative teaching and working with curriculum in non-traditional ways, may not require purpose-built spaces, nor indeed modern furniture and mobile, digital technology. What it would require, however, is to give up teaching solo to work in a team. What would this mean, in reality?

Lecturing teams (or, more correctly, 'facilitation teams') would have to collaborate on all course preparation and planning; together, team members would have to find ways of engaging students' interest in using digital technology in intellectually stimulating ways; and course papers would have to be rewritten to engage with curriculum differently. It may be missing the point that if all teacher educators do differently is stand up and lecture about these non-traditional approaches. If student teachers are to grasp the possibilities—and challenges—presented by non-traditional approaches, then their university teachers must model these in the classroom. And in their teams, as the school practitioners mentioned in this book indicated, they would have to engage in critical, reflective thinking and practice. In short, university teachers would have to partake of the pain themselves, not just talk about it.

What would be some of the challenges if ITE providers and teacher educators attempted to provide a model of technology-rich, flexible learning environments and innovative teaching practice? For one, significant levels of 'buy-in' amongst teaching staff as well as leaders and administrators would be required. Success in this regard will be more likely to follow from a bottom-up, democratic process of change management. Material and moral support, including opportunities to engage university teachers in professional learning, would have to be provided to effect the changes mentioned above.

A significant challenge, however, would lie in obstinate bureaucracy, which pervades all levels of the teaching profession. In the New Zealand context, this would include the teacher licensing body, the Education Council, which has a stake in teacher education, by approving, reviewing and monitoring ITE courses. Any significant course changes must be able to meet the standards set by this body, thus courses must be written with this body in mind. Within universities are layers of course approval and accreditation bodies and committees that also have a vested interest in closely scrutinising suggested courses.

Nevertheless, given the direction being taken by the shifting tides of education reform globally, teacher educators will better to grapple with these changes and challenges, rather than ignoring them. The reality is that school leaders, bureaucrats and politicians may tire of the unwillingness of teacher education providers to change, and greater responsibility for teacher education provision will shift to the schools themselves, with potentially dire consequences for the long-term health of teaching as a *profession*.

Lessons for Policy-Makers

Policy ought not to be a blunt instrument; yet frequently it appears to emerge in this way. Under-researched, under-debated and over-rushed, policy sometimes really does appear out of the blue, in spite of what Ball (1993) suggested. This has the effect of blunting its value. Even when there is research, policy appears to come under the cover of deception rather than making a well-prepared entry to life. The attitude of some teachers to the notion of flexible learning environments, digital technology and non-traditional pedagogies can be dismissive, regarding these initiatives to have no grounding in research, and unable to point to other jurisdictions where such initiatives have been a success.

Considering what was proposed in Chap. 8 regarding ways change could be effected, policy-makers have to be open to the possibilities for a tide of change in relation to the development of modern or innovative teaching and learning practice occurring at the micro-level, that is, the level of individual schools, and groups of schools. Indeed, this may be a preferred model for policy-makers such as the Ministry of Education. It provides no professional learning to support teachers through the difficult changes underpinning policy shifts towards a digital and innovative education experience for students, the Ministry of Education opting for 'locally developed' pedagogies instead. Arguably, in the New Zealand context, the policy of Communities of Learning (COL) is a model to enable such micro-level change, which may spread to the centre (the meso- and macro-levels of policy-making). The COL potentially opens the door for a participatory, 'bottom up' momentum. Whether this is borne out in practice, and whether this strategy is more likely to be successful than imposed change, is a matter for future investigation.

There is a lesson too for the Ministry of Education in respect of implementing its school building strategy. Clearly, to bring about holistic change demands sufficient budgets for new builds—the early experience of building the experimental learning studios, reported in Chap. 5, reflected difficulties at several levels, many attributed to the Ministry of Education itself, particularly in relation to budgets, inflexible requirements and poor communication. It may be hoped that the Ministry of Education will have learnt its own lessons from those early experiences. A (potentially controversial) strategy it has put in place is the public private partnership (PPP) model (2016d), in terms of which the Ministry outsources to a private consortium, which has the task of designing, financing, building and maintaining the facility, usually for a 25-year period. The Ministry has a quarterly financial obligation to the consortium; the consortium has an obligation to maintain the building to Ministry of Education requirements. Under thee arrangements, questions remain, such as the skill, competence and ability of the consortium to hold up its end of the agreement, and the whether private consortia of any kind have any business managing state educational facilities on behalf of the state. This raises questions of profit motives, and what benefits accrue to the 'private' segment of the PPP. Furthermore, to what degree can local communities and educators be guaranteed of any input under a PPP?

As Moore and Lackney (1993) noted, it is important to work with children and teachers to transform both learning spaces and pedagogical approaches. This provides an impetus for designers to support school communities as they rethink school design and develop spatial pedagogies. The Ministry of Education would be well advised to ensure the widest consultation process possible is put in place for the creation of new school design. Within these communities, the re-shaping of pedagogies may also be a matter for wide agreement. As was seen in the case of the BYOD implementation at Holyoake College, students and parents may simply not understand where teachers are going to, or coming from, when new approaches to teaching and learning are adopted without adequate consultation and re-education.

In relation to the development of new buildings in which to develop modern teaching and learning practice, a perception may be created by the Ministry of Education property strategy (2011) that it is not in the business of consultation. The strategy intends all schools to conform to a 'Modern Learning Environment' standard by 2021. This strategy is surprisingly uniform given the intent of the Ministry to create a diverse, engaging and vibrant education for the 21st century, with the help of modern facilities. Put differently, questions may be raised as to whether the Ministry of Education is imposing a 'one size fits all' prescription over all New Zealand schools. This suggestion was raised by Morris (2015), ex-Head of Auckland Grammar in one of the media reports mentioned in Chap. 8. Thus the reality may be the Ministry of Education appointing designers who offer up suggestions to establishment boards and school communities, rather than the impetus coming from the other direction.

Lessons for Designers

Optimistically, design considerations should be in tune with what practitioners and communities ask for. Certainly, there is the possibility to learn by the errors of earlier projects—a hope clearly expressed by the *Learning Studio Pilot Review* (Ministry of Education 2012). A point Chap. 5 made very clear though, is the importance of shifting the emphasis away from the technical aspects of building, such as those likely to be highlighted in post occupancy evaluations (POE).

How can it be ensured that retrofits, modifications and renovations, or new school builds, will meet educational and pedagogical aims, rather than simply meeting technical standards? It is a valid and pertinent question to ask whether these buildings and technologies improve teaching and student academic achievement. The solution may be in trying to come to terms with the tension between the view that only 'good teaching' matters, thus the environment plays little or no part; and the view that the changed environment will lead to changed practice. It seems the former is a position that is less open to change, while the latter seems either deterministic or naïvely optimistic. It may be that some designers and the Ministry of Education fit into the latter camp.

Relatedly, critical questions arise then in relation to whether designers are leading the changes in educational thinking, or whether educators are, with designers following by providing expert guidance and planning to put into effect modern and innovative approaches to teaching and learning. These comments apply equally to buildings, digital technology and educational furniture. To educators, the point must be made that they in turn will profit by retaining an open mind to expertise from fields of design and health, for example, when considering how new pedagogies might be implemented and executed. It will help both sides to take note of the argument suggested at the end of Chap. 5 that, space is an enabler of new and evolving pedagogies—it does not determine those pedagogical practices, and, in turn, making those changes in pedagogy will depend on willing and able teachers.

The Final Word

This book set out to create understanding and awareness of, and to raise significantly the level of critique and critical thinking in relation to, the trend to 21st-century learning. It has presented the narratives and responses of real practitioners in real schools dealing with the daily life of implementing policy. It has, through working on the margins of phenomenology, sought to make sense of how the participants make sense of their lifeworld. By working in the paradigm of interpretation and critical theory, it has attempted to deconstruct the policies and the change processes affecting teachers' lives in specific contexts, each interacting with a specific phenomenon. The people in these contexts—the participants—are practitioners who make do as best as they can with their tools-at-hand, as they each craft a new way of being with their lifeworld. It is my hope that I have done justice to their work, and in the process, suggested appropriate arguments and justifications in support of that work, helping to make sense of their emergent being in a constantly evolving pedagogical reality.

References

Ball, S. J. (1993). What is policy? Texts, trajectories and toolboxes. *Discourse, 13*(2), 10–17.
Bolstad, R., Gilbert, J., McDowall, S., Bull, A., Boyd, S., & Hipkins, R. (2012). *Supporting future-oriented learning and teaching: A New Zealand perspective. Report prepared for the Ministry of Education*. Wellington: New Zealand Council for Educational Research and

References

Ministry of Education. Retrieved August 8, 2015, from http://www.educationcounts.govt.nz/publications/schooling/109306

Ministry of Education. (2011). *The New Zealand school property strategy 2011–2021*. Retrieved from http://www.education.govt.nz/assets/Documents/Primary-Secondary/Property/SchoolPropertyStrategy201121.pdf

Ministry of Education. (2012). *Learning studio pilot review*. Retrieved from http://www.education.govt.nz/assets/Documents/Primary-Secondary/Property/School-property-design/Flexible-learning-spaces/LearningStudioPilotReview.pdf

Ministry of Education. (2016d). *Public private partnerships to build schools*. Retrieved November 19, 2016 from http://www.education.govt.nz/ministry-of-education/specific-initiatives/public-private-partnerships/

Moore, G.T., & Lackney, J.A. (1993). School design: Crisis, educational performance and design applications. *Children's Environments, 10*(2), 99–112. www.jstor.org

Morris, J. (2015, May 15). Grammar wise to steer clear of the 'one size fits all' classrooms. *New Zealand Herald*. Retrieved from http://www.nzherald.co.nz/nz/news/article.cfm?c_id=1&objectid=11448816

Vagle, M. D. (2014). *Crafting phenomenological research*. Walnut Creek, CA: Left Coast Press.

CPSIA information can be obtained
at www.ICGtesting.com
Printed in the USA
BVOW06*2127140317
478533BV00008B/42/P

9 789811 037818